▶

Social Work Practice with Families
A Diversity Model

Lonnie R. Helton
Cleveland State University

Maggie Jackson
Cleveland State University

Allyn and Bacon
Boston • London • Toronto • Sydney • Tokyo • Singapore

Editor in Chief, Social Sciences: Karen Hanson
Series Editor: Judith Fifer
Editorial Assistant: Jennifer Jacobson
Marketing Manager: Joyce Nilsen
Editorial/Production Service: Chestnut Hill
  Enterprises, Inc.

Composition Buyer: Linda Cox
Manufacturing Buyer: Megan Cochran
Cover Administrator: Suzanne Harbison
Cover Art: Robert O. Evans, Jr.

Copyright © 1997 by Allyn & Bacon
A Viacom Company
Needham Heights, MA 02194

Library of Congress Cataloging-in-Publication Data

Helton, Lonnie R.
     Social work practice with families : a diversity model / Lonnie
  R. Helton, Maggie Jackson.
       p.   cm.
     Includes bibliographical references and index.
     ISBN 0-205-16704-7 (pbk.)
     1. Family social work. 2. Problem families—Counseling of.
  3. Family—psychological aspects. 4. Family assessment.
  5. Pluralism (Social sciences) I. Jackson, Maggie. II. Title.
  HV43.H44   1997
  362.82—dc20   96-12687
                                                                            CIP
Printed in the United States of America
10 9 8 7 6 5 4 3 2   01 00 99 98

Photo Credits:

1.2 © *Robert Harbison*   6.2 © *Robert Harbison*
3.3 © *Robert Harbison*   7.1 © *Robert Harbison*
4.1 © *Mary Ellen LePrunka*   8.1 © *Robert Harbison*
5.1 © *Robert Harbison*   9.1 © *Robert Harbison*
6.1 © *Robert Harbison*

Dedication

To our fathers, Luther R. Helton and Willie D. Jackson (both deceased) for their insight in developing our potential through their wonderful stories of our family heritage throughout our childhood years

To our mothers, Mollie Helton and Hattie Mae Jackson, for their wonderful sense of humor that provided both energy and inspiration in moments of trial and tribulation. Two women, two cultures, two paths that were destined for their offspring to cross; they provided for us the sensitivity to embrace our similarities and differences in our passion to understand the significance of family that led to the genesis of this book

To our siblings, Willard R. Helton, Billie Sue Ratliff, Glenn David Helton, George L. Helton, Willie James Jackson, Franklin Jackson, and Geneva Jackson, we extend our appreciation for having had the privilege of growing up as "middle" children

To our extended family members, living and deceased, who provided the initial curiosity toward learning about how families cope, support one another, and survive. These values were passed on to our parents, who then passed these same values down to us. To them we are forever grateful.

CONTENTS

Preface   vii
Abstracts of Case Studies   ix
Foreword   xii

1   **The Family: Yesterday and Today**   1

Introduction and Evolution   *1*
Changes in Family Structure   *2*
Theoretical Foundations   *5*

2   **Perspectives and Assumptions of Families**   15

Diversity in Communication   *15*
Differences in Power Structure   *18*
Strengths of Relationships   *22*

3   **Understanding Families: The Four-R Model of Family Dynamics**   29

Rules   *32*
Roles   *34*
Relationships   *38*
Rituals   *41*

4   Intervention Strategies Through Utilization of the Four-R Model of Family Dynamics   49

Engagement   49
Interviewing   50
Assessment   51
Planning and Contracting   54
Implementation and Action   55
Termination   57
Evaluation and Follow-up   59

5   Application of the Four-R Model   63

Rules and the Thomas Family   63
Roles and the Romano Family   71
Relationships and the Jones Family   78
Rituals and the Johnson Family   86

6   Families: Issues In Diversity   95

Ethnicity and Culture   95
Sexual Orientation   99
Diverse Parenting   102
Women's Roles and Gender Issues   105

7   Fields of Social Work Practice: Beginning Intervention with Families   113

Social Work with Older Adults   113
Social Work Practice with Children   120
Developmental Disabilities   126
Community/Neighborhood Services   131

8   Trends in Policy and Practice   139

Introduction   139
Foster Care and Adoptions   139

Family Preservation   142
Deinstitutionalization   144
Health Care   146
Women in the Workforce   148
Children's Day Care   151
The Impact of Social Work Licensure and other
    Regulatory Statutes   154

9   Implications for Social Work Practice with Families:
Current and Future Challenges   161

The Four-R Model of Family Dynamics and Future
    Adaptations   161
Recommendations for Research   165
Practice with Families in a Multicultural Society   166
Longevity and the Impact of Better Health   167

Appendix   173

Glossary   175
The NASW Code of Ethics   183
Supplemental Exercises   195
    Jones Family Eco-Map Analysis   195
    Eco-Map Exercise   197
    Analysis of Johnson Family Genogram   198
    Genogram Instructions   199
    Process Recording of Romano Family Session   199
    Family Sculpture Exercise   205
    Family Communication Exercise (Satir's Model)   205
    Family Contract Exercise   205
    Family Systems Exercise   206

Index   208

▶

Preface

This book is about social work practice with families and includes theoretical methods for understanding and working with a diversity of clients in generalist practice. The development of this work evolved from the authors' experiences in practice in various settings as well as from their classroom teaching. The organizing theme is the Four-R Model of Family Dynamics, which may be used in the helping process on an ongoing basis, from engagement through evaluation and follow-up. The Four-R Model includes the concepts of rules, roles, relationships, and rituals that the authors view as the basic family dynamics inherent to all family functioning. The authors' conjecture is that one of the four dynamics, that is, rules, roles, relationships, or rituals, will emerge in any family as the dominant or guiding force. This dynamic may be identified by practitioners and utilized as a means for helping family members to better understand themselves and to work toward enhanced functioning. The Four-R Model of Family Dynamics may be applied to any family system regardless of structure, status, age, gender, ethnicity, culture, religious orientation, worldview, social class, sexual orientation, or any other way in which a family may define itself.

In the first chapter, the authors examine the evolution of the family as a social grouping, addressing historical perspectives and changes in family patterns. These patterns (i.e., extended to nuclear to extended) are assessed through utilization of two theoretical paradigms: communication and systems theory. Examples are provided to clarify incongruent and congruent modes of communication based on the work of Virginia Satir. This chapter and all to follow include a summary, questions for discussion, significant terms, and references for the chapter.

In the second chapter perspectives and assumptions of families are explored in depth. Three areas are investigated: (a) diversity and communication; (b) differences in power structure; (c) strengths of relationships.

Under each of these areas, four assumptions about families and family functioning are described and clarified. An example is given to refute each assumption or myth about family life.

In Chapter Three, the authors define and elucidate the Four-R Model of Family Dynamics. The authors hypothesize that rules, roles, relationships, and rituals are inherent to all families. A case study is introduced to illustrate each type of family configuration. Each illustration includes a working definition of the dynamic in focus and provides a unique case example.

Chapter Four addresses the problem-solving process applied to the stages of intervention. These stages include: engagement; interviewing; assessment; planning and contracting; implementation and action; termination; and evaluation and follow-up. Each of these stages is defined using family dynamics. In Chapter Five the authors develop detailed case studies, each representing a family that is dominated by one of the dynamics (rules, roles, relationships, or rituals) of the Four-R Model. A special feature of this chapter is a group exercise wherein students are asked to choose one of the family types discussed and apply their knowledge of the stages of intervention to that particular family.

In Chapter Six diversity is examined from many different perspectives. Four types of diversity in families are discussed: ethnicity and culture; sexual orientation; diverse parenting; and women's roles and gender issues. Each form of diversity is described through specific areas unique to that type, and concrete examples are provided for understanding the challenges of family living.

Chapter Seven addresses fields of social work practice commonly confronting beginning, generalist practitioners. These fields of practice are divided as follows: work with older adults; practice with children; developmental disabilities; and community/neighborhood services. These fields of practice are addressed from several perspectives: definitions, issues and problems, service delivery systems, and significance for social work practice.

In Chapter Eight trends in policy and practice are highlighted. These trends include: foster care and adoption; family preservation; health care; women in the workforce; children's day care; and social work licensure and other regulatory statutes. These trends are further subdivided into the following topics: description; essence of trends; and significance for social work practice.

In the ninth and concluding chapter, the authors analyze current and future challenges facing social work practice with families. Implications of the Four-R Model are provided along with ideas for future adaptations. The chapter is further subdivided into topics including recommendations for research; practice with families in a multicultural society; and longevity and the impact of better health.

ACKNOWLEDGMENTS

The authors would like to acknowledge those key individuals who have helped with this project. First of all, we would like to thank Karen Hanson, senior editor, for her foresight in approving the initial prospectus for this important work and for her patience in assisting us in broadening the scope of the original proposal. Also, we would like to extend our appreciation to Judy Fifer, our assistant editor, for her guidance and support in the final stages of manuscript preparation. Next, we would like to thank the Department of Social Work faculty at Cleveland State University for their continuous support and encouragement throughout the writing of this manuscript. Special thanks go to Dorothy Loretz for assistance in preparing the diagrams and figures, and to Gail Witherspoon in preparing the final manuscript.

We want to give a special, special thanks to Steve Moody, our student assistant, who spent many long, hard hours completing library research and initial proofreading. Steve, a senior social work major, read the manuscript as a consumer and was therefore able to provide valuable suggestions.

We want to thank Robert O. Evans Jr. for his ability to design our cover art work through our description and thoughts regarding the intent of this book.

We also want to express our appreciation to those professionals in the community, Edith Anderson and George Tsagaris, Cuyahoga County Juvenile Court trainers, and Sonia Winners, Cleveland Marshall College of Law, for providing special insights and references for documentation regarding boot camps and mediation programs, and our reviewers: Brad Sheafor, Colorado State University; Louise C. Johnson, University of Wisconsin-Madison; and Alvin L. Salles, New Mexico State University.

To our families, significant others, and friends we want to extend our deepest gratitude for their loyalty and patience during the long hours of work and "eight-day weeks" required for the completion of this project.

ABSTRACTS OF CASE STUDIES

Case Study One—The Culliver Family
The Culliver family is a two-parent, middle income, African American family consisting of Ella, the mother, (40); Bill, the father, (41); Franklin, a son (20); Sarah, a daughter (16); and Louise, a daughter (12). A major issue confronting the Culliver family is that of the mother's having volunteered for the father to sing in the Christmas Cantata at their church, with-

out consulting him first. Family communication patterns are addressed as each family member responds to this family dilemma.

Case Study Two—The Davis Family

The Davis family is a two-parent, low income, caucasian family of five. The family consists of John, the father, (36); Marie, the mother, (35); Terry, a son, (13); Henry, a son, (8); and Marie's mother, Minnie Adams (63). Both Mr. and Mrs. Davis work and conflict has arisen over Mrs. Davis' spending time helping Henry with homework and caring for her mother. Minnie is later diagnosed to have Alzheimer's disease.

Case Study Three—The Thomas Family
(A Rules-Dominated Family)

The Thomas family is a single-parent, low to middle income, caucasian family. The family consists of Beverly Thomas, the mother, (35); Samantha, a daughter, (15); Lewis Jr., a son, (12); and Richie, a son, (4). Beverly, a diabetic, has developed strict rules regarding diet, family time together, discipline, and housekeeping. Samantha is experimenting sexually and has contracted a sexually transmitted disease (STD) and is also is anorectic. Lewis is bright and obedient whereas Richie has a visual problem causing other developmental delays. Richie also has difficulty understanding the divorce.

Case Study Four—The Romano Family
(A Roles-Dominated Family)

The Romano Family is a two-parent, extended, upper middle-class family of Italian-American heritage. The family consists of the following: Victor Romano, the father, (58); Julia Romano, the mother, (54); Mario Romano, the oldest son, (35); Angelo Romano, a son (33); Veronica Romano, a daughter, (25); and Frances Romano, the youngest daughter/child, (20).

Victor Romano has just been laid off from his job as vice president of an oil company due to downsizing. Being unemployed has led to family problems. Julia, the mother, is resisting her husband's tendency to control the family. Mario Romano, an attorney, has requested family intervention with the agreement of his mother. Angelo, a medical internist, is engaged to Sue, a fundamentalist believer, and plans to marry her outside the Roman Catholic tradition, an additional family stressor. Veronica and Frances are experiencing financial difficulties with college expenses at this time. Both Mario and Angelo have offered to help the family financially.

Case Study Five—The Jones Family
(A Relationships-Dominated Family)
The Jones Family is a blended, caucasian, working-class family. The family consists of Barbara, the mother (38); Joe, the stepfather (40); and Carl (14), Barbara's son by her previous marriage to Hugh Barker.

Barbara works as a nurse's aide and wants to return to school to earn her RN diploma. She is six months' pregnant by Joe Jones. Joe has an associate degree and works as a computer programmer. Barbara has eleven siblings, all of whom are college educated. She is the middle child, and a family expectation is that she complete college and have at least three children. Hugh Barker is incarcerated and Carl is pressuring his mother and stepfather to visit Hugh. They are reluctant to grant his wish because Carl has recently been in trouble with the authorities. Barbara and Joe have been married for two years. A close relationship is developing between Joe and Carl.

Case Study Six—The Johnson Family
(A Rituals-Dominated Family)
The Johnson Family is a lower-middle-class, extended, caucasian family. The family consists of Wayne, (31); Margaret, his wife (30); Eric, a son (12); Michelle, a daughter (8); Ron (61) and Clara (60), the paternal grandparents; Eva, (81), the widowed, paternal, great-grandmother (Ron's mother). Ron has two brothers and a sister, all of whom live some distance away; and all of them have children.

Wayne Johnson works as an air traffic controller and Margaret is starting her own private tax business. They were high school sweethearts and have struggles financially. Their second child, Michelle, was born via in vitro fertilization with Margaret's single sister Jenny being the egg donor. Eva lost her husband five years ago. A retired real estate broker, she volunteers regularly at a hospital gift shop. Eva plans her life around the weekly family dinners and other family rituals, which she hosts. Family conflict has emerged because all family members would like Eva to "slow down."

FOREWORD

The Family

By
Lonnie R. Helton

From stone age to space age,
Her energy prevails,
A haven for care,
When all else fails.
From pain to joy and back again
She holds us close and fast,
A bastion of strength,
Amidst turmoil and change,
Seldom tiring,
Sometimes failing
Listening beyond the call,
Gathering us into her branches
When wounds are fresh
All pride vanquished,
Curing and healing,
With magical power unspoken.
She alone is there,
And we for her,
We inside her and she in us,
She is the family.
Encouraging, prodding,
Yet anchoring,
She is the glue that binds us,
She knows our wants and needs.
Never abandoning, always giving,
When none is left to give.
She is the teacher,
Yet learns from each age
New lessons for coping,
Enduring each challenge,
Passing each test.
Warm and resilient,
Always familiar,
Nurturing our hopes and dreams.
Her door always open,
In sunshine and in storm,
Beyond boundaries and expectation,
She gathers her fold.
Life triumphs in her arms,
She is the family.

▶ 1

The Family: Yesterday and Today

INTRODUCTION AND EVOLUTION

Families have always been identified in our society as the most basic social group. Historically, the family has changed through the years. From the beginning, individuals grouped themselves around like kinship features and kinship bonds. These groupings evolved from informal to formal arrangements as reflected by environmental needs.

Individuals arrange themselves in groups as a way to meet basic physiological needs, safety and security needs, and to foster psychological development (Maslow, 1968). In addition, such groupings or constellations provide a cadre of emotional sustenance and ongoing social support. Therefore, families serve as a link to the past with the ability to provide continuity between yesterday and today. As a linking force, the family serves as a pathway to the future.

Another major need served by the family is that of socialization. Socialization may be defined as the process of shaping an individual's social behavior to fit the expectations of the culture in which he/she lives (Brigham, 1991). Family members are enhanced socially within the context of the family. The nurturing function of the family elevates the self-esteem of all its members. It is also through this process that individuals establish the capacity for relationship development. As individual family members interact with one another, they learn what is acceptable and unacceptable in human relationships. This protective enabling environment permits practice of interpersonal skill building and boundary setting.

Given the multiple needs that are met by the family, the family may be defined as the primary unit of caretaking for its members. Such caretaking includes ongoing concern and love, and the ability to provide a protective environment for all family members. As mentioned earlier, protection includes support for both physiological and mental development. Childrearing represents a major area of supportive intervention within the family. It has been said that the family is essentially the "headquarters" for human development (Garbarino, 1992, p. 72).

A traditional definition of family by the U.S. Census Bureau is: "a group of two or more persons related by blood, marriage, or adoption"(U.S. Census, 1990). Reiss (1980, p. 29), however, defines the family as "a small kinship-structured group with the key function of nurturant socialization." Considering the definitions of family provided by the U.S. Census and Reiss, the family in this text will be defined as a small group that serves as the developer and caretaker of its members.

In view of the above definition, this text is being written to help undergraduate students to better understand the nature and complexity of families. With this understanding, practical explanations will be given on how to work with families. Without clarity of definition, students cannot fully understand families, nor will they be able to develop strategies for practice with families.

Inherent in the knowledge of families is understanding how family members communicate with each other and function as a microcosm within the larger society. That is, the family is the primary social unit that provides an arena for human development and the fulfillment of nurturant drives.

CHANGES IN FAMILY STRUCTURE

In the early beginnings of family life, families lived in an extended family arrangement. Families inevitably depended on each other for basic survival and support. The extended family format developed in early times, as many individuals were needed to meet family responsibilities. Having additional individuals available provided assistance for the tasks required of families. And, it stood to reason in those days, as well as today, that the larger the family the more secure the unit would be in meeting its own basic needs. Consequently, the extended family constellation developed out of the necessities or requirements of family life.

The nuclear family arrived as human beings made advancements in their existence. As technology replaced manual labor, fewer bodies were needed to meet the obligations of family life. Conversely, the responsibilities of families changed in relation to societal development and

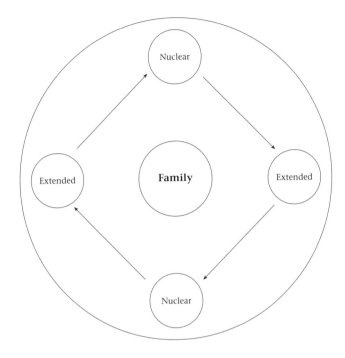

FIGURE 1.1 Historical Progression of Families

upkeep. Families also had to depend more on society to ensure their continued contributions.

One might say, then, that the development of families has moved full circle (see Fig 1.1). The circle moves from extended to nuclear and back to extended. In today's fast-moving environment of the twentieth century, the extended family is operating at full force once again. The visibility of the extended family is largely due to the economic crisis within our present society. Family members must band together out of necessity. These necessities include food, clothing, shelter, and psychological support. Another example of this phenomenon occurs when adult children and their children must return home to live with the family of origin. The economic environment is difficult for those individuals without solid, independent financial means. The entire (total) family, therefore, continues to be a haven for emotional sustenance and well-being. The presence of this trend is also signified through media images of the American family. Interestingly, a study of families depicted on television between 1950 and 1990 indicated that since 1960 the extended family has been the most frequently occurring type of household, followed by nuclear families and single parent families (Skill & Robinson, 1994).

Prior to the Industrial Revolution, the extended family was the accepted format. Individual family members simply could not function on their own. Therefore, individuals were forced to group themselves for supportive and survival needs. During this era, society was primarily agrarian, and families depended upon an internal division of labor. It was appropriate for family members to adopt the extended family format in efforts to meet the demands of day-to-day living. The agrarian society family demanded a division of labor in which every family member had a contributing role to play.

In addition, the bartering system was in full force during these times. This can be observed through the exchange of fresh garden produce and home canned goods, as well as manual labor (e.g., building barns, meeting deadlines for planting). Not only did this exchange occur within large extended families, but it was also a common system of survival among neighbors in small communities. This indicates that the extended family network had another vital component. It was a time when people in general assisted one another as much as possible; this, in essence, formed a type of "kinship" bond among them.

As society advanced from an agrarian economy to the Industrial Revolution, the family format changed to nuclear. With the technological advancements of the machine age the necessity of having large families

FIGURE 1.2   The Family of Yesterday

decreased. Although families maintained the development and nurturing roles, the primary parenting figures had the responsibility for implementing family tasks. Grandparents were given the role of temporary caretakers (child care providers) to assist the primary parenting figures. With the ongoing roles and responsibilities of the family, significant others were utilized. For example, babysitters and housekeepers were hired, and ministers and social workers were often engaged to provide supportive services. With the nuclear family type, parents had to take the initiative to create new helping relationships for assistance with development and nurturing responsibilities.

After the Industrial Revolution the intervening years brought wars, economic depressions, and other catastrophic events (e.g., fires, floods, hurricanes), which inevitably led family members to continue to "revisit" the extended family reality. Of course, in times of great need people often naturally will revert to past modes of coping and survival. And, society gives permission to its members to utilize various means of operating for survival purposes. To illustrate this concept, during times of war, young mothers and their children often move back into the home of their parents or parents-in-law. Another reflection of this dynamic is that during times of unemployment, family members often provide financial support for meeting basic needs.

During the latter part of the twentieth century, families have returned to utilizing the extended family format. This era represents a highly technological environment wherein computerization of institutions has led to increased unemployment. With unemployment comes the need for the sharing of resources for survival purposes. In addition, this period of history reflects increased acceptance of multicultural differences. Within these subgroupings (e.g. African American, Hispanic, Native American) the extended family format has remained in operation over time. This crisis situation has ultimately forced the majority into adopting values and practices of these ethnic/cultural subgroups. This typifies the phenomenon in American society in which the majority culture creates a standard that subgroups lack the power to establish. Even though the majority culture represents the ability to change standards in American society, they nonetheless represent a minority within the context of world societies.

THEORETICAL FOUNDATIONS

Social work with families requires an understanding of basic theoretical concepts that will serve to guide everyday practice. Communication and systems theory are the theoretical underpinnings being utilized here to understand the nature and dynamics of families. These two frameworks will enhance the reader's understanding of how family members relate to each other and to society.

Modes of Communication

First, communication theory, as seen through the work of Virginia Satir, identifies five modes of communication common to the dynamics of family interaction. These five modes are: *placating, blaming, super-reasonable, irrelevant,* and *congruent.* The first four modes are viewed as blocking or incongruent forms of communication. These five modes of communication are inherent within all human relations, according to Satir (Satir, Stachowiak, & Taschman, 1990).

These five modes of communication will be addressed as they are observed within the context of family life. These five modes are useful in understanding the communication flow in families. One's ability to assess communication patterns within families will be greatly enhanced through the use of these modes. They specifically are useful in helping professionals to understand basic communication styles. These styles portray various possibilities of communication blockage that commonly occur within the context of family life. Communication, therefore, may be totally blocked when two individuals persistently use opposing styles of communication.

First, placating can be defined as complete agreement among family members. Members agree completely with everything that is said; that is, there is no challenging of each other's statements. Placaters will always comply outwardly, although they may inwardly be strongly opposed to what is being communicated. Still, in the placating style, total submission is the norm (Satir, Stachowiak, & Taschman, 1990). (See Example A.)

Blaming is the second mode of communication. Blaming is defined, quite simply, as invariably placing fault for one's actions onto other family members. Blamers feel that they must always assume a position of authority, and they enjoy throwing their weight around. The blaming style of communication is used by the individual regardless of whether he/she feels that this position is right or wrong within the given context. (Satir, Stachowiak, & Taschman, 1990). (See Example B.)

Next, super-reasonable is a communication mode assumed when "the words bear no relationship to how one feels" (Satir, Stachowiak, & Taschman, 1990, p. 44). Super-reasonable individuals communicate content (i.e., make statements) inconsistent with their feelings at the time. They tend to express ideas without any regard for their underlying feelings. These individuals express nonverbal communication that is the exact opposite of their verbal communication (Satir, Stachowiak, & Taschman, 1990). (See Example C.)

Fourth, the irrelevant mode of communication is defined through the inability to show any relationship to what is taking place. This is a cover-up and derailing style of interaction to avoid having to focus on the issue at hand. It serves to stall and postpone movement within relationships. The physical body is in constant motion, which serves as a deterrent to enabling family members to connect with one another (Satir, Stachowiak, & Taschman, 1990). (See example D.)

Congruent is the fifth and last mode of communication described here. The words spoken relate to reality in all congruent communication. There is clarity between what is being said and what is being felt. Therefore, the highest level of communication has been reached among family members. Both parties, the initiator and the receiver, are clear about the message. The lines of communication are clear, open, and mutually understood (Satir, Stachowiak, & Taschman, 1990). (See example E.)

The five modes of communication discussed above will now be portrayed through the case example of the Culliver family. The Culliver family is a middle-income African American family of five, consisting of Ella, the mother (age 40), Bill, the father (41), Franklin, a son (age 20), Sarah, a daughter (age 16), and Louise, a daughter (age 12).

Placating (Example A)
The Culliver family has always been loyal to church attendance. When issues are raised regarding church attendance, every member of the family agrees, for the Cullivers are a religious family with deep values illustrating that conviction. Although his views are not shared verbally, Bill inwardly is not as deeply committed to religious expression as the other family members. To convey this stance, on one occasion Bill was asked to join the church choir and did so. Although he had strong feelings against membership, he remained silent. Bill's reluctance to be in the choir was manifested by his showing up late for the Christmas cantata at which he was to perform a solo. Thus, the back-up vocalist finally had to take his place, after the concert had to be delayed for thirty minutes.

Blaming (Example B)
When Ella confronted Bill at home about the incident, she discovered how unhappy he had been in the church choir. He blamed her for having added his name to the nominating list for possible choir members. Bill informed Ella that he is the

head of the household; therefore, she had no right to nominate him for choir membership.

Super-reasonable (Example C)
As Franklin overhears the conversation between his mother and father, he walks into the room where they are and says: "I'm going to join Hell's Angels [motorcycle group]." He hesitates but then proceeds slowly to walk out of the room. Without speaking to one another, Bill and Ella, suddenly embrace one another.

Irrelevant (Example D)
Meanwhile, Sarah is playing the piano in the next room with the door open. Her response to her parents' discussion is one of losing focus in her music. Her disciplined rendition of Beethoven's *Fifth Symphony* immediately gives way to a loud, raucous, and erratic version of "Twinkle, Twinkle, Little Star."

Congruent (Example E)
Louise is working on her stamp collection in the den and is proud of her accomplishments in stamp collecting. She has just discovered that she is the owner of a rare nineteenth century-stamp. She dashes into the family room and shares this find with her parents. As she tells her story, in walk Franklin and Sarah; they are listening attentively, and at the conclusion of her story they express how proud they are of her stamp-collecting genius. One by one, they embrace her and continue to give accolades of how they feel about her sleuthing abilities. If one could be a fly on the wall, one would observe communication in which everything is clearly understood, both verbally and nonverbally.

Discussion
In working with families, the primary goal is to move toward establishment of congruent communication patterns among all family members. When this is achieved, family members are able to have a deeper level of trust because what they say is verified through their nonverbal communication (e.g., facial expressions, gestures, posture). What is most difficult for family members is their general lack of awareness of which blocking or incongruent mode of communication they have assumed within the family. Thus, the blocking positions assumed prevent open communication. One role to be played by practitioners is to enable family members to become aware of various incongruent communication patterns, as well as to assist them in developing strategies for clearer communication.

In some families complete congruence is not achievable. However, greater understanding will provide crucial insights for working toward increased congruence within all family communication. A typical intervention strategy is the use of role rehearsal or role-plays. The positive outcome of this strategy is that it enables family members to demonstrate skills in responding differently to each other. The method also includes family members' being able to test out their true feelings in daily communication.

Systems Theory

Systems theory is another framework by which to understand the inner workings of families. It has the capacity to portray the parts and how these separate parts are connected to the whole. Systems have the ability to explain how the parts are able to maintain or destroy themselves in relation to the whole. The family as a system may be analyzed in terms of its own internal functioning as well as how it relates to larger social systems.

The parts within a system are simultaneously independent and interdependent. Understanding the dynamics of independence-interdependence enables practitioners to provide role-modeling to those in need. Stability within the family can best be described as functioning that occurs when individuals are able to provide a supportive network for all members. Therefore, this functioning becomes the glue that holds the parts together. It is this cohesion that lends itself to the use of systems theory as a recognizable tool for the analysis of family functioning. Systems theory lends itself also to readily understanding the existence or lack of supportive networks within the family unit.

First, it seems important to further define the concept of a system. Berger, Federico, and McBreen (1991) have defined a system as simply a whole made of mutually interdependent parts. They elaborate that all parts of a system will be influenced when any change occurs in a given part, and that systems influence each other through the exchange of resources. Similarly, Kirst-Ashman and Hull (1993, p. 4) view a system as a "set of elements which forms an orderly, interrelated, and functional whole."

Basic to understanding this concept of systems are these key terms: *input, output, homeostasis, subsystems,* and *boundary. Input* refers to energy, information, or communication received from other systems, while *output* refers to a like flow that is discharged by a system into the environment. *Homeostasis* is a term that alludes to the affinity of a system to maintain equilibrium or balance (Kirst-Ashman & Hull, 1993).

A major advantage of applying systems to understanding families is the clarity it yields in helping us to see the various groupings or subsystems within families themselves (White & Woollett, 1992). The parents form a dyad that interacts constantly with their children, who will also form identifiable alliances. For example, it is not uncommon for same-sex children who are close in age to support each other's opinions in family matters. Moreover, the two oldest children may be given joint positions of authority in looking after younger siblings when the parents go out for the evening. Still, father/son and mother/daughter groupings are natural in recreational activities and may be also be expected by practitioners in family sessions. *Boundary* is a line of demarcation separating the family from the environment.

Pincus and Minahan (1973) developed a systems model for assessment in social work practice. They identify the practitioner (including his/her agency) as the change agent system. The client system (individual, family, group, or community) comprises the individual or individuals actually requesting help from the change agent system. The client system engages with the practitioner in developing an intervention contract. The target system involves the individual or individuals whom the client and change agent systems decide to target as needing to be changed if intervention goals are to be met. One target may be the client who may need to alter individual perceptions or behaviors. Finally, the action system comprises persons who are engaged on behalf of the client to assist with the achievement of goals.

An example of a systems perspective is provided to clarify how the family operates as a system. This illustration involves the Davis family, a low-income caucasian family of five: John, the father (age 36), Marie, the mother (age 35); two sons, Terry (age 13) and Henry (age 8); and Marie's mother, Minnie Adams. John works night shift (five nights per week, including rotating weekend work) in a local steel mill and Marie works part-time as a dry cleaning attendant on weekday afternoons and all day Saturday. Terry, a seventh grader, has always made straight As and has invariably been on the honor roll. However, Henry, a second grader, has had to struggle with schoolwork. In fact, despite substantial help at home from his mother, he failed second grade and again has Ds and Fs in all the language arts course work.

> John and Marie are at their wit's end. They have had one conference after another with Henry's teacher, but recently have not been able to go in for parent/teacher conferences together, as John has to sleep during the day. Marie always had learning problems herself in school, and secretly blames herself for Henry's having "inherited" her poor learning abilities. She also feels that she should have been at home for Henry, as she had been for Terry at the same age. Nevertheless, the family's

finances have been dwindling over the past few years, since John was laid off from his job at the auto plant. The family is just beginning to get back on its feet financially, although John resents having to work the graveyard shift at the plant. And, to complicate matters further, Marie's mother, Minnie Adams, has moved in with the family, due to her failing health.

John and Marie have been yelling at each other daily, over the slightest matters. Every night, Marie finds herself sitting for hours over the kitchen table, helping Henry with his homework. Still, he cannot remember simple words, gets confused with directions, and reverses some words and letters. And, whatever Marie does at home to help Henry with homework, he inevitably leaves his spelling book at home and fails every exam. His teacher, Mrs. Burton, has said that without a doubt Henry is at the bottom of his class, and she does not know where to go next with him. Sometimes, Henry puts his head down on his desk and cries at school.

Meanwhile, at home the tension is forever mounting, as John is beginning to feel neglected by his wife. He has accused her of spending more time with Henry, stewing over his homework, when she could be ironing his clothes for work or packing his lunchbox. He has had to assume these duties at home in order to keep the family functioning. Terry is also contributing to Henry's bad grades and poor performance by calling him "lamebrain." Last night, Henry retaliated by throwing a softball at Terry that inadvertently struck and cracked Marie's antique mirror that her mother gave her. She became furious and yelled at the boys before going to her bedroom in tears. She feels alone in her struggle to help Henry and, at times, even blames him for "messing up" the family. Afterward, she feels guilty, because she remembers how hard it was for her in elementary school. Moreover, she is beginning to feel the added pressure of caring for her mother.

Discussion
To further explain the use of systems concepts through the Davis family case study, one must consider those outside events that influence the inner workings of the family. The parents' communication with the school has consistently been limited, that is, there have not been ongoing conferences between parents and teachers in an effort to maintain balance between the parents and Henry's teachers. So, in an effort to

maintain balance (homeostasis), the Davis family attempted to arrange a conference on behalf of the family. However, John seems to have created a "balanced" state for himself by sleeping most of the day. This is done largely in response to his nighttime work schedule, but it also serves as a vehicle to quietness. When he is sleeping, he does not have to generate energy to address family issues.

To reiterate, *boundary* in this context represents the limits placed upon the family by family members and outside forces (e.g., work schedules and school conferences). Finally, *output* refers to those things that the Davis family gives back to the community. At this time, the family continues to maintain relative self-sufficiency and independence. John endures a difficult work schedule, Marie has taken on the added responsibility of caring for her frail mother, and the children attend school regularly.

SUMMARY

This first chapter is designed to help the reader reflect on the evolution of the family yesterday and today. In reviewing the trends involved in this evolutionary process, the authors have traced the family structure from nuclear to extended, back to nuclear, and then back to extended. There is a distinct, circular pattern within the evolution of the American family.

Besides evolutionary patterns, the theoretical frameworks selected, communication and systems theory, serve as the conceptual guides to understanding the nature and dynamics of families. The case examples illustrating these principles are based on real-life situations most likely to be encountered by beginning social work professionals and other practitioners. In addition, these case examples, among others, will be used in later chapters to further aid the reader in understanding the nature of practice with families.

QUESTIONS FOR DISCUSSION

1. Trace the evolution of your own family, using the concepts *nuclear* and *extended.*

2. Describe Satir's five modes of communication and apply them to your own family or one with which you are familiar.

3. What adaptations will be necessary to accommodate the issues that you identify within the Davis family system?

GROUP EXERCISE

Arrange the class in groups of three to four students. Have each group discuss the differences in family life of yesterday and today. Ask the students to think about how families arranged themselves as units of support and managed to meet their needs. Students should describe families as they existed one hundred years ago, seventy-five years ago, fifty years ago, twenty-five years ago, ten years ago and five years ago. Given the range of opportunity in describing family life, how will the family of the future manifest itself? Each group should describe environmental conditions and the impact of these issues influencing family structure and coping. Each group might discuss an era or take one of the six. Each group should describe the family of the future. Encourage students to be vivid in describing families and the means utilized in maintaining equilibrium.

SIGNIFICANT TERMS

family	congruent
nuclear family	system
extended family	subsystem
communication	input
placating	homeostasis
blaming	boundary
super-reasonable	output
irrelevant	

REFERENCES

Anderson, R. E. & Carter, I. (1990). *Human behavior in the social environment: A social systems approach*, 4th ed. New York: Aldine de Gruyter.
Berger, R. L., Federico, R. C., & McBreen, J. T. (1991). *Human behavior: A perspective for the helping professions*,. 3rd ed. New York: Longman.
Brigham, J. C. (1991). *Social psychology*, 2nd ed. New York: HarperCollins.
Garbarino, J. (1992). *Children and families in the social environment*, 2nd ed. Hawthorne, New York: Aldine de Gruyter.
Kilpatrick, A. C. & Holland, T. P. (1995). *Working with families*. Boston: Allyn & Bacon.
Kirst-Ashman, K. K. & Hull, G. H. (1993). *Understanding generalist practice*. Chicago: Nelson-Hall.
Maslow, A. H. (1968). *Toward a psychology of being*, 2nd ed. Princeton, N. J.: Van Nostrand.

Parsons, R. J., Jorgensen, J. D., & Hernandez, S. H. (1994). *The integration of social work practice*. Pacific Grove, Calif.: Brooks/Cole.

Pincus, A. & Minahan, A. (1973). *Social work practice: Model and method*. Itasca, Ill.: F. E. Peacock.

Reiss, I. (1980). *Family systems in America*. 3rd ed. New York: Holt, Rinehart, and Winston.

Satir, V., Stachowiak J., & Taschman, H. A. (1990). *Helping families to change*. New York, N.Y.: Jason Aaronson.

Skill, T. & Robinson, J. D. (1994). Four decades of families on television: A demographic profile, 1950–1989. *Journal of Broadcasting & Electronic Media*, 38(4), 449–464.

U.S. Department of Commerce, Along with Economic and Statistics Information, Bureau of the Census (1990). In *General Population Characteristics of Ohio*.

White, D. & Woollett, A. (1992). *Families: A context for development*. London: The Falmer Press.

Zastrow, C. (1992). *The practice of social work.*, 4th ed. Belmont, Calif.: Wadsworth.

▶ 2

Perspectives and Assumptions of Families

In thinking about families it is important to understand various perspectives and assumptions within families. To provide understanding of these assumptions, this chapter is designed to give the reader an overview of major perspectives and assumptions. Three categories—diversity in communication, differences in power, and strengths of relationships—will be explored.

DIVERSITY IN COMMUNICATION

Assumption I. Communication is top-down in families.

This assumption is based on the historical organization of families in American society. Traditionally, the person at the top is considered to be the starting point for all communication to occur within the family. This is undeniably a myth, because families in which communication starts from the bottom up or from a partnership stance appear to exist in just as great a number. As families are examined today, much more diversity is found in family communication patterns. However, the myth of top-downward communication is strong, due to the predominance of societal norms. That is, the average individual perceives communication to take place along a vertical line, with few exceptions. The power of societal norms greatly influences the top-downward mode so that throughout social institutions—for instance corporations, courts, schools, churches—one may find this intrinsic form of communication.

In families where the father is the controlling force, communication is defined through his position. The mother generally takes her cues from the father, and the children often take their cues from the mother. This is the traditional model of family structure utilizing the top-downward style of communication. In today's world one may generally find communication to occur more along the lines of a partnership format. That is, the responsibility for communication is shared by the mother, father, and the children, which points to the abolition of the top-downward communication style within families.

> Example
> In the Culliver family the father, Bill, was incensed because his wife, Ella, had submitted his name to be a member of the church choir. He had not been given the opportunity to decide whether he wanted to make such a commitment. The Culliver family is a traditional family wherein communication is top-downward. Bill felt it should have been his decision, and his alone, to take the necessary steps toward joining the choir, had he been interested in the first place. In this example, however, communication around choir membership began with Ella, not Bill, which indicates he was not allowed to assume his usual role of initiating the communication.

Assumption II. Being related by blood automatically provides understanding of family communication.

Being related by blood is considered to be a spontaneous connector for family communication. In most instances, bloodline is the legal boundary for determining the direct channel for communication in families. Closely related to this concept of communication being automatic is the belief that blood paves the way for direct linkages in communication. The truth, however, which dispels this myth, is the reality that family members are often unable to communicate about even the simplest matters. As ascertained by Satir, Stachowiak, & Taschman (1990), inadequate communication is a primary contributor to family conflict. Therefore, the myth is further disproved through systematic research and evaluation of families. In biological families it is considered that members' strongest connections are their blood ties. These families are thought to always have clear and open communication. In actuality, these families will often become distraught, overwhelmed, and conflicted because of their lack of communication. There seems to be a prevalent belief that blood ties alone create an openness among all family members. Merely having the same blood is thought to enhance communication in a special way. Nevertheless, this myth is dispelled by the realization that family members related by blood will often have as many or even more serious conflicts in daily communication as any other family members.

> Example
> In the Davis family case scenario, Terry calls his younger brother "lamebrain" because he is slower at learning. It is assumed that being related by blood eliminates name calling through the members' understanding of the specific nature of problems within the family. Even in those families where name-calling occurs, it is often done in an innocuous or joking manner. Although Terry and Henry are brothers, Terry is still unable to comprehend and show sensitivity toward Henry's school problems.

Assumption III. Communication creates understanding among family members.

Many believe that communication creates openness among individual family members. Communication in essence establishes exchanges between individuals but does not always guarantee understanding. The ordinary expression of words does not necessarily provide emotional insight. To clarify, words in and of themselves do not provide the clarity and frankness desired by all family members. The myth of confusing understanding with communication is diluted when individuals gain insight into the technical qualities of these two concepts. That is, communication does not always create understanding, and conversely, understanding does not always create clear communication. Moreover, communication may be verbal or nonverbal, which also addresses the myth. Nonverbal communication might generate understanding, but understanding might then be confused through verbal communication. Therefore, in working with families, one needs to be aware that blind spots can occur when family members equate communication with understanding of one another's concerns or problems. In working with families one needs to be clear that various steps ought to be taken to ensure good, open communication.

> Example
> In the Culliver family Franklin overheard an argument between his parents, Ella and Bill. Even though Franklin has

been able to communicate in the past with his parents, on this occasion he makes an outrageous statement: "I'm going to join the Hell's Angels." Franklin has previously been able to express his feelings to his mother and father, but in this stressful event he cannot do so. Thus, the above assumption is nullified, for at the moment there is no indication that Franklin has any capacity to comprehend his parents' predicament.

Assumption IV. Communication is in the eye of the beholder.

In working with families, practitioners must recognize that there is invariably an initiator and a receiver in all communication. Therefore, the myth that communication is in the eye of the beholder is quickly refuted. The aforementioned assumption speaks to a one-dimensional or unilateral pattern of communication. By definition, communication is always two-way. It is particularly problematic in today's diverse society to work with families using a one-dimensional perspective. A major way to combat this unilateral pattern is to encourage strategies whereby one develops approaches to understand the inherent two-way phenomenon of all communication.

Example
In the Davis family, Henry accidentally broke his mother's antique mirror when he threw a softball at his older brother, Terry. The mother, Marie, became furious and yelled at both boys as she rushed to her bedroom in tears. Therefore, this event represents one-way communication. Marie quickly leaves the room without giving the boys an opportunity to respond to her verbal outburst regarding their behavior. Regardless of Marie's feelings, her sons were left to assume that she was angry only at their behavior. However, due to her mother's Alzheimer's disease, Marie may have associated their breaking of the mirror with the potential loss of her mother, as her mother had entrusted her with this treasured antique.

DIFFERENCES IN POWER STRUCTURE

Assumption V. The male is at the top of the hierarchy.

In the socialization process, the male has been the traditional individual to be placed in the top position within a family. That is, the male is the person or the agreed upon individual to lead and direct the family. Throughout the socialization process, individuals are taught to accept the male as the person in authority positions. In the childrearing process, the male child is traditionally given responsibilities to represent the decision-making function among the sibling group. This myth has been perpetuated by both males and females. To perpetuate this myth human service providers have generally referred to the male as being at the top of family structure. Moreover, in the literature there are examples of human service providers' enabling the male to maintain this role in all family contexts (Toman, 1976; Hesse-Biber & Williamson, 1984). Even in therapeutic methods (Haley, 1976), the male has been placed in the role of the primary spokesperson. Techniques utilized sometimes dictate a structure directing the helping person to address the male first, based on his hierarchical position.

On the contrary, reality demonstrates that women share being at the top of the family hierarchy. With the onset of the women's liberation movement the myth declined even more (Friedan, 1974). Women are able to take on the responsibilities delegated to men. The sharing of the hierarchy is acceptable in the childrearing effort. As children are being reared, they learn from the socialization process that either gender may assume a power position. Therefore, as we position ourselves to enter the twenty-first century we will further observe and participate in reordering the role of gender in relation to the hierarchical position in families. In the coming generations, the articulation that "the male is at the top of the hierarchy" will continue to dissipate and perhaps totally vanish.

Example

In the Davis family, John, the husband, perceives his position as being at the top of the hierarchy. His questioning as to why his lunch was not prepared and his clothes not ironed are prime examples of male dominance and an attitude of superiority. As John perceives himself at the top of the family's power structure, he has little patience for those family activities that might preclude his needs from being met. After all, if one is in control, he/she should be able to get their requests answered first.

When his wife, Marie, takes on the responsibility for helping her son with his homework, it is interpreted as a violation of the perceived structure of the family. Again, even though Marie works also, John feels that it is her responsibility to respond first to his needs, wishes, and desires.

Assumption VI. One person or family member will always assume control.

In family structures someone will assume control; this is inevitable. As families arrange their unique ways of being, someone emerges as the leader. Leadership is not necessarily based on gender, but the individual is given permission or assumes the leadership position in a family. These dynamics, of course, happen in all groups.

> Example
> In the Culliver family the mother, Ella, volunteered her husband, Bill, to be a member of the church choir. In making this decision she assumed control over the family's participation in choir. Ella acted on behalf of all family members without getting permission. Through this action Ella displayed absolute control. She responded based upon her assumption that she had the authority and right to make this decision.

Assumption VII. Birth order of offspring determines roles and responsibilities.

In families it is perceived that the oldest child takes the position of authority with his or her siblings. Through the socialization process parents often defer to the oldest sibling to take care of the others. These roles and responsibilities are given when parents are present in the home, as well as when they are away. In most families the position of the oldest child, especially a male, is seldom questioned. In two-parent families the oldest female sibling is often given the nurturing, supportive role. Largely due to gender stereotyping, this role is often not given to a male child. Moreover, the middle child is too frequently viewed as being in a precarious position, simply due to birth order (Ernst, 1983). This view of the unbalanced nature of the middle child is based simply on his/her not being the oldest, nor the youngest.

Throughout the literature there are examples referring to the middle child's not being given the responsibilities of the oldest nor the special treatment shown to the youngest child or the "baby." There are studies that suggest children born first excel academically and possess greater leadership skills. These studies indicate that later-born children excel in popularity and social acceptance (Steelman & Power, 1985; Lamb & Sutton-Smith, 1982). These studies support the thrust given to middle-born or later-born children that firstborns possess academic and leadership skills. But, middle children are treated in a manner wherein they are able to practice social interactions skills and are not given the burden of leadership responsibilities. This unsteady position creates within the middle child a sense of not belonging or feeling unique, due to the clear roles assigned to the eldest and the youngest. The youngest child is given special privileges by each family member. In most families, the youngest is heavily protected and sheltered, primarily due to birth order alone.

In families today, the socialization process has been refocused to consider not so much birth order but the sibling most able to take on the roles and responsibilities as caregiver. The relaxing of this stereotypical view has made the caregiving role less gender-oriented. Consequently, the refocused nature of birth order enables agency practitioners to be more inclusive in selecting and maintaining participants in intervention. Due to the rapid, changing characteristics of modern families, such as step and blended, encouraging siblings to adjust to diverse roles and responsibilities is seen as being more normative than stereotypical.

Example
Due to birth order in the Davis family, Terry, the oldest son, is given the responsibility to care for his younger brother, who has learning problems at school. This caregiving role is expected of Terry by the parents because of his being the older child. Moreover, since Terry has consistently done so well in school, the parents may have minimized their contacts with the school. This seeming preferential treatment might also be perceived as being related to birth order.

Assumption VIII. Structure determines family strength.

In American society strengths of families are often determined by structure. Structure in the American family network includes father-dominated, mother-dominated, extended family–dominated, single parent–dominated, and alliance-dominated patterns. The norm in American society is for the father to be at the head of the family. Therefore, those families where the father is absent are often determined to have a weakened structure. Throughout the literature there are examples of structure as the basic determinant of family strength or weakness. For example, Bogulub (1989) acknowledges the literature's movement toward postdivorce families being able to create safe and supportive environments for children. In addition, through the extended network grandparents often assist in providing backing to families such as babysitting, financial assistance, advice, and emotional support. As modern trends are born, there is a shift away from the view that structure is the primary determinant of family functioning to the attitude that the structure of the family determines the level of interaction

(Vosler, Green, & Kolevzon, 1987). Structure is reinforced in the couple's defining the manner in which focus and commitment are given to the family that they are establishing. This process distinguishes them from their families of origin (Lewis, 1986).

If strengths were defined only by structure, then the existence of varied family structures in today's world would refute this assumption. In reality, structure in and of itself does not determine strength in families (Richards & Schmiege, 1993; Hanson, 1986). What determines strength in families is based on the strengths and the potential of individual participants. The gifts and talents of each family member provide the guiding force for the level of functioning within a family. The responsibilities implemented by family members speak to the strength of families.

Example
In the Culliver family the shared leadership of the parents, Ella and Bill, creates a high level of respect. The respect between them enables the fabric of the family to be strengthened. The mere fact that Ella was able to sign Bill up as a choir member, as well as get him to attend rehearsals, leads one to believe that there is a strong family foundation. Strength is shown through the couple's ability to support each other even when there is disagreement within the context of a family decision.

STRENGTHS OF RELATIONSHIPS

Assumption IX. When there is clarity in communication, family members have closer relationships.

Clarity in communication provides the opportunity for family members to have clearer exchanges of energy. Therefore, in those families in which members work toward sending clear messages to each other, a framework is provided for the possibility of close relationships. Relationships are established whereby individuals create exchanges that are not only clear but also have an emotional dimension. Trust is another essential element that is present where closeness is developed. Family members who are able to transmit clear messages display an emotional dimension, and if they consistently demonstrate trust there is a greater possibility that a close relationship will exist. Consequently, the myth remains if we define clarity in communication as the *only* criterion for the development of close relationships. This is not only true for family members but also for people in general. Therefore, clarity in reality does not guarantee closer family ties.

Example
In the Culliver family during a family argument between the parents, the children are able to provide words for support of the youngest child, Louise. At the time of an argument, there is usually a lack of clarity in communication. Therefore, within a confused environment closeness remains intact among all family members. This example further dismisses the myth of clarity in communication as being necessary for close relationships.

Assumption X. Being physically present in the family means that one has an integral role.

Whether or not one is physically present in the home or lives in a far-away place does not ensure a central role within family functioning. Due to technology and mobility families are as close or as far apart as they participate in the modern world. To illustrate, one might live in Australia and still E-mail instructions to Cleveland each morning regarding a family member's medication. However, a family member might live on Cleveland's West Side and never contact close family members living twelve miles away in East Cleveland. The above myth is thus refuted, because distance clearly does not establish the level of involvement of family members. Rather, how involved one is with his/her family is based upon a commitment to the ongoing care for and maintenance of the family.

Example
The Davis family is an example of an extended family system. In such families the extended family member has the opportunity to become an integral member. Whether this occurs depends upon the specific family organization and interactional dynamics. In the Davis family, Minnie, the grandmother, does play important roles within the context of family life. However, being physically present does not guarantee that an integral or central role will be provided for every family member. Despite Minnie's failing health the family has centered its energies on the special needs of Henry, who is learning delayed. Therefore, Minnie's role is not as central as it might be at another time. Due to Minnie's Alzheimer's dis-

ease, she is unable to assume a central role. Furthermore, family members are unable to support Minnie in a primary role, as they are surrounded by problems and issues relating to Henry.

Assumption XI. Family members have the same shared values over time.

As families address the issues of daily living, they establish a pattern of values and beliefs. In building their identity they share a set of common values that are similar if not identical for each family member. These values serve as an anchor for family living. But as individuals within the family develop other social relationships within the outside world and/or through the educational process, their values are often modified. As persons adapt to environmental influences, shifts occur from the basic family value orientation toward a more individualistic expression. Therefore, the myth of family members' having the same shared values over time is an incorrect assumption. In reality, family members develop identities reflected by the myriad of societal customs, traditions, and mores to which they are exposed. Another important variable to be considered is the chronological age and/or developmental transitions being faced by each family member.

Example
In the Davis family the oldest son, Terry, is insensitive to Henry's (his younger brother) learning difficulties. Name-calling may be a response to Terry's feelings regarding Henry's learning difficulties. In addition, the response from family members toward Henry may represent to Terry a feeling of being left out. Terry may feel as if his role within the family has been totally overlooked and that Henry is receiving favoritism from the mother. Neither the father nor the mother seems to understand Terry's view of the situation, and consequently they have begun to continually blame him for not being willing to help his brother with his homework, since he, after all, is "so intelligent." One would suspect that as Terry matures he will look at his brother differently and may become a protector rather than a perpetrator regarding Henry's problems. Being an early adolescent, Terry is dealing with identity formation and is therefore unable to fully appreciate issues confronting his school-aged brother. We can expect that as Terry moves further toward late adolescence and young adulthood, he will develop additional understanding of, and show more empathy for, Henry's learning prob-

lems. Therefore, Terry might show signs of supportive acceptance of his brother's learning challenges.

Assumption XII. One family member can be hurting or have a problem without other family members' being impacted.

Another myth is that family members can somehow experience pain and other concrete problems without influencing other family members. This assumption has little credence in the context of family relationships. When physically present in a family, the behaviors, feelings, and thoughts of members will inevitably affect everyone within the living environment. Therefore, it is an impossibility for individuals to conceal these expressions from others. The family represents a safe haven for displaying the range of emotions operating in a person's life. Through the socialization process, the drive for independence and individualism overrides the necessity to include others in sharing difficulties being experienced. When a family member is unable to share difficulties, messages are given to other family members. These messages tend to display the true feelings of the individual, however negative or positive, and they will inevitably impact other family members and significant others.

Example
In the Culliver family Bill, the husband, is unable to talk with his wife, Ella, about his wish not to sing in the church choir. Instead, he acts as if he enjoys singing with the church choir. He attends rehearsals and even commits himself to a solo performance. But, on the day of the performance he does not appear on time. This behavior is the first indication to Ella that Bill does not wish to be a choir member. It is during this exchange that she is observed to be hostile toward him. Therefore, the above assumption about families is disclaimed, as Ella is vividly hurt when she learns of Bill's dissatisfaction with singing in the choir. All family members need to remember that when one individual is hurting others will experience discomfort and react accordingly.

SUMMARY

There are three major categories describing assumptions of families. These classifications include communication, differences in power, and strengths of family relationships. The major myths within these assumptions have been addressed and refuted. The realities dispelling these assumptions provide a foundation for understanding the functioning of families. Given the understanding of how families operate, one may be able to plan strategies for enhancing the overall well-being of families. Furthermore, individuals will be able to interpret and design strategies and interventions for families based around the manner in which they arrange their state of being.

Society has always developed rules for family structure and functioning, but one must realize that families have their own internal rules or norms that will describe the roles that various family members will play. Through identified roles, relationships emerge from the outset of family living. Given rules, roles, and relationships, another variable essential to understanding family dynamics is family rituals. Rituals may be defined as those habitual patterns of interaction within the family; these actions may be conscious or unconscious.

In next chapter the Four-R Model of Family Dynamics (based on rules, roles, relationships, and rituals) will be presented and described in detail. This model is designed by the authors to especially help practitioners to better understand family dynamics and functioning, and thus be able to plan effective family interventions.

QUESTIONS FOR DISCUSSION

1. Why do myths of families exist in our society?

2. How have modern societal and cultural trends affected family structure and family dynamics?

3. Describe your own personal experiences with family myths.

GROUP EXERCISE

Arrange students in groups of three to four. Assign each group one of the myths about families. Have students discuss ways in which the myth might exist in their own families. Each group should recommend ways of eliminating the myth assigned. That is, the students should discuss how families may be able to dispel myths about themselves, and they should also consider how they as practitioners may contribute to eliminate societal myths and sterotypes about families.

Have students report back to the class and present a definition of a myth, followed by examples of myths from their own families, and concrete ways of dispelling myths. Encourage creativity in presentations to class. For example, some groups may choose to role-play their responses, debate, use another medium such as a play.

SIGNIFICANT TERMS

diversity	leadership
myth	structure
socialization	alliance
power	rule
hierarchy	role
sibling	relationship
assumption	ritual
control	

REFERENCES

Bogulub, E. (1989). Families of divorce: A three generational perspective. *Social Work*, 34(4), 375–76.

Ernst, C. (1983). *Birth order: Its influence on personality.* New York: Springer, Verlag.

Freeman, D. S. (1976). The family as a system: Fact or fantasy? *Comprehensive Psychiatry*, 17(6), 735–746.

Friedan, Betty (1974). *The feminine mystique*, 10th anniversary ed. New York: Norton.

Haley, J. (1976). *Problem-solving therapy.* San Francisco: Jossey-Bass.

Hanson, S. M. H. (1986). Healthy single parent families. *Family Relations*, 35(1), 125–132.

Hesse-Biber, S. & Williamson, J. (1984). Resource theory and power in families. Life cycle considerations. *Family Process*, 23(1), 261–278.

Lamb, M. E. & Sutton-Smith, B. (Eds.) (1982). *Sibling relationships* (pp. 153–165). Hillsdale, N. J.: Lawrence Erlbaum.

Lewis, J. M. (1986). Family structure and stress. *Family Process*, 25(2), 235–247.

Richards, L. N. & Schmiege, C. J. (1993). Problems and strengths of single-parent families. *Family Relations*, 42(3), 277–285.

Satir, V., Stachowiak, J., & Taschman, H. (1990). *Helping families to change.* Northvale, N. J.: Jason Aronson.

Steelman, L. C. & Powell, B. (1985). The social and academic consequences of birth order: Real, artificial, or both? *Journal of Marriage and the Family*, 47(1), 117–124.

Toman, W. (1976). *Family constellation: Its effects on personality and social behavior*, 3rd ed. New York: Springer.

Vosler, N. R., Green, R. G., & Kolevzon, M. S. (1987). The structure and competence of family units: Implications for social work practice with families and children. *Journal of Social Service Research*, 9(2/3), 1–16.

▶ 3

Understanding Families: The Four-R Model of Family Dynamics

The Four-R Model includes four dimensions: rules, roles, relationships, and rituals. In describing family dynamics, each of these major components is present within all families. Families arrange themselves to display one of these four dimensions as the predominant characteristic or guiding force for meeting the responsibilities of family living. Included in these major responsibilities are caretaking and nurturing. Families will implement these significant functions through operating from one of the four areas within the model. The uniqueness of families will determine which dimension will dominate or prevail within a specific family system. Furthermore, the uniqueness will be determined by the participants within a given family. These participants will also bring social experiences to the family that will help to shape their ways of being. In addition, their distinctiveness will determine what they can become as a family. Therefore, the Four-R Model enables families to describe who they are and helps them to be goal-oriented by assisting practitioners to capture the dominant orientation and then assist them with strategies to achieve the highest level of family well-being.

In reflecting on the major responsibilities of family members, one must realize that caretaking and nurturing are major facets. Caretaking can be defined as those supports that provide security and basic needs of

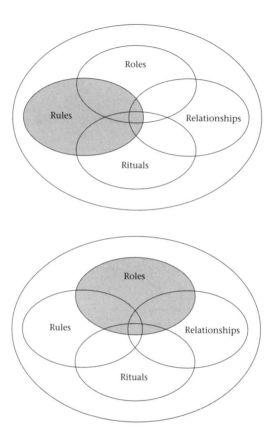

FIGURE 3.1   Four-R Model of Family Dynamics

individual family members. On the other hand, nurturing includes the emotional support for all family members. This emotional support is a requirement for growth and development, especially the fostering of self-esteem. Family members thus provide the protective environment empowering individual members to maintain a sense of well-being. It is this environmental protection that determines the degree to which one's self-esteem may be developing. Likewise, family members create the opportunity for them to experience security. This experiencing of security creates the foundation for collective self-development. Consequently, one must consider the importance of security for the development of one's well-being.

As family members arrange themselves in unique patterns relating to

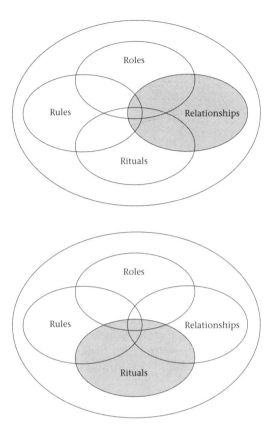

FIGURE 3.2   Four-R Model of Family Dynamics

rules, roles, relationships, and rituals, their socialization to the external environment is also being developed. Therefore, there is a reciprocal response to the unique manner in which families govern themselves. Individuals learn to respond or react to their environment based on the socialization style of their family orientation. This means that a family member's connection to the outside world will be influenced by the specific prevailing style of family living. The prevailing style of family living is uniquely important for family members' insight into understanding their dominant family pattern and its influence over their lives. The depth and breadth of understanding one's social world creates the opportunity to bridge the distance between one's own family and the external environment. Consequently, upon acquiring insight into the specific guiding force within their family, individual members may become better prepared for the processes involved in carrying out their responsibilities. In addition, this guiding force will determine the level of understanding of each individual family member in simply living his/her life.

RULES

All families, of course, have rules, but in some families rules will be the dominant force for family functioning. Jantzen and Harris (1986) stated that family rules might be described as relationship agreements impacting the manner in which the family functions. Brown (1990) indicated that adolescents in families with well-defined rules participated more in family decision making.

Rule development in families may be generally grouped into three types: rules developed to ensure maximal family functioning in a single-parenting structure and/or during a parent's absence; rules developed for overall daily governance and overseeing; and rules developed in response to societal demands/pressures. In general, rules are related to how family members grant permission. Rules also relate to how family members should behave. Rules create boundaries for living and environmental functioning.

In all those families where fewer members exist, oftentimes a greater number of rules will be established. For example, in a single-parent family the need might exist for a greater number of rules, due to the necessity for a clearer governance structure. However, this is not meant to imply that family structure is the only determinant in setting the guiding force within a family. If one adult person has the responsibility for governing a family, there is a greater need for assistance in determining parameters. This is not meant to stereotype the single-parent family but simply addresses the likely need for further assistance when one is given the responsibility as the sole head of household. Moreover, to understand the responsibilities of a single parent, it is helpful to know that rules might be explicit or implicit (Kirst-Ashman & Hull, 1993).

Rules are established to create the governance or overseeing structure of the family. For example, there are rules that grant permission to children regarding curfew; rules establishing a specific time for meals; rules granting permission for bedtime. Another major reason for rules is that of supportive nurturing. These attributes enable families dominated by rules to receive constructive support toward self-advancement and optimal family development. Among these attributes are creative climate, supportive embracing, and dynamic encouragement toward goal achievement. These attributes are present in those families in which readiness for involvement is important. Therefore, rules can easily be utilized as the guiding force within some families. This would indicate that rules may be used as a positive force for the well-being of families. However, rules may have a negative or detrimental impact on family life essentially managed by rules. The negative impact will most likely arise from rules that are too strict or too permissive.

Furthermore, rules exist in families in response to societal demands. The environmental domain contributes to the shaping of rules necessary for a family's response to external conditions. These rules further create parameters by which family members protect themselves from the onslaught of avalanche political decisions. The avalanche effect forces families to respond quickly by developing rules without the benefit of self-evaluation. For example, when public school lunches are discontinued, family members may no longer be able to provide for the once-a-month family outing. Instead, every penny may have to be utilized to meet basic family needs.

Illustration of a Rules-Dominated Family

Case Study C—The Thomas Family
Beverly Thomas is a 35 year old caucasian, divorced parent with three children. The children are: Samantha (15); Lewis Jr. (12); and Richie (4). Beverly is a diabetic and works as a secretary for a utility company. She has developed strict rules regarding diet, family time together, and discipline. She expects the entire family to maintain a diet consistent with her own diabetic regimen. The enforcement of this strict diabetic diet has led to problems with the children, especially with Samantha. Consequently, because of this special diet, which includes frequent, small meals, Samantha sees herself as obese. On the contrary, she is actually approaching being anorectic. Moreover, her low self-esteem has led her to countless sexual interactions aimed at helping her to feel wanted and accepted by her peer group. Through this experimentation, Samantha has already contracted a sexually transmitted disease (STD). These behaviors have emerged from Samantha's response to family rules.

On the other hand, Lewis Jr. is an obedient, bright child. His response to strict discipline has been to overachieve. He believes that by his maintaining an A average in school, his mother will relax the rules. Lewis Jr. has shared with his peers that he wants to become a physician, an endocrinologist, so that he will be able to treat his mother's diabetes and other people with problems like hers.

Richie, the youngest child, has experienced the greatest difficulty with his mother's divorce. He simply does not understand why his parents are not still together. However, he has managed to grow and develop as he should. But a complicating factor is his partial blindness. Despite this disability and his sadness over the divorce, Richie is an energetic, inquisitive four-year-old.

Beverly, the mother, is insecure regarding her chronic diabetes. The elaborate rules established are designed to insulate the entire family from the environmental factors impacting upon them. She is fearful of losing her income as a result of her ongoing struggle to keep her insulin level within a healthy range. This worry over her diabetes is directly related to the possibility that her current employer may decrease her health care benefits. In that event, she does not perceive a way to stretch her budget any further. Beverly is also aware that public support for specialized preschool may not be available next year for Richie. She has established additional rules in a desperate effort to cope with current stressors, as well as impending problems that might jeopardize the family's security.

ROLES

Families dominated by roles are likely to be characterized by regimentation, gender orientation (male/female), specific expectations, and a division of labor. Roles have been referred to as concerning both the status differential and the behavioral expectations that family members have for each other (Kirst-Ashman & Hull, 1993). Classic research on role orientation within nuclear families identified family roles as fitting into two categories, instrumental and expressive (Parsons & Bales, 1955). Men were identified with instrumental roles, that is, roles that focused on goal accomplishment, whereas women were identified with expressive roles, or roles related to raising group morale and maintaining positive feelings. Nonetheless, researchers contested this theory with strong contentions that men and women assume these roles interchangeably, depending on the needs of the family (Slater, 1961; Udry, 1974; Bernard, 1981). Family roles might include parenting or contributing to the family's performance of maintenance tasks. Moreover, roles may be more informal and originate from individual personalities or interactional patterns (Kirst-Ashman & Hull, 1993). In a study of parents with both biological and stepchildren, Voydanoff et al. (1994) noted that family organization (i.e., delineation of work and family roles) and family structure are independently related to the quality of family living.

Families in which roles reflect regimentation tend to be characterized by structure, deliberate actions, extreme consistency, unvarying patterns, and uniform construction. Within these characteristics are examples of families' implementing prescribed roles. These roles are agreed upon by individual family members. Regimentation creates the parameters within which family members operate. Parameters represent the invisible boundaries for carrying out assigned roles. Family members tend not to question assigned roles, as the invisible safety net provided by this structure has already been defined and accepted by each family member.

The second characteristic is gender orientation. Whether a family is headed by a male or a female, roles are established toward the identified head of household. The person in charge determines roles given to each family member. Gender is an issue, as prescribed roles are those that are determined by the gender within a given family. That is not to stereotype families by gender but a way of describing assigned roles within families. Therefore, society has already established roles for each gender in the culture wherein a given family may reside.

However, in recent years roles have become more inclusive. Women have become much more autonomous, both psychologically and economically. Female and male role socialization is becoming more relaxed and less traditional, especially among the middle class (Kravetz, 1995). This inclusiveness creates diverse participation by both males and females in a range of family roles. Diversity enables gender to play a lesser role in determining what will be carried out by individuals. In addition, gender orientation creates clarity regarding what roles may be carried out by various members. Clarity stems from a cultural interpretation of gender-delivered roles.

Gender-delivered roles are those roles that societal members have sanctioned. For example, it is readily agreed upon that females are naturally nurturing individuals. This does not mean that males cannot be nurturers. It speaks to a sanctioned role assigned to women through cultural socialization and conditioning. Likewise men are conditioned to be the breadwinners of their families. Again, this does not mean that females cannot be breadwinners. Rather, these gender-delivered roles are roles sanctioned by society to be carried out by either males or females. The reader might deduce that these two examples on the surface represent gender stereotypes. But one must look beyond the mere surface to a broader interpretation to comprehend the true meaning of the sanctioned roles of society that continually influence and guide human behavior, including behavior in families.

The third characteristic is that of specific expectations within families. These expectations reflect the uniqueness of all families and individual family members. Therefore, specific expectations define for family members their precise responsibilities. These interpretations will of course dominate the exact nature of assigned roles. This concept might be illustrated by a child within the family being given the responsibility to put the garbage out on the curb on garbage pickup day. It is expected that the child will carry out this responsibility without having to be reminded. The task is an implicit expectation shared and respected by all members of the family. Specific expectations are agreed upon and accepted by all family members. Therefore, the agreed upon roles are carried out as a reflection of shared purpose and family unity.

The fourth and final characteristic of roles is the division of labor. Division of labor is the attempt to share the roles and responsibilities within the context of the family. The sharing nature of distribution provides clarity of what is expected from individual family members. This clarity creates security within the distribution wherein members can remain focused on their assigned roles. Remaining focused provides support for enabling family members to be productive in completing designated roles. This division of labor serves as the glue that binds the family together and instills a sense of wholeness. The importance of togetherness contributes to the well-being of the family through the use of roles defining the division of labor. Therefore, each role contributes to a major function that leads to the entire working system of family living.

Illustration of a Roles-Dominated Family

Case Study D—The Romano Family

Victor, the father (age 58), was laid off from his job due to downsizing in his oil company where he had served as vice president for the last twelve years. In modeling an extremely regimented style, Victor insisted that all subordinates under his division have a specific time and manner in which to make their monthly reports. Now being unemployed, he has assumed this regimented role within the home. Julia, the mother (age 54), works in the home and babysits for her four-year-old grandson, Mario Jr. Julia had already established a pattern for Mario Jr.'s daily routine. This routine, however, has been interrupted with Victor's being home during the day. Victor is attempting to create another routine for little Mario, based on his own regimented model. He believes that all children should be on a rigid time schedule. He believes that Julia allows Mario Jr. to eat his lunch when he feels like it. Consequently, Victor is strongly suggesting that a four-year-old should have lunch at noon whether he is hungry or not. Julia has explained to Victor that the pediatrician has recommended that Mario Jr. not be forced to eat if he is not hungry. Furthermore, the pediatrician has cautioned Mario Sr. that feeding children when they are not hungry may lead to obesity. Julia is caught between the wishes of her son and her husband. Victor is attempting to take on Julia's role as caretaker for her grandson as a way of responding to his displacement from his primary role as breadwinner for the family.

Being laid off from work has enabled Victor to take a stronger position in dictating what roles should be carried out by Julia. Throughout the marriage she has assumed the nurturing role for all four of their children. Julia was taught by her mother to behave in a specific manner based on simply being female. It is important to remember that Julia grew up in the late 1940s and 1950s when females were given defined roles generally centered around being a wife and mother. Prior to Victor's being laid off, he had never interfered with Julia's role as mother.

The Romano family is strong in its Roman Catholic beliefs. Specific expectations exist around any grandchildren being raised Roman Catholic. However, Angelo Romano (age 33) is a medical doctor in private practice as an internist. He is engaged to Sue, a fundamentalist (Pentecostal) in religious affiliation. She is insisting that any children born to them be raised Pentecostal. Thus, the entire Romano family, except for Veronica, is encouraging Angelo to break off his engagement to Sue unless she agrees that any children born to them be raised Roman Catholic. Angelo is confused because he really loves Sue but is also committed to obeying parental and family guidance. He has been reared to carry out assigned roles expected of a loyal son and brother.

On the other hand, Veronica, Angelo's sister (age 25) is engaged to Michael Corsini, a strong Roman Catholic. Veronica's engagement has been embraced by the entire Romano family and therefore serves as a constant reminder to Angelo of a child who is obedient to the expectations of the family.

Moreover, within the Romano family the distribution of labor has led to high academic achievement and professional development. During their early childhood, the Romano children were given specific roles within the family. These roles led to the development of excellent work habits at home and at school. The results of the collective distribution of labor may be observed in Veronica's and Frances's continued help with household responsibilities. Both still living at home, Veronica (age 25) is a graduate student working on her MBA degree and Frances (age 20) is studying to be an early childhood educator. Although they are completing university degrees they are home to assist Julia, the mother, with the family dinner each Sunday. The sons, Mario and Angelo, display the same level of work commitment in their respective professional positions as a corporate lawyer and medical specialist.

RELATIONSHIPS

The third component of the Four-R Model is relationships. Relationships can be characterized by power orientation, communication, configuration-structure, and accentuation. Power orientation includes the dimension to control someone within a relationship. Power within itself means having the ability to act (Moore, 1991). Therefore, in relationships the possibility exists for one person to control what takes place within the bond. For example, a husband might dictate what his wife may wear out to dinner. His wife will wear what has been recommended by her spouse. This pattern in their relationship has been developed over time. The response to power in the relationship leads to strengthening the relationship or weakening it. Conflict in relationships may emanate from a reaction to power.

Another important aspect of relationships is communication. It is through the ability to communicate that individuals strengthen or weaken the existing relationship. When communication is clear, relationships tend to be stronger. The ideal description of communication is that the message sent is received by the receiver in the same manner in which it was intended. Open and clear communication fosters trust and respect. This clarity may also lead to openness within the relationship. To illustrate, when communication is clear between a mother and father, a strong model exists for siblings to understand the importance of the clarity of communication in family relationships.

The configuration or structure of a family comprises the third component of relationships. Whether a family is nuclear, extended, blended, or alliance-based will determine the types of relationships that will develop. That is, the specific type will affect the pattern that will prevail over time. Another factor determining the configuration is the participants within a given family type. For example, in a blended family, children may develop a close relationship with the stepfather. The degree of closeness is generally based upon the pattern of communication established by the nature of interaction among family members. Another example is one wherein a mother remarries yet does not agree for her new husband to assume the role of disciplinarian until six months into the marriage. Therefore, his role is neutralized from day one. He enters the system with no power or authority, which means he has no authority as a parent.

Finally, there are those family relationships which members feel they need to accentuate for further clarification. Family relationships may be emphasized to show the exact nature of the bond, whether it is strong or weak. For example, a child who feels insecure in his relationship with his father may constantly refer to "my dad" in all situations. This accentuation within the relationship may actually bring them closer. Moreover, stepsiblings will often refer to themselves as "stepbrother" or "stepsister", "half-brother" or "half-sister." These relationships may change over time, that is, they are dynamic in nature. It is important to remember that the outset or beginning of a relationship will create the manner in which accentuation may be determined and carried out. An example of this would be when a woman decides to marry again and introduces her new husband to her children as "Bill," instead of as "your new dad, Bill." Within this illustration, Bill is given a lesser role than his spouse from day one. Another unique component of accentuation of the relationship can be observed in alliance-based families. In most instances, members will highlight or place emphasis on the person best known within the configuration. To illustrate, in lesbian families where there are children, both women might be refered to as "mother." However, by the way in which the word *mother* is said, the listener will usually know which one is the birth mother. This is due to the special accentuation of the word *mother.*

Illustration of a Relationships-Dominated Family

Case Study E—The Jones Family
The Jones family includes: Barbara, the mother (age 38); Joe, the stepfather (age 40); and Carl Barker (age 14), Barbara's son from her first marriage to Hugh Barker. In describing power within relationships, it is important to note that Hugh Barker represents the typical, powerful male spouse. He had control over Barbara, which led her to accept extravagant gifts from him that she later discovered had been stolen. Hugh's power over Barbara was such that she never questioned anything he ever said or did. Barbara knew Hugh was not employed at the time, yet she did not take issue with his regu-

lar gift giving. It was a pattern within their relationship for Barbara to accept whatever decisions or actions Hugh displayed. Since Hugh dominated Barbara, she accepted his excuses for consistently getting home late. She had been conditioned not to question his behavior. This eventually led to the divorce, initiated by Hugh, as a result of an ongoing extramarital affair.

Another example of the power that Hugh had over Barbara can be illustrated through Carl Barker's seeing his father with another woman. Carl conveyed this observation to his mother, who excused this behavior, telling Carl that his father was only a friend to this unknown female. Barbara was unable to connect this observation with the consistent absence of Hugh from the family. This inability stems from the conditioning Barbara had undergone not to question any of Hugh's behaviors and motives.

Communication style within the Jones family may be observed through Joe, the stepfather. Although he has been married to Barbara for two years, he is not sure of his role within the family. Thus, his inability to tell Barbara how he really feels about her desire to return to school for her RN diploma is indicative of his reticence to be open with his feelings. He fears that telling her will create conflict between the two of them. As Barbara is six months' pregnant and is already experiencing swelling, Joe does not wish to do anything that might create additional stress for his wife.

Failure to communicate may also be demonstrated through the feelings of both Joe and Barbara in their reluctance for Carl to visit his biological father. These feelings have never been expressed, due to Hugh Barker's having been incarcerated for eight months on breaking and entering charges. Joe and Barbara believe that to tell Carl how they feel will jeopardize any present and future relationship with him. Carl has often wondered how his mother and stepfather really feel about his father. He has little memory of family discussions regarding his natural father. He has observed no response to questions raised regarding his father.

Moreover, Barbara cannot tell her parents about her desire to return to school to complete her RN diploma, as she is expecting a child in three months. She was always able to share with her parents during her years at home. Being married to Hugh and now to Joe has compromised her ability to have open communication. Now her ability to communicate is affected by her yielding to dominance within her marital relationships. Therefore, her parents are completely unaware of her strong desire to return to school as soon as she delivers her child.

Because Barbara was the middle child, she was made to feel different from her older and younger siblings. All of her siblings received a college degree. This has led her to feel that she has disappointed her parents. Her strongest desire is to complete her nursing degree as a way of pleasing her parents. It is Barbara's feeling of failure, rather than her parents' feeling. Barbara feels inadequate in comparison to her siblings and therefore she accentuates her relationship with her parents a way of feeling equal to her siblings. Barbara has an innate need to stress her feelings to her parents by overemphasizing any interaction with them. This need has led to stress between her older sisters and her.

RITUALS

Rituals represent those habitual activities performed over time within families. Family rituals have been described as "the repetitious, highly valued, symbolic occasions or activities observed or undertaken by a family" (Tseng & Hsu, 1991). Some types of rituals are: mealtime grace; celebrations; religious participation; and specific family activities. These rituals may be characterized by having a specific sequence and an unchanging character. Rituals occur within every family, and like other family phenomena they may be implicit or explicit.

There is some evidence that practitioners and researchers are paying closer attention to the importance of rituals in the lives of families. The family ritual has been referred to as one "whole family process," which is gaining more notice in the field of family counseling, and it has been suggested that rituals may even be "prescribed" by practitioners to address limitations or conflicts in the ritual lives of families (Subrahmanian, 1992; Levick, Jalali, & Strauss, 1981). Rituals might be applied as a resource in helping a family cope with the placement of an older adult family member outside the home (Schneewind, 1993) or in maintaining marital bonds (Berg-Cross, Daniels & Carr, 1992). Laird (1984) noted the merits of considering ritual in family assessment and intervention and highlighted several family "ritual" situations: the underritualized family; the family undergoing rites of passage; the family wherein spouses have conflicting rituals; and the family that uses rituals in austere and demeaning ways. Laird stated:

Through the medium of ritual, families can be helped to express their traditions and values; to achieve coherence; to adapt to transitions, unsettling life events, and catastrophes; and perhaps dismantle dysfunctional patterns of rigid behavior that are perpetuated by certain rituals (Laird, 1984, p. 125).

Wolin, Bennett, et al. (1980) reported that in families in which one or both parents are alcoholic, their offspring are more prone toward alcoholism if family rituals are disturbed during the period of the parents' most intense drinking.

There are many rituals that occur in families and are expected by all family members, yet no one is able to define the origin of these vital family activities. Still, there are family activities that are visible to all family members, as well as to outsiders. Although these events are seen by family members and others, they may not be perceived by the family as rituals. This relates to the routine nature of rituals to family members. This would indicate that rituals are performed in such a relaxed manner that little conscious focus is given to them. In other words, some rituals are invisible. Another implicit variable of rituals is their unchanging

FIGURE 3.3   A Family Ritual

character. There is a built-in course of events. An example of this unchanging character is the family in which the Christmas tree must be put up before any other holiday decorations.

Rituals have a specific sequence, and in order for them to be classified, one must be able to observe the sequence. For example, some families always pray or have grace before eating. No one is allowed to eat anything before grace or a prayer has been spoken. This leads to one of the primary rituals within families, mealtime. Eating represents the primary activity within families in which there is agreement regarding routine actions. The commonality within families is the nurturing that is obtained through sharing a meal. Through nurturing, specific patterns are established enabling family members to maintain the sequence without questioning. To illustrate these dynamics, family members may take turns in saying grace. It is often during the saying of grace that family members provide verbal support for one another by addressing individual needs of all members. These needs create the unconscious desire to maintain the ritual of a family mealtime.

Another type of ritual is the family's celebration of itself. Some examples of family celebrations are marriages, anniversaries, birthdays, baptisms, holiday gatherings, and funerals. Each one of these rituals represents an opportunity for a family to create a routine based on family interaction. An example is the family that celebrates each birthday with a cake baked by the mother of the family. The difference is that on the mother's birthday a cake is purchased by the family.

Religious participation reflects an agreed-upon representation regarding rituals. Rituals within this context provide spiritual meaning for all family members. Kneeling, standing, bowing, singing, raising hands in unison, or reading in unison all represent rituals. In each of these, the element of spirituality is present. In religious rituals mental alertness is required and expected by all family members of each other. Participants will drive great distances to be a part of a worship service. It is not unusual for a family to drive by five or six churches before entering one where they hold joint membership.

Within families there are special family activities that are classified as rituals. These special activities represent events that are born within families and represent the uniqueness within a given family. This can be represented through the family that eats peanuts every night before bedtime. It is an activity that describes sharing among family members. This ritual is performed every night at the same time, in the same room, and with the same proportions being allotted to each family member. Another special activity might be watching the same television program or renting a videotape on Saturday night. Story time represents another special activity. In families story time might be every night, once a week, or on special occasions. The story might be read by the identified story-teller within the family (e.g., the father), or this role might be transferred from one family member to another, depending on who is available.

Illustration of a Rituals-Dominated Family

Case Study F—The Johnson Family
The Johnson family is an example of a multigenerational family. The nuclear family members are: Wayne, the father (age 31); Margaret, the mother (age 30), Eric, their son (age 12), and Michelle, their daughter (age 8). The extended family includes: Ron, the paternal grandfather (age 61), Clara, the paternal grandmother (age 60), and Eva, the paternal great-grandmother (age 81). Also in the extended family are Ron's two brothers and a sister who live far away.

Every Sunday Eva makes dinner for all extended family members. This includes her son and daughter-in-law, Ron and Clara, her grandson, Wayne, and his wife, Margaret, and the great-grandchildren, Eric and Michelle. Sunday dinner is served promptly at 1:30 p.m. Prior to dinner's being served, Ron always provides the mealtime grace. He has a standard prayer from which he never deviates. This prayer was taught to him by his father, now deceased. This prayer is: "Father, bless this food that we share and may it be used to strengthen our bodies and our souls. We ask for your ongoing support for each person around this table. Amen." As the prayer is being said, all family members join hands around the table, with their eyes closed.

The Johnson family has a yearly celebration during the Christmas season. This celebration is initiated by the annual Christmas tree trimming party at Eva's house, followed by a potluck dinner. Each family unit brings its favorite holiday dish. Eva always provides stuffed cornish hens, her favorite recipe, for this event. Ron and Clara always bring the same dessert, French apple pie. Wayne and Margaret's contribution is the vegetable, broccoli casserole. Eva's other children contribute additional dishes. One son living in the south provides southern venison stew. The son living out west brings sourdough bread. Finally, the daughter living in Europe brings gourmet Danish pastries.

During this celebration the tree is trimmed first, followed by everyone sipping eggnog around the fireplace. Thereafter, dinner is served, with Ron, the eldest son, saying grace and serving the cornish hens. This yearly celebration ends with the family gathering around the fire and singing carols, and addressing Christmas cards to be mailed to other relatives.

The Johnson family's religious participation is character- ized by Eva's going to early morning Mass at 8 a.m. each day. This is a daily ritual; she misses only when she's ill. After Mass she faithfully goes down and lights a candle in memory of her husband, Ron Sr. Eva insists that each of her children attend midnight Mass with her on Christmas Eve, so that they too may share as a family in the candle-lighting ritual in memory of the father. This event has represented a highlight in Eva's life since the death of her husband. No one is ever permitted to miss this special occasion in the family. Prior to the death of Ron Sr., not one midnight Mass had been missed by Eva and him. The importance of this ceremony is reflected in Eva's special emphasis on everyone's being present, even the grand- children and great-grandchildren, for the Christmas Eve Mass. During the year, however, Eva is satisfied if the family attends Mass together weekly on Sunday morning.

In special family activities, Clara, Ron's wife, is the one who takes the lead for each birthday celebration. Therefore, birthdays are always celebrated at her house. Clara is from a family in which storytelling was an important pastime. So, she always insists upon all family members' sharing in story- telling during each birthday celebration. After birthday cake and ice cream have been served, family members arrange themselves in a circle in comfortable positions in the living room. Starting with the person being honored for his/her birthday, each family member contributes to telling a story. Once the story topic is initiated, each person takes turns adding the plot and sequencing of events without previous preparation. It is spontaneous and is influenced by what has been stated before by other family members. No birthday cel- ebration is complete within the Johnson family until the storytelling ritual has taken place.

Throughout the discussion of rituals, the unchanging character and specific sequencing of events have been integrated. These two aspects of rituals are blended into the specific types of rituals practiced. This indi- cates that the nature of these two characteristics are present in all rituals. This means also that a ritual cannot exist unless it follows a specific sequence and has an unchanging character.

SUMMARY

Families are designed to meet the two primary needs of caretaking and nurturing. These two functions can be better understood through the Four-R Model of Family Dynamics. All families have these four dimensions: rules, roles, relationships, and rituals, but one of these dimensions will be dominant within the context of a specific family. This chapter has described the unique attributes of the Four-R Model of Family Dynamics. Although these four dimensions are innate to every family, one dimension will invariably serve as a guiding force for family functioning.

Examples of attributes within each of the four dimensions have been described. The major components of each dimension have been clarified through specific case illustrations of families. Students should be able to perceive this model as a tool for understanding the totality of family dynamics. The reality that a given family is basically dominated by one dimension of the Four-R Model (e.g., rules) does not mean that this family unit would not reflect the other three dimensions (i.e., roles, relationships, and rituals). If at a given point the dominating or guiding force within a family creates inordinate conflict between family members, the other dimensions may be utilized to help the family understand its unique style of operation and thus serve as a foundation for intervention planning.

QUESTIONS FOR DISCUSSION

1. Describe the dimension of the Four-R Model of Family Dynamics that is dominant in your family of origin.
2. Describe the dimension of the Four-R Model that is dominant in your current family grouping.
3. Which dimension might lead to conflict within your family (i.e., family of origin and/or current family grouping)?

GROUP EXERCISE

Arrange the class in groups of three to four students. Assign each of the four guiding forces of family dynamics (rules, roles, relationships, and rituals) to each group. Each group should then develop a plan to present a five-minute role play of a family scenario depicting how a family might approach a problem when dominated by one of the forces. These examples might be real or imaginary. The role plays will be followed by a full class discussion on how it felt to be in a given role as well as insight gained from observing each of the role plays. Of course, students might be asked how different these roles might be in relation to their own families.

Class members should be given specific questions to think about as presentations are made. For example, what are the influences of income, educational status, social class, interethnic or transcultural marriage, aging and life transitions, on the ways in which families define and arrange themselves.

SIGNIFICANT TERMS

collective self-development
governance
regimentation

division of labor
parameter
gender-delivered roles

REFERENCES

Berg-Cross, L., Daniels, C., & Carr, P. (1992). Marital rituals among divorced and married couples. *Journal of Divorce and Remarriage*, 18(1/2), 1–30.

Bernard, J. (1981). The good provider role. *American Psychologist*, 36, 1–13.

Brown, J. E. (1990). The relationship between family structure and process variables and adolescent decision making. *Journal of Adolescence*, 23(1), 25–37.

Jantzen, C. & Harris, O. (1986). *Family treatment in social work practice*. Itasca, Ill.: F. E. Peacock.

Laird, J. (1984). Sorcerers, shamans, and social workers: The use of ritual in social work practice. *Social Work*, 29(2), 123–129.

Levick, S. E., Jalali, B., & Strauss, J. S. (1981). With onions and tears: A multidimensional analysis of a counter-ritual. *Family Process*, 20(1), 77–83.

Kirst-Ashman, K. K. and Hull, G. H. Jr. (1993). *Understanding generalist practice*. Chicago: Nelson-Hall.

Kravetz, D. (1995). Social work practice with women. In T. M. Morales and B. W. Shaefor (Eds.), *Social work: A profession of many faces*, 7th ed., 303–330. Boston: Allyn & Bacon.

Moore, L. L. (1991). *Release from powerlessness: A guide for taking charge of your life*. Dubuque, Iowa: Kendall/Hunt.

Parsons, T. & Bales, R. (1955). *Family socialization and interaction process*. New York: The Free Press.

Schneewind, E. H. (1990). The reaction of the family to the institutionalization of an elderly member. *Journal of Gerontological Social Work*, 15(1-2), 121-136.

Slater, P. E. (1961). Toward a dualistic theory of identification. *Merrill-Palmer Quarterly, 7*, 113–126.

Subrahmanian, C. (1992). *Rituals in family life: A qualitative study of clinical and non-clinical families.* (Doctoral Dissertation, Purdue University, 1992). *Dissertation Abstracts International, 54-01,* 0335-A.

Tseng, W. & Hsu, J. (1991). *Culture and family: Problems and therapy.* New York: The Haworth Press.

Udry, J. R. (1974). *The social context of marriage,* 2nd ed. Philadelphia: J. B. Lippincott.

Voydanoff, P., Fine, M. A., & Donnelly, B. W. (1994). Family structure, family organization, and quality of family life. *Journal of Family & Economic Issues, 15*(3), 175–200.

Wolin, S. J., Bennett, L. A., Noonan, D. L., & Teitelbaum, M. A. (1980). Family rituals: A factor in the intergenerational transmission of alcoholism. *Journal of Studies on Alcoholism, 41,* 199–214.

▶ 4

Intervention Strategies Through Utilization of the Four-R Model of Family Dynamics

Families are grounded in rules, roles, relationships, and rituals. The uniqueness within a family determines the dominant force within the Four-R Model. In intervening to provide assistance to families, the helping person may use the Four-R Model as the instrument for intervention. This chapter will describe the following intervention steps (sometimes referred to as the problem-solving model). These steps are: engagement; interviewing; assessment; planning and contracting; evaluation, and follow-up.

ENGAGEMENT

Engagement represents the point of contact between the worker and the client system. In working with families, this moment represents the introduction of the worker to the family. This represents the socialization stage (Haley, 1977) of family intervention. During this phase, beginning trust is established between the worker and the family system. It provides the opportunity for the worker and family members to check out one another. Engagement is also the phase in which mutual opinions are being shaped; the worker forms opinions about the family and the family forms opinions about the worker. Rapport building takes place in this initial phase of intervention. It is through rapport that the established barriers begin to diminish. These barriers represent preexisting ideas or reservations that the family and the worker may have had about each other and/or the helping process. Moreover, rapport provides the climate for understanding to emerge within the beginning connection between the worker and the family system. Mutual understanding enables the worker and family system to relax and focus on the tasks at hand.

Engagement is not time-limited but is contingent on the individuals involved. However, it is also based on the nature of the issues within the context of a specific family. This suggests that the urgency of need will inevitably drive the timing element during engagement. Conversely, the worker's social agency may control the pacing of engagement as one of the most crucial steps of intervention. Policies governing intervention steps are important elements in working with families. In family violence shelters, work with the family, generally the mother and children, must be initiated immediately and progress rapidly for safety and security reasons. Moreover, in family preservation programs the window of intervention is structured by the agency's rules and regulations. Funding constraints often dictate how long the family worker may interact with a family. A specific example is a family presentation program wherein the agency guidelines determine the length of intervention by a worker. Initially programs were designed to offer ninety days of home-based family intervention. But, today some programs have been limited to sixty days as stipulated by agency rules and regulations.

Another aspect of engagement is setting the ground rules for working together. These rules provide the clarity that is necessary for the mutual understanding of all participants. Mutual understanding guides the investment of each party in entering into an ongoing helping relationship. The importance of mutuality or bilateral understanding cannot be overlooked. Bilateral understanding provides equal partnership, thereby removing the top-down intervention mode. In other words, the worker does not determine or dictate what the intervention process should include; rather, the worker and the family jointly determine the essentials of their relationship together.

INTERVIEWING

Within this stage of intervention the worker utilizes information gathering as a way to clarify issues and/or problems within the family. These issues and/or problems provide the information for describing the dynamics within the family. These dynamics represent those ingredients that are necessary to the worker for understanding the issues within the family. Within these dynamics, such as communication patterns, uses of power, and closeness in relationships, clarity is developed for comprehending family functioning. Interviewing creates the opportunity for data collection, which outlines the complexity within the family. That is, interviewing enables the worker to probe for understanding the vast nature of this complexity. This includes the nonverbal as well as the verbal expressions of the entire family system. As families connect or join with the worker, they may be able to look more carefully at the nature of the interaction and thus gain additional insights.

Throughout the interviewing stage, family members are also learning from each other. As Satir (1990, p. 35) points out, "The family is the main learning context for individual behavior, thoughts, and feelings." They will continue this vital learning process as they become more able to see and hear interaction that was perhaps heretofore invisible. The visible nature of these once hidden areas may now be addressed by family members. Consequently, the questions asked by family members of each other serve to enlighten the worker about the issues within the family that are causing the most distress. With this information being made available, the worker may now begin to emphasize leading the family toward narrowing the focus to key issues. This would indicate that the worker must have the ability to listen attentively during this intervention phase. Listening is a skill that will enable the worker to be more directive in assisting family members to pinpoint and consolidate their concerns.

In addition, in this phase of intervention, the worker has the responsibility to ensure equal participation by each family member present (Haley, 1977). The importance of equal participation gives some assurance that each family member is equally respected. The worker has the responsibility to ensure balance in the interview to prevent family members from feeling that they are not being respected or that their views are insignificant.

ASSESSMENT

During this phase of intervention the worker processes and interprets information, both nonverbal and verbal. This process occurs not only within the initial phase of intervention but also throughout the worker's involvement with the family. The worker must analyze nonverbal processes such as eye contact, facial expressions, gestures, and body positioning (aka body language) among family members. Verbal expression specifically includes word choice, tone of voice, emphases, style of speech, and cultural expressions. Also, in assessment, the worker must consider the following processes: developing a clear picture of family issues; determining family leadership configurations; interpreting family dynamics to the participants; and examining reactions by family members to problem identification.

Developing a clear picture of family issues

Assessment enables the worker to develop a view of the issues confronting the family. An understanding of these issues is necessary to enhance the worker's knowledge of how the family operates. Having this understanding is supported by Sheafor et al. (1988, p. 222), who define assessment as, "the process of interpreting or giving meaning and conceptual order to data; it is an attempt to make sense out of the data that have been collected." Developing the skill of ordering data is a crucial step in learning how to assist families. Ordering this information enables the worker to stay focused as well as to provide a clearer vision for all family members as to which problems may need immediate attention.

Determining family leadership configurations

Another important component of assessment is leadership configuration. Within this component of assessment, leaders within the family may be identified. Having an understanding of leadership patterns enables the worker to describe strengths and limitations of leadership. The strengths may be utilized by the worker to aid families in addressing those issues that may be creating barriers to effective family functioning. Likewise, limitations noted may be outlined in order to assist families in correcting those areas that prevent successful functioning. That is to say, upon identifying limitations, the worker is better positioned to create with the family changes that will enhance overall family functioning. During this phase of assessment it is important to create the opportunity for family members to participate fully in identifying leadership roles.

The worker should maintain a "bottom-up" approach rather than a "top-down" approach in examining leadership patterns. This bottom-up approach provides avenues for each family member to have direct input in identifying leaders within the system. The bottom-up approach simply means equal participation by each member involved. Equity is the goal within determining leadership configurations. Within this approach, potential leadership may be lifted and placed in a recognized position. This would suggest that family members are able to use an avenue for development that will maximize the contributions of every family member. However, the worker must not confuse existing leadership patterns with potential for leadership. By also focusing on the leadership potential of each family member, the worker should be able to identify implicit leadership patterns and roles.

Interpretation of family dynamics

In the assessment process the worker is also provided a forum for interpreting certain dynamics occurring within the family unit. These dynamics are described as a part of data collection. These dynamics include: relationships among family members; leadership patterns; the manner in which issues are described; communication styles; problem-solving strategies; and other unique displays of interaction. Of particular concern to the worker is the dynamic of how the family describes or approaches issues. In observing this dynamic, the worker is in a unique

FIGURE 4.1   Multi-Faceted Images

position to utilize visual images displayed by the family. These images assist the worker in developing a picture of issues being addressed. Utilizing a camera effect, clarity is provided for understanding how each facet contributes to the whole, like the snapshots of a photographer.

For example, to demonstrate various interactions among members, snapshots (observations) are taken at various intervals. To have a holistic understanding of family functioning all snapshots (observations) must be placed together. The importance of placing observations (snapshots) together will eliminate "fuzzy" pictures that may still be in the process of emerging into wholeness. The totality of these snapshots or observations is achieved over time. That is, one snapshot or observation will not provide clarity and precision for the worker. However, placing all the snapshots together should optimize the worker's chances to obtain the clearest picture possible in interpreting family dynamics.

Reaction by family members to problem-identification

The last aspect of assessment is the appraisal of how family members react to problem-identification. During this component of assessment the worker may be able to describe how family members respond to issues being highlighted. The benefit to the worker is his/her being able to interpret concretely how members react to the issues or problems being described. The worker might gain insight by regarding family members' interaction with one another. Likewise, family members may gain insight regarding how they each perceive the issues at hand. These perceptions provide understanding relative to individual interpretation and differences of opinion. With these interpretations family members are better positioned to move forward in committing themselves to action. Being positioned implies that action will follow. Action might indicate family members' physically repositioning themselves during the meeting, verbally attacking or challenging each other, or jointly making decisions as a family with all members being in agreement. Action refers to steps being taken by family members in addressing the identified issues or concerns.

PLANNING AND CONTRACTING

Planning as a component within the intervention process may be defined as deciding what to do as a result of information obtained in the initial assessment phase. The first aspect of planning is reaching agreement on the specific nature of family issues and/or problems. The worker and family members' being able to do this is that it brings about a mutually negotiated process. The importance of mutuality is that it leads to investment on the part of the family system and the worker. The worker must ensure that each family member has input into and understands the agreement.

The second component of planning and/or contracting is reshaping the problems into workable goals. Ambiguity or lack of precision and clarity must be eliminated in order for the plan to be most effective. Ambiguity in planning might lead to confusion at a later date as to agreed-upon goals at the outset. During the planning process, problems identified must be reframed into achievable goals. Moreover, each broad plan or goal must be broken down into behaviorally stated, specific objectives. The worker must lead the family in developing goals that are broken down into specific activities/objectives that are realistic. Objectives should be specific enough in order to ensure measurement of progress over time, as well as eventual outcomes of planned change efforts.

Mutual expectations comprise the third component of planning and contracting. Mutual or bilateral expectations will enhance accountability. There has to be common understanding between the worker and the family concerning what is expected from each party. Efforts must be made by the worker and family to reach understanding regarding expected behaviors. The rationale for mutual understanding is simple human dynamics. Without this understanding little progress will occur. Included in these expectations are such factors as: time of meeting; place of meeting, length of meeting; agreement to attend all meetings; agreement to share verbally; and commitment to carrying out assigned responsibilities.

The last aspect of planning and contracting is that of formatting and establishing priorities. Each meeting must be guided by established boundaries. This is the format of the family session. This formatting would include such factors as creating a therapeutic climate, reporting on assignments, and discussing issues placed on the table for that specific meeting. Priorities are established to provide focus toward the agreed-upon crucial issues. Prioritizing enables the worker and family members to address the most pressing or urgent issues or problems first. As the most stressful or pressing issues for family members are addressed, they will then be able to deal with other family problems that are less threatening to overall family safety and security.

IMPLEMENTATION AND ACTION

During this phase of social work practice with families, the worker is attempting to help the family with issues and/or problems that are preventing optimal functioning. There are four areas to be explored regarding implementation in practice. These are: (1) the process of carrying out goals; (2) the family's interaction with outside systems; (3) the family's utilization of resources; and (4) the roles assumed by the family social worker. The worker's goal in implementation is to lead the family through a process to meet established goals. This is the action phase of intervention. This is the "doing" aspect of practice. It is the time in which the worker and the family members decide to eliminate the barriers confronting the family's well-being. During this phase both the worker and the family coalesce and engage all available energy to bring about planned change.

The second concept is the interaction of family members with outside systems in the community. This provides the opportunity for family members to share feelings and support one another as they address agreed-upon issues needing attention. The worker is able to introduce the family to outside systems. These outside systems/institutions may include the school, religious institutions, social agencies, governmental programs, employment agencies, health care centers, and recreational programs. These systems represent the primary formal support systems and institutions most likely to become involved with families. The informal support systems addressed by the worker may include other families with similar problems, naturally formed support groups, extended family networks, close friends, and understanding co-workers.

Utilizing Resources

The third component of the implementation and action stage of intervention is utilizing resources. The worker helps families to develop creative ways to use available resources, formal and informal. Sometimes family members lack the information essential to utilize existing resources. The worker has the responsibility to assess this lack of knowledge. It is expected that the worker will know where the resources exist and also that he/she will have the capacity to connect families to those resources. In addition, the worker must introduce family members to new resources, as well as help them to discontinue poor or unworkable relationships with agencies. Another task of the worker is to teach family members to use community resources effectively.

The fourth and last issue to be considered during the implementation and action stage is the exploration of diverse roles to be assumed by the worker in helping the family fulfill their needs. These roles might include: mediator; broker; facilitator; enabler; teacher; coordinator; and advocate. These roles are designed to help workers act in a holistic and systematic manner on the behalf of families. In addition, these roles are designed to focus the work of the social worker. They serve as mechanisms for planned intervention in helping the family face issues both inside and outside the family.

To clarify these roles further, one might consider the function of the mediator. In this role the worker attempts to resolve conflict that might be existing between family members. An example of this role may be illustrated in a divorced couple with children. As the parents negotiate joint custody arrangements, the family worker assists in trying to get them to be realistic in their expectations of one another. Therefore, it is not unusual in today's society that men are taking care of their children at least part of the time. This example illustrates how important it is for the social worker to be clear about major tasks. When clarity exists with the worker, it enables greater understanding to be transmitted to the client. In this transmission, clients are more likely to be able to reach planned goals. This does not mean that change is guaranteed, but it simply means that a greater opportunity will exist for planned change to occur where clarity in purpose and goals exists.

TERMINATION

The unstated goal from the outset of intervention is that of termination. Each practitioner needs to enter the helping relationship with families with the unstated desire to "work him or herself out of a job." Within this thought rests the idea of terminating as one begins intervention. The characteristics describing termination include: (1) recognition of enhanced well-being; (2) reasons for termination; (3) planning the end of interaction; and (4) closure of the relationship. These four steps are recognizable by social workers implementing the termination phase.

First, the practitioner must recognize the enhanced well-being of the client system (Hartford, 1971). For termination to be facilitated, the social worker should acknowledge the client's skills in self-development and his/her current level of functioning. Within the recognition of client functioning is the worker's ability to see and understand the client's ability to function independently. That is, the client system will have developed skills that enable it to function or cope with problems. Within this recognition each family member must be given the opportunity to share and receive specific comments regarding his/her level of functioning. The feedback must be twofold; that is, there will be comments related to development within the family as a whole. And the worker has the enormous charge of clearly describing to family members their current level of coping.

The second aspect of termination is examining the set of possible reasons for ending the intervention (Hepworth & Larsen, 1993). Sometimes a worker leaves the agency due to having been laid off, taking a new job, retiring, or dying. For each of these reasons, there is no alternative but termination. Next, one must also consider the possibility of the agency's closing. Families are thus customarily referred to another agency or their cases might be terminated at that point. Or, the family simply improves to a healthy state, thereby leading to a joint decision with the worker for termination. Mutuality is essential during this decision-making process. This step should be inclusive of input from both the social worker and family members. Also, some interventions are time-limited. At the time of contracting, family members and the worker may agree on the length of time for intervention. This is further complicated by agencies wherein programming is done within a thirty-, sixty-, or ninety-day period. Moreover, insurance companies will often dictate a coverage period. In these examples, the length of time for intervention has been predetermined. Another reason for termination is simply that the client system dropped out or quit. In these cases the worker is compelled to terminate due to a lack of access to the client. If the client disappears there is no option but to terminate services. It is important to note that client drop-out may be abrupt or gradual over time. As social workers, it is important to remember that dropping out does not always imply negativism or a lack of client motivation. Rather, it might relate to the absence of financial means or a lack of commitment on the part of one or more family members.

The third characteristic of termination is planning the end of an action. Termination does not occur within planned steps by the social worker. The worker must help the family to be involved with the planning of termination. Both parties must bilaterally agree upon the content describing the end of the working relationship. A recognized ending should be planned (Hartford, 1971). This event might include a celebration as the recognized ending, or the date of the last meeting may be established as the recognized end. The important factor to remember is the crucial need for mutuality and/or inclusiveness between the worker and the family members in working through this process.

The fourth and final characteristic of the termination process is the actual closure of the relationship. This aspect represents the finite completion of face-to-face interactions between the worker and the family. This process includes discussion regarding actual emotional feelings and thoughts about terminating on the part of the worker, as well as the family. Schwartz (1971, p. 573) refers to this process as "the dynamics and skills in the ending and transition phase." Within this phase comes the recognition of denial and anger that may occur within family members simply as a result of working through the reality of ending.

.ocess represents the highlight within the steps
client into independent living or the ability to
rvention by professionals. Termination is to be
1 by the social worker. It is a natural phenomenon
elationship. Termination must be accepted as a
)le part of intervention. With this understanding
-w phase may be accomplished by the family.

EVALUATION AND FOLLOW-UP

Evaluation and follow-up comprise a vital component of the helping
relationship. These two concepts are being described together because
they are connecting links. Several characteristics are utilized to describe
these two significant concepts in intervention. One cannot evaluate a
family adequately without referencing the future, that is, what is to follow. First, the worker must determine the level of functioning within the
family system. Mutuality must be an important dynamic. The level of
functioning should not be determined by one party but by all family
members.

The second characteristic of evaluation and follow-up is the identification of resources for helping the family to maintain equilibrium. As
family members understand how they operate and identify those ingredients enabling maintenance, they develop insight regarding specific
resources available within the system. As family members visibly recognize resources they may then preserve those elements that provide supportive resources for functioning. As these resources are identified,
equilibrium is maintained. Resources, of course, include both internal
and external sources of support for overall family well-being. External
resources might include extended family support, and institutional support from schools, religious organizations, and governmental programs.
Internal resources may include components provided by family members themselves, such as enhanced communication, joint decision making, and problem-solving abilities.

The final characteristic of evaluation and follow-up may be described as the identification of future steps. Follow-up is the major aspect
of planning for the future. The primary question here is whether the
client system is continuing to function independently, should be rein-
troduced to the agency system, or perhaps might need to be referred to
other supportive services. The major expectation or ideal of the social
worker is to find the client coping independently without further need
of professional assistance.

SUMMARY

In working through the framework for the interventive process, the social worker should outline for himself/herself the primary concepts to be addressed within each phase of helping. Preparation must be done prior to meeting family members. Clarity must be present in the mind of the worker in order to have a keen vision of issues and concerns confronting the family. Outlining concepts enables the worker to have a guiding direction for assisting families. These guiding directives are absolutely necessary to determine where and how to intervene in dissecting family problems and/or concerns. Once this dissection has occurred, the worker is better positioned to help the family understand the issues and problems needing attention.

QUESTIONS FOR DISCUSSION

1. Discuss in detail your understanding of the intevention stages involved in working with families.
2. Create an example of the snapshot approach to family assessment.
3. Discuss power configurations within families in relation to the top-down approach and the bottom-up approach.
4. Write a goal for helping a family resolve a problem.
5. Develop three objectives for the above goal that you have developed for family problem resolution.

GROUP EXERCISE

Have the entire class create a role play or short play demonstrating the stages of family intervention. Each stage may represent an act or one theme. Members of the class should be creative in arranging the set for the production.

Students should describe what is the most challening part of the role play for them as individuals and as beginning practitioners to implement. Encourage thought for how ideas will unfold and how characters or content may be presented. A coherent presentation should be the goal of the class. Group development is one of the goals to be accomplished. Class members should be asked to describe group interaction and how this exercise might help them enhance their practice skills with families.

SIGNIFICANT TERMS

engagement
interviewing
assessment
planning
contracting
implementation
termination
evaluation
follow-up
rapport
top-down approach
bottom-up approach

goal
objective
internal family resources
external resources
snapshot approach
mediator
broker
teacher
enabler
coordinator
advocate

REFERENCES

Haley, J. (1977). *Problems-solving therapy: New strategies for effective family therapy.* Jossey-Bass.

Hartford, M. E. (1971). *Groups in social work.* New York: Columbia University Press.

Hepworth, D. & Larsen, J. (1993). *Direct social work practice: Theory and skills,* 3rd ed. Belmont, Calif.: Wadsworth Publication.

Satir, V. (1990). *Conjoint family therapy,* 3rd ed. Palo Alto, Calif.: Science and Behavior Books.

Schwartz, W. & Zalba, S. (Eds.) (1971). *The practice of group work.* New York: Columbia University Press.

Sheafor, B. W., Horejsi, C. R., & Horejsi, G. A. (1988). *Techniques and guidelines for social work practice.* Boston: Allyn & Bacon.

▶ 5

Application of the Four-R Model

In discussing the Four-R Model of Family Dynamics, each type of family will be utilized to demonstrate the use of problem solving within the intervention process. The authors will describe how the Four-R Model may be applied to each stage of the intervention process—from engagement to evaluation/follow-up. Moreover, the rules-dominated, roles-dominated, relationships-dominated, and rituals-dominated families introduced in Chapter 3 will be examined in reference to how they might respond to the social worker's strategies during each stage of intervention. The utilization of the Four-R Model will further elucidate the tenets of this conceptual framework and present practical considerations for social work intervention.

RULES AND THE THOMAS FAMILY (SEE CASE STUDY THREE)

Engagement

The Thomas family (see Abstracts for Case Study Three) is a rules-dominated family. The first step in the intervention process is engagement. The mother, Beverly, contacted the agency seeking assistance with issues relating to her three children. These concerns stem primarily from unresolved issues related to her divorce and the response of the children to the mother's strict rules for governing the family. As a worker has the first face-to-face contact, the opportunity arises to check out Beverly and her family, and for the Thomases to check out the worker. The social worker may start by expressing his/her understanding of the issues present within the Thomas family. The worker should be prepared for a slow start with this family. Being rules-dominated, Beverly is more likely to have a protective wall established against outside suggestions concerning her style of running her family. This wall may impact initial intervention efforts, as she will perhaps consider outside intervention as an intrusion into her parenting domain. Although Beverly has requested counseling, she has already established rules that she feels are the core for her family's coping and maintaining equilibrium. The worker representing the agency has power and authority, thereby raising red flags for Beverly during this crucial rapport-building phase of intervention. The rules already in place within the Thomas family represent preexisting reservations that families often bring into the helping process.

Interviewing

In interviewing a rules-dominated family, the worker must remember the guarded nature of this family system. The least threatening interviewing technique is furthering (Hepworth & Larsen, 1993). This "low-level" approach involves the worker's using minimal prompts, such as "Ummh," "I see," "Okay," or the repetition of short phrases used by the client, that is, the family members. As questions are asked to clarify issues/problems within the family, several inquiries may be necessary in order to obtain clarity regarding a single issue or concern. In responding to the guarded nature of the mother, Beverly, the worker must ask open-ended questions. This approach will enable Beverly to speak freely and yet not push her into a corner. Having the freedom to speak in such a manner provides Beverly with the opportunity to maintain a level of control with which she feels most comfortable. In addition, Beverly's responses may constitute a circular pattern to questions asked. The worker must, consequently, be prepared to raise multiple closed-ended questions in order to secure needed information.

Other techniques the worker may use in the interviewing phase with the rules-dominated family are summarizing and paraphrasing. In summarizing the worker will use Beverly's exact wording to reflect his/her understanding of the family issues. This technique will communicate to the mother that the worker has heard what she has said and respects her style of presenting her issues. Paraphrasing, moreover, enables the worker to use his/her own language as well as that of the Thomas family to restate what has been said by family members. With paraphrasing the worker may move gradually toward helping the family to have a different view of its issues and concerns. It enables the worker to move the family forward in reflecting upon its problematic experiences within the home. The worker must not be pushy in asking questions of a rules-dominated family. That is, if the worker is too direct with questions, he/she may be perceived as too threatening or overpowering.

Another interviewing technique to consider with the rules-governed family is that of providing/maintaining focus (Hepworth & Larsen, 1993). For example, Beverly Thomas must be supported in her efforts to maintain balance within the rules she has worked hard to establish for her family. In this interviewing technique the worker's questions enable the mother or any head of a rules-dominated family the freedom to determine when to expand information to be shared. In all families, support in providing and maintaining focus can be offered within the interview. But in a rules-dominated family the sensitive nature calls for a more careful design of information gathering to ensure proper spacing in the approach to asking questions.

Assessment

In working with any family, the practitioner will find that the assessment provides a clearer picture of family issues/problems. However, in a family that is rules-dominated, such as that of Beverly Thomas, obtaining a more vivid picture of family issues must be centered around the nature of existing rules. Rules may prevent an openness to sharing issues and concerns among family members. In the worker's view the rules-dominated family might appear to pose extreme obstacles for his/her visualizing the operational patterns of family life. From Beverly's point of view, the rules in her family provide a way of describing family functioning. From her perspective, she has given the worker all that is needed to understand the problems in her family. For Beverly, rules mean clarity.

In assessing leadership configurations within a rules-dominated family, the pattern is top-downward. A top-downward model of leadership maintains structure and authority within the family and keeps all rules intact. In order for Beverly to remain in control she has to maintain authority over all family members. Her functioning as a parent hinges on her ability to remain in the most powerful position. The primary way in which Beverly illustrates her power is through developing and enforcing stringent rules for all family members.

Given Beverly's disposition toward family governance, the worker must assist the family in understanding the rules operating within the context of all family interactions and activities. The worker may facilitate family interaction and create the opportunity for family members to have input into describing and explaining how they see overall family dynamics. The worker may also have as a goal helping Beverly to become more aware of her behavior as the head of a rules-dominated family. Likewise, the Thomas children may be assisted to better understand how an emphasis on rules has become an integral and essential factor in family coping.

Planning and Contracting

In looking at the rules-dominated family in the stage of planning/contracting, agreement has to be reached on the focus for change among family members. Beverly Thomas has to be assisted in permitting other family members to have input on the problematic concerns confronting the family. When rules dominate a family, such as the Thomases, the worker has to take firm steps in directing the family toward a set of common goals. As a rules-dominated person, Beverly is accustomed to being authoritative in her position within the family. Therefore, the worker needs to be aware of the importance of Beverly's position and its impact on family dynamics. Early in the planning stage, recognition should be given to working with Beverly in enabling other family members to have input.

During this planning phase the worker should help Beverly in reshaping problems into workable goals. Those areas that might be ambiguous, or in which a lack of clarity exists, should be revisited. The purpose for revisiting these issues is to enable the rules-dominated family to share in the reshaping of initially stated goals. This represents the opportunity for the children, Samantha, Lewis Jr., and Richie to experience inclusion in shaping the direction of their family. Children should be included in the decision-making process. The worker must take the responsibility in the planning phase to ensure equity among family members. If equity can be developed by the worker among all family members, the investment will be higher in working toward stated goals with each family member. Expectations and accountability rank highly among issues to be addressed in the planning-contracting phase. Beverly Thomas has high expectations for herself and all family members. High expectations are often present in rules-dominated families. Since Beverly occupies the top position in the family, she is positioned to dictate outcomes. These outcomes are often predicated upon levels of productivity. When one is in authority he/she may give directions to other family members. However, the accountability component can be used by the worker as the vehicle to assist Beverly in being realistic with her expectations. The worker may assume a teaching role in order to assist family members in understanding the importance of having realistic expectations. Therefore, the worker may connect expectations and accountability in a positive framework for assisting Beverly and her family toward working for consensus. The last component in the planning stage involves formatting and prioritizing. In formatting the worker assists Beverly and family members to write out family objectives. In writing down their views, family members should prioritize all expectations. This prioritizing of objectives enables Beverly, family members, and the worker to develop a clear focus for their work together. This collaborative planning step enables the Thomas family to soften the strict dictation of what ought to occur within the family system. Thus, rules are present, but they are workable due to the partnership established between the worker and all family members.

Implementation and Action

Beverly Thomas and her family can be assisted by the worker in carrying out the goals within the family system. With this step comes interaction of family members with outside systems. Beverly has to interact with the school system to address those issues impacting the children; the health center, addressing those issues relating to the family diet; and the Center for the Blind to address the issue of Richie's visual problems. The worker must enable Beverly to utilize resources that are available to the family. During the implementation phase the worker has the responsibility to operationalize various social work roles. In a rules-dominated family the worker's role as mediator is crucial to enhancing family dynamics.

Beverly, as the ruling authority in the family, has to be assisted through mediation to be more inclusive in addressing family expectations. An example of this style might be reflected by Beverly's involvement with the school system. She typically assumes an overpowering stance regarding any matters dealing with Richie's visual problems and his need for ongoing specialized programming. The worker may play an important role by intervening with school officials in order to help the mother feel more confident that the school system will indeed be able to address Richie's special needs and maximize his developmental potential.

The worker will also function in the role of a facilitator within a rules-dominated family. Given the strong nature of Beverly Thomas's personality, that is, her need to be in control, the worker must facilitate or bring about other family members' being able to have input and express their individual concerns to their mother. In addition, the facilitating role is critical in connecting Beverly with outside resources, such as the health center. This effort is due to the mother's strong will and tendency to function independently as the final authority in all matters pertaining to the family.

Moreover, within the implementation stage, the worker utilizing the Four-R Model must support the family in understanding that there are three other important dimensions impacting family life. Beverly Thomas needs to understand that her family is basically rules-dominated. This mode of day-to-day living may seem to meet Beverly's needs, but she must be able to perceive how roles, relationships, and rituals also figure into general family dynamics and functioning.

Understanding how roles, relationships, and rituals also play a part in family contentment and coping abilities should enhance family members' ability to carry out their responsibilities. In looking at the dimension of roles within the Thomas family, each child is given a specific role to implement. Samantha, the oldest, has either assumed or been assigned the role of caretaker for her younger siblings. Lewis Jr. is often given the role of man of the house, as he is the older male in the household. Richie is given the role of the baby because he is the youngest. Beverly assumes the role of overseer because she is the only adult within the family. Still, one must be continually aware that roles of family members may be restricted by the strong rules that govern all family functioning in the Thomas household. Children need to experience variety and flexibility in the roles that they play within the context of family life, which will contribute to their successful assimilation into adult roles within society. Beverly must be made aware during the intervention process that children must also be given the freedom and time to choose some roles for themselves within the family. This process should help them to be more resilient in social relationships at large and should also enhance their overall contentment with their position within the family. Resiliency in family roles inevitably involves Beverly's growing awareness of the children's need to exert their own individuality within the family, while still supporting each other in the fulfillment of family tasks.

Furthermore, relationships are strong within the Thomas family, as demonstrated through the degree of support among family members. This support is well demonstrated through the discussion of divorce issues. Beverly, Samantha and Lewis Jr. are also able to help Richie as he struggles with not fully understanding the meaning of divorce. The nurturing and support shown to Richie stem directly from these close family ties. On the other hand, the worker needs to be aware of the downside of the rules-dominated family system. As family members attempt to strengthen relationships, established rules may impact their ability as a family to become closer in their family ties.

Also, rituals, the last dimension of the Four-R Model, will help the family members to better understand themselves. Beverly has established strict, even stringent rules regarding the family's diet. These rules have led to a ritual within the Thomas family that affects all members. This ritual is that the family always eats "proper" foods at dinner time. Junk food is never served during the evening meal in the Thomas household. This daily ritual of always eating totally nutritionally balanced meals has led to depression and resistance among the children. This problem is especially observed on weekend evenings. The children are never allowed to have pizza or other fast foods, even on Friday and Saturday. The worker needs to remind the family members that rituals are not always enjoyed by everyone. Beverly's diet stems from her diabetic condition, and she has draped the family system with this rigorous regime. The worker may use this example to help the children develop their own rituals, such as eating at a fast-food restaurant of their choice once per week. In addition, Beverly might be assisted by the worker to be less strict about the family's eating patterns and allow the children to establish their own ritual around dinnertime. The worker may also remind the mother that an increasing number of fast-food restaurants also serve balanced meals, thereby allowing her to join the children in this newly formed ritual.

Termination

In planning termination, the end of the interaction, with a rules-dominated family, the worker must communicate with clarity the enhanced sense of well-being and skills that have been achieved by family members. Beverly needs assistance in understanding the movement within the family that has enabled termination to occur. The importance of clear communication toward improvement within the family system is crucial in preventing Beverly from reverting back to previous behaviors upon the exiting of the worker. The purpose for such clarity is to help Beverly gain insight into the family's current level of contentment with its life and to discourage the reestablishment of rules that will stifle family communication and cooperation.

In discussing termination with Beverly and the Thomas children, the worker has to facilitate a primary focus on improvement by all family members. In the facilitation process, family members should be encouraged to share their views and perceptions of family functioning. The worker's purpose here is to ensure clarity and congruence among family members so as to provide the opportunity for each member to articulate his/her concerns, desires, or wishes. During this stage of intervention, the worker must enable all family members to understand that the family is not being denigrated because it is a rules-dominated system. Rather, this is the perfect time to demonstrate to the family that rules have helped it to survive and function despite many obstacles. Termination is the time to sum up and bridge the Thomas family to a new beginning.

Evaluation and Follow-up

As the worker approaches closure in working with the Thomas family, due to the fact that stabilization has been accomplished, steps must be put into place for evaluation and follow-up. The first step is to determine the level of functioning of the Thomas family. Family members and the worker must attempt to work toward mutual understanding of their growth and progress because of the worker's involvement and their own commitment to bring about change through the achievement of stated goals and objectives. The Thomas family and the worker should have some understanding of the necessary rules that the family developed to govern family functioning over time. Those rules that have been restrictive in nature must be looked upon as having been functional, at least in part, within the family context. Still, rules must be operating at a level to provide the family with both stabilization and satisfaction regarding its own functioning. Mutuality in understanding and purpose provides the common focus essential for the family and the worker to be able to connect and move forward to a different level of functioning.

Identifying resources for maintaining family equilibrium is another important component to evaluation and follow-up. The Thomas family and worker must work together and identify specific resources to be utilized in future efforts to help the family maintain the stability it has worked hard to achieve. For equilibrium to be maintained within the family, both family members and the worker should be clear about the necessary resources needed to ensure maximal family coping. These resources should reflect concrete strategies and mechanisms by which the family will continue to create and utilize internal and external family supports when needed. To illustrate, the Thomas family and the worker may identify the importance of setting aside money each week for a weekly dinner at a fast-food restaurant. Such collaboration and strategizing will be important in keeping alive the new ritual of a child-oriented family outing each week at a fast-food restaurant.

The realization of the importance of working hard to support the continuation of this family ritual should create a warmer, more supportive environment within the family. This expected event or ritual each weekend should help Beverly to be somewhat more relaxed about her dietary regimen. In turn, it will help the children to feel that they have more of an accepted role in family decision making.

The worker also has the responsibility during evaluation to assist the family in outlining various concrete examples to help them further appreciate their accomplishments and their readiness to maintain an ongoing healthy existence. For instance, although a full-time working mother, Beverly has followed through with all the family meetings and has never lost her enthusiasm about getting help. Meanwhile, the children have supported their mother throughout this process by helping out more with household tasks on the days of the family meetings and by listening carefully to their mother, the worker, and each other during the sessions. The facilitation role on behalf of the worker is vital to helping the Thomas family comprehend the nature of its functioning. If the worker provides leadership during this transitional period, it is more likely that the family will continue to function well without the worker's intervention.

Finally, the worker has the responsibility to help the Thomas family identify future steps for follow-up. Follow-up represents those items to be revisited after the worker has evaluated and has oftentimes already terminated with the family. The Thomas family members should, at this point, be able to articulate what they perceive to be necessary for their continued satisfaction within the family. This step ought to be carried out in consultation between the Thomas family and the worker. The rationale for this consultation is to provide recognition of mutual input in deciding what should follow the initial intervention process. Such understanding among both parties is crucial to the relationship that has been established. An example may be observed through the request from Samantha, the daughter, to have the worker come out to visit the family again in one month. The entire family agreed that the worker make such a visit. In addition, Samantha is to report back to the worker and her mother about her progress in the support group for anorectic teens, to which she has been referred. Moreover, the worker has explained to the mother that she would accompany her to an Individual Educational Plan (IEP) meeting at school next fall concerning Richie.

ROLES AND THE ROMANO FAMILY (SEE CASE STUDY FOUR)

Engagement

The worker was introduced to the Romano family because of the problem of unemployment. The company of the father, Victor Romano, has decided to downsize and lay off a large portion of its staff. Victor, a senior management staff member, has been targeted for layoff. Mario, his son, a successful corporate attorney, has attempted to assist his parents financially during this difficult period. As a result of his own concern about his parents' stress level, Mario has requested that the worker visit the family at home. The worker from the agency was somewhat hesitant to respond to this request from Mario, who is married and lives elsewhere with his own family. Nevertheless, she consented to visit the Romanos after having a telephone conversation with Mario's mother, Julia, who welcomed the worker's intervention. During this telephone conversation Julia shared with the worker her anxiety about her husband's feelings of depression and worthlessness about being laid off from his job.

Interviewing

In interviewing the roles-dominated family, it is important to remember the definition of a role. Roles signify specific behaviors expected from family members. The family member designated to be the head of the household would be addressed first. In communicating with family members, the worker must keep in mind the hierarchy within the family structure, based on assigned and/or assumed roles.

The flow of the interview, including the pattern of questioning, will be largely determined by the respect shown by the worker for family roles. The worker would most likely begin with open-ended questions tailored to enable family members to function within established roles. That is, when family members respond to open ended questions, they will respond from their assigned roles rather than from positions that have not yet been established. Furthering is another interviewing technique that is designed to help family members express themselves about family issues with acknowledgement from the worker. Since the head of the household in a roles-dominated family may tend to control the initial phase of the interview, the worker may want, at first, to summarize what family members share and then move to paraphrasing as a method of giving feedback.

In the first interview, it is important for the worker to establish a role for himself/herself. That is, the family members should be able to realize through the interview with the worker the nature of the role that the worker will most likely assume. This is a crucial ingredient of the first interview with a roles-dominated family. If the worker's position is not clarified at the outset, his/her role in future sessions may be compromised or even undermined by the family. In a roles-dominated family the worker should allow members to provide the focus for the interview.

Assessment

The Romano family pattern of interaction may be described as that of top-down, with the father, Victor, being the head of the family. The males in the Romano family occupy the power position. The strongest role within the Romano family is that of decision maker, and no one has the authority to question the decisions made by the males. Leadership configuration is clearly identified in families dominated by roles. Therefore, the strong breadwinner role is delegated to the male. Age and position are also important variables in carrying out the responsibilities of caring for other family members. For example, Mario was successful in reversing the role of his father and himself. Mario took on the responsibility to find professional support services for his parents, since his father had rejected financial help from him. He felt that he could at least help his parents out in this important way.

During this assessment phase, the worker begins a thorough exploration of family dynamics. Until now, the Romano family has always had sufficient financial means. Moreover, Victor has been able to support the college-education plans of all his children. It is devastating to Victor not to be in the position of providing financial support to his younger children, Veronica and Frances. The financial crisis being experienced by Victor has created a sense of unworthiness and self-defeat. It has been documented that Victor is not to blame for the downsizing that took place in his oil company. Because Victor had been vice president of the company, he had believed that his family would always be financially safe and secure. Nevertheless, the layoff has shaken Victor's self-confidence and is impacting his ability to function in the role he has always identified for himself—that of the leader and head decision maker. He is unable, at this time, to move to a comparable position in the working world, perhaps due to his age and the economic climate. Thus, his view of himself has diminished to a negative perception of his role as the primary provider for the family. In other words, Victor's role as breadwinner has always been considered by the family as a bulwark of strength and support for the family.

Another dynamic that is emerging within the Romano family involves Angelo, the second-oldest, who is an internal-medicine specialist in private practice. Angelo is engaged to marry Sue Wheeler, a fundamentalist Christian. The problem arises from the fact that the Romano family is Roman Catholic, and all family members are devoted to their faith, which they practice together regularly as a family. Victor is especially against the marriage, since Sue will make no real commitment toward agreeing that any children they might have be raised Roman Catholic. The situation is further complicated by the strong friendship between Sue and Veronica, Angelo's sister. This friendship has grown even closer, because Veronica is also engaged and the two women have joked about having a double wedding. Consequently, Victor feels that he has lost not only his job and primary role as family provider, but also his important decision-making role within the family. Victor has had lengthy discussions with his wife, Julia, about his ardent feelings toward "mixed" marriages and is embarrassed and disappointed by his inability to direct his children toward acceptable behavior in line with family and cultural traditions.

Furthermore, a significant area of assessment is to determine how family members are reacting to the problems that are being identified through the intervention process. Frances, the younger daughter, is concerned that her college education will suffer, that is, she will no longer be able to depend on her family's financial backing. She had always viewed her father as the epitome of power and strength; to her he was "unshakable." Observing his response to his layoff has affected her confidence in her father's ongoing financial support. Frances feels that she has always been able to rely on her father and never expected him to be without a job. Still, she has not shared these feelings with her father. Also, Julia, the mother, has taken on the role as babysitter for Mario's son as a way of being able to accept money from him. The money she receives from Mario is being utilized to help the family with the costs of daily living. At this point, Victor is unaware of the amount of money (quite substantial) that Mario is giving her to care for Mario Jr.

Planning and Contracting

The worker has the responsibility to focus on changes that the family members wish to see occur within their family. Planning should serve to help the family reshape its concerns over problems into workable goals. In those families that are dominated by roles, the worker should attempt to direct the family toward clarification of messages that may be confusing. For example, in this case the worker should assist Victor, the father, in finding ways to search for a comfort level that would lead to acceptance of his current status as an unemployed corporate vice president. The worker must help to bolster Victor's self-esteem and assist him in achieving a stronger sense of usefulness as a person, despite his unemployment and his perception of having lost his key role as the family's power broker and decision maker.

Due to Victor's strong role orientation, the worker might attempt to find some fundamental ways for Victor to become involved with planning and contracting to rectify the family's problems. Such an intervention strategy should bolster his sense of inclusion and provide avenues for him to be able to assume a more comfortable role within the decision-making process. In addition, expectations of family members should be shared openly and outlined for further clarity. These expectations should provide guidance for designing and prioritizing the steps that are to follow.

Implementation and Action

At this time, the worker will begin the process of helping the Romano family to implement established goals. These goals and objectives will imperatively involve intrafamily and extra-family strategies. That is, the Romanos must be able to realize that while they may concentrate in intervention on problems inside the family system, they may also need to consider possible resources outside the family. The worker has to facilitate the Romano family's discussion regarding obtaining alternative financial support for the whole family, particularly during this time of crisis. Victor has to be assisted by the worker to accept his current role as breadwinner not as being "compromised" or "less than" before, but merely as being different. Likewise, the issue of religiously mixed families must be explored in depth with all family members.

Facilitation by the worker will include having all family members address to Victor and each other how they perceive his current and past role within the family. Such dialogue should center around the reality of the family's need to face difficult issues and decisions and should reinforce the need for all family members to be as open as possible in sharing their views and feelings. The worker, of course, must be accountable for helping to create an environment whereby everyone will feel relaxed and respected in imparting their innermost concerns. To illustrate, Victor might be encouraged to discuss openly with the family his feelings of disgust and disappointment with himself for having earlier invested large portions of past family income in stocks that later failed. Thus, Victor seems to be blaming himself for the family's present financial dilemma and seems convinced of the family's ability to overcome its money problems today if only he had been more cautious with his investments. Julia, his wife, has shared that he often muses to himself about this, almost as a form of self-chastisement. He has shared with Julia that with the investment income alone that he lost, he could have taken an early retirement. As family members begin to respond to one another during this interaction phase, they must be encouraged by the worker to be supportive and to emphasize family strengths and positive traits, such as strong kinship bonds, as opposed to dwelling on past or present shortcomings.

During the implementation and action stage the worker must assist the family members to utilize resources available to them. For instance, Mario and Angelo Romano, the sons, have been most successful in their careers and are financially secure. They both attribute much of their own success to the financial and emotional support that has always been extended by their parents. Despite Victor's contention that they will compromise their capacity to provide for their own families, they realize that they are in a position to assist their parents financially. Nevertheless, Victor is having extreme difficulty in accepting financial support from his sons. To Victor, it is unthinkable, as he does not perceive any degree of financial success by his sons as being sufficient enough to assume also the financial support of his family.

During this family intervention the worker is able to help the family members move toward acceptance of how they might be financially supportive of one another. It is through such family discussions that Victor becomes somewhat more receptive toward receiving financial help from his children. In addition, Frances has moved her thinking to a less selfish position and thus is willing to get a part-time job to take care of her personal needs. This family discussion enables the Romanos to establish new roles for themselves in an effort to enhance family functioning.

During the implementation phase the worker has the responsibility to explain to the family how it is organized as a working family system. In the Romano family, roles are the dominant force within family coping. Still, family members must also realize the importance of their understanding the functions of rules, relationships, and rituals within family functioning. Rules, roles, relationships, and rituals are four major forces existent in all families. Once the worker has decided which of these forces dominates within a given family, the task is to describe how the other three forces also operate within overall family dynamics.

For example, rules within the Romano family must be altered or compromised in order to move the family toward a healthier state. The rule was that Victor had to always assume the breadwinner role within the family. Fate would have it that Victor would lose the family's investments and his job as well. Therefore, all the family rules must change, and these changes will inevitably affect the roles typically assigned to or assumed by all family members. Also, relationships will be affected by changes in roles. Relationships will likely be strengthened by virtue of the Romano family's need to redefine or renegotiate its rules and roles. Moreover, these changes in major family variables will impact family rituals. In the Romano family, rituals are imbedded in religious beliefs and practices. Being a strong Roman Catholic family, the Romanos view marriage as a sacrament and one of the most important rituals within their Italian cultural heritage. With Angelo's proposed marriage to a fundamentalist believer, the marriage ceremony will perhaps not take place in the Roman Catholic church. However, the worker might help the family to understand that the marriage can still be conducted within the Roman Catholic church, with a fundamentalist minister co-officiating. However, in this case Sue has requested that the wedding take place within her church. Consequently, a rich tradition within the Romano family is being disrupted by this marriage. The worker must assume roles as facilitator, enabler, and mediator to help the family grasp the impact of rituals on the family's responses to issues and to each other.

Termination

The worker has to assist the Romano family in recognizing it own sense of well-being. The skills achieved for growth and self-development will serve as bridges to renewed stability as the family members are able to understand and appreciate the roles that enable their existence as a unique family system. Termination may occur only after the family is able to reach a level of satisfaction regarding the identified problems of unemployment and mixed marriage, and related issues causing role changes or redistribution of family roles. These difficult challenges must ultimately be resolved by the Romanos themselves, with the persistent guidance and support of the worker. The major task of the worker in this phase of intervention is to help each family member understand the egalitarian effort of all family members and their commitment toward maintaining this renewed state with some level of contentment. The worker must help the family become confident in its ability again to exist comfortably without her involvement and intervention.

Throughout this process the worker must help the Romano family to maintain its cultural identity. For instance, Victor may need to be reassured that by helping his wife at home with household chores or by agreeing to his son's wish to have a non-Catholic wedding he will not diminish his continued commitment to his cultural heritage nor his family's core identity with each other as a family unit. The worker must also continually be aware of her own personal values and appreciation for cultural differences while concurrently helping the family gain insight into inevitable shifts in family values and ways of being that may result from cultural assimilation and responses to environmental crises.

Evaluation and Follow-up

The last step in discussing intervention with the roles-dominated family focuses upon the need for evaluation and follow-up. The worker must help the Romano family to achieve a level of functioning that leads to success and self-fulfillment for all family members. Obviously, they will not always agree with each other's decisions, but they will learn to respect each other's right to have an equal say in family concerns and decisions. It is during this phase that resources are identified and mobilized to help the family maintain equilibrium. Though Mario and Angelo Romano are financial resources for the family, Victor, with his years of experience and expertise in corporate leadership, may be encouraged to seek a consulting position in his field. But, first, the worker has to assist in providing the insight for Victor to see and understand that he still retains these skills to succeed in a related area of employment. The challenge for the worker is to establish guidelines that will enable the entire family to recognize resources and support one another in utilizing them.

Follow-up is recommended at the appropriate time by the worker. Follow-up is the time at which the worker will determine whether the family has been able to accept the financial support from Mario and Angelo as well as concede to the marriage between Angelo and Sue. Another question of merit is whether all family members have been, in their own way, able to deal with the necessary changes in their roles as a consequence of Victor's unemployment.

RELATIONSHIPS AND THE JONES FAMILY (SEE CASE STUDY FIVE)

Engagement

The worker's introduction to the Jones family came about as a result of Barbara Jones's concern for Carl, her fourteen-year-old son. Barbara is seeking help because of her son's desire to have a relationship with his incarcerated father from whom she is now divorced. Barbara, being from a family of twelve children with close family ties, is committed to having family members visit one another. Now remarried, she is disturbed because of the uncertainty about the influence that her ex-husband, Hugh, might have on Carl.

Interviewing

In interviewing the relationships-dominated family, the worker should phrase questions so as to capture the social/emotional aspects of family interaction. How family members arrange relationships ought to be the driving force for interactions between the worker and the family. The seating arrangement may provide clues for the worker regarding degrees of interaction and closeness among family members. For example, if Barbara and Joe always arrange themselves apart from Carl, this might signify a close relationship between the mother and step-father and perhaps a weaker relationship between the parents and their son. As a result of this observation, the worker should be careful not to exclude Carl in family discussions.

The format of information gathering by the worker should include open-ended questions to enable all family members to respond freely. Being able to respond in this manner should allow family members to speak as they so desire, thereby enhancing family relationships. In relationships-dominated families the worker should attempt to maintain focus through the creative use of summarizing. This technique will assist family members to realize those areas about which they agree and disagree.

Assessment

In the assessment phase the worker attempts to develop an accurate picture of family issues. The worker's introduction to the Jones family resulted from Barbara's request for help. In addition to the issue of Carl's renewing his relationship with Hugh, his natural father, Barbara is six months' pregnant and is having some problems with swelling. She is being followed very closely by her doctor, who has requested to see her weekly until the birth of the baby. She is being seen at the neighborhood health center. Barbara is presently working as a nurse's assistant and is experiencing some difficulty with being on her feet so many hours per day. She has a strong will to work because she is competitive with her siblings. All her siblings have college degrees, but Barbara never went to college. She has a strong desire to someday earn her diploma as a registered nurse.

The assessment enables the worker to describe leadership within the family. As relationships dominate the Jones family, it stands to reason that leadership will be a shared task, given the close interaction and open communication between the parents. The stepfather, Joe, plays an important role in assisting with governance of the family due to the close relationship between Barbara and him. Barbara has insisted that Joe take an equal role in the overall parenting of Carl. This has been the arrangement since their engagement. Joe is beginning to view Carl as his own son, and Carl has recently started calling him "father." They attend baseball games together; in fact, Carl has asked Joe to go to more games with him, but Joe has had to work overtime in his job as a computer programmer. He has an associate of arts degree and was the first in his family to have gone to college.

An issue that Joe faces relates to Barbara's broad interpretation of family relationships. Joe is deeply concerned about Carl's proposed visit with his natural father in prison. Barbara is also skeptical of this visit but her reservations are overshadowed by her firm belief in and commitment to close family relationships and their impact on family members' well-being.

Another issue for Barbara is the seeming appearance of Joe's replacement of Hugh in Carl's life, that is, the strengthening relationship between Carl and Joe. Barbara is especially concerned about Carl's visit with his father because Carl himself has recently gotten into trouble with the authorities by hanging out with a gang of teen-aged boys who broke into a hardware store. Moreover, it has been learned that Carl has been skipping school at least once per week. Barbara, Joe, and Carl have recently had a meeting with the Juvenile Court counselor and they have agreed that Carl will be grounded and maintain a 9 p.m. curfew for one month. If Carl honors the decision made with the counselor, he will not have to appear before the Juvenile Judge. This is extremely frustrating for Carl because he has already missed one baseball game and cannot go out with his friends.

Barbara is fearful that because of his jealousy, Hugh might somehow try to dissuade or hinder Carl's growing trust in his stepfather. Moreover, Barbara is nervous because of not knowing how Carl is going to react when she and Joe have their first baby. This feeling grew out of Carl's reaction whenever the baby is mentioned; he always leaves the room and slams the door. She is anxious that the new baby might pull Carl and Joe apart, just when they seem to really be reaching out to each other. Barbara's feelings of uncertainty seem to be intensifying as the birth of the baby approaches.

These issues are particularly affecting Barbara because her whole world is dominated by relationships. Consequently, the interactions that occur among family members may appear to be blown out of proportion, but then one must continually be mindful of Barbara's being totally absorbed in family relationships. That is, she is sensitive to how other family members perceive their relationship with her and likewise how she perceives herself within these connections.

Planning and Contracting

The planning focus with the Jones family is to enable family members to agree on how to address their most pressing issue. The worker has to help family members concentrate on the strengths of their relationships to approach their problems. In attempting to reach the agreed-upon focus for intervention, the worker has to provide facilitation leading to reshaping problems into workable goals. In this time of reshaping the Jones family should receive feedback from each other and the worker. An example of reshaping is Barbara Jones's strong views about the nature of family relationships. These views have created mixed emotions regarding her son's proposed visit with his incarcerated father. The worker has to help Barbara redefine or reframe this issue of visitation within the context of her own philosophical belief in the power of relationships. In other words, Barbara has to sort out whether she is truly supporting Carl's visit with his natural father for Carl's sake, or because she feels that the father-son relationship must be encouraged despite the consequences.

Other areas of concern that must be addressed are expectation and accountability on behalf of family members. Barbara expects strong ties among all family members despite distance. The worker has to work with family members in clarifying expectations that might be unrealistic. In this time of contracting the worker has the opportunity to assist the Jones family in sorting out expectations regarding change within the family system. Sometimes it is difficult to distinguish between issues because of the confused and diffuse boundaries that exist in relationships-dominated families (Minuchin, 1981). Such family members are enmeshed; that is, they are so close to one another that they cannot pull themselves far enough away from a problem to make unique, individual contributions toward how to resolve it. Jones (1992) noted that due to the ideology and structure of American families, parents often become enmeshed with children as they seek validation, self-esteem, and intimacy from them. Such family relationships may tend to be as bewildering as those wherein family members are disengaged; that is, they are so isolated and distant from one another that any move toward consensus leads to much dissension and disagreement over which goals must be established (Minuchin, 1981).

The final consideration involves both designing and setting priorities. The worker has to assist the family in outlining the agreed-upon plan of action. This will help family members in reaching their stated goals and objectives. Within a relationships-dominated family it is important that the written plan enable them to feel comfortable with the use of relationships in accomplishing set goals and objectives. An example is Barbara's struggle to maintain close relationships regardless of the proximity of family members to each other. Also, Barbara's struggle to maintain a job without a college degree has been problematic. Being from a family of twelve wherein she was the only one not to go to college has caused Barbara much pain and anxiety. The close-knit family has served as a source of both pain and joy for Barbara. Therefore, at this time of setting priorities, the primary struggles Barbara has to face are those of maintaining self and nuclear family while continuing close ties with all other family members regardless of the physical distance involved. Barbara's perception of family relationships has created additional anxiety because of her desire to "do the right thing" where Carl is concerned. She feels that he is entitled to have a relationship with his natural father, regardless of the consequences, yet worries that a visit to the prison at this time might be detrimental to her son and inhibit the relationship he has developed with his stepfather.

Nevertheless, Barbara has become even more perplexed recently about how to respond to Hugh's requests that Carl be able to visit him in prison. Hugh has been working very hard on his rehabilitation in prison and has earned a vocational certificate for advanced skill development in auto mechanics. Hugh has stated that he plans to return to the same town upon his release and set up his own auto repair shop. He wants to see Carl regularly and thus wants to begin their new relationship before his prison discharge in six months. Joe and Barbara have had a recent argument about Hugh's having called to speak with Barbara about this matter at 2 a.m.

Implementation and Action

Barbara is a strong believer in carrying out goals and objectives within the family. She has always avowed that families who work together as a whole will be able develop stronger relationships. Being from a family of twelve children, she has always asserted that she plans to have at least three children of her own. The worker has to assist Barbara in understanding that having three children is not absolutely necessary just because she came from a large family. Barbara has her own family now and must realize that the relationships within her nuclear family at this time will naturally take on different characteristics and unique issues. She must be able to realize that she cannot always use her family of origin as a rule of thumb for measuring her success in creating and maintaining family relationships. Moreover, the worker must help Barbara to clarify for herself the reasons behind her strong aspiration to achieve an educational status similar to that of her siblings. She must focus, instead, on her accomplishments and successes in life, for instance, having remarried and having achieved a close, trusting relationship with her new husband, Joe, who also is dedicated to Carl. Having more children may impact Barbara's ability to return to school and, in the long run, may not necessarily strengthen her relationship with her siblings and parents. A primary focus of the social worker's actions in helping this family might be to concentrate on helping Joe and Barbara to better understand and define Joe's relationship as husband and father.

In implementing the goals and objectives, the worker must aid the family in utilizing outside systems. This is an added advantage for relationships-dominated families who generally value and attempt to maximize relationships in their best interests. The worker has to help the family members to use their strong skills in relationship-building to establish connections with outside resources. That is, such family members may be able to approach outside resources with the same relationship focus that they adhere to so closely within the family system. Such an approach should strengthen their capacity to establish and maintain priorities in seeking help from human service agencies.

Effective utilization of resources by family members may lead to the desired outcomes. As the Jones family is able to reach some understanding regarding vital issues they will be carrying out agreed-upon goals and objectives. Nevertheless, as the worker intervenes with the relationships-dominated family, he/she must achieve the ability to move inside and outside the family as an important resource without becoming overly involved. Since relationships-dominated families may tend to overaccentuate any relationship with another person, the worker may feel that he/she is at times walking a tightrope in an effort not to become enmeshed or submerged in family problems. Family members are more likely to experience difficulty in dealing with a professional, as they may expect the professional to take sides or may feel rejected if the professional has to use confrontation in problem solving. Still, the worker must be forever cognizant of the power inherent within the helping relationship and the special opportunities afforded by this bond in assisting a relationships-dominated family.

Termination

In a relationships-dominated family the worker may use recognition of the family's enhanced well-being through the use of relationships in describing growth and self-development. In preparing the family for termination, the worker must help the family to realize the growth and progress it has made, thus enabling family members to cease regular visits. More specifically, the worker may need to outline for the family several specific reasons that termination is appropriate at this time. For the Jones family, these reasons may include further clarification or explanation regarding their major concerns, for example, deciding on Carl's visit with his incarcerated father, dealing with the birth of the new baby, and additionally clarifying Joe's role as stepfather.

Moreover, in closing the helping relationship with a relationships-dominated family, the worker must realize that there may be more resistance to the termination process than with other family types. This is because of family members' tendency to define their existence through strong relationships. In fact, their conditions of worth may stem from their perception of the need to prolong relationships. Therefore, they may find it almost impossible to examine those dynamics that define family functioning. The worker has become an important asset to the family, and it will inevitably highly value this new relationship. With this type of family, members may also have difficulty in perceiving how they might continue to function and maintain their gains in problem solving without the worker's presence.

Evaluation and Follow-up

In determining the level of functioning, the Jones family members must define mutuality as reflected in their relationships with each other, as well as with the worker. Mutuality, that is, mutual understanding, will define for the worker and members of the Jones family whether or not termination may be implemented. Termination may be addressed only if an agreed-upon, satisfactory level of family functioning exists. In the relationships-dominated family, mutuality occupies the commanding position for termination. Relationships involve interconnecting emotions and interactions. To terminate means to discontinue these processes that tie the family to the worker. Therefore, it may be vastly difficult to bring to closure that relationship which has been joined by intensive sharing of one's whole being. That is, the driving force for the relationships-dominated family is to maintain and nourish the relationship.

Follow-up is an agreed-upon step in intervention that will enable the Jones family and the worker to reevaluate family functioning as necessary. The major issues addressed in the family will need to be reviewed. This review or evaluation will provide avenues for future intervention. The relationships-dominated family may be expected to have greater difficulty in realizing the finiteness of termination. Therefore, if defined appropriately, follow-up may be seen as a way that the family members may continue to utilize the worker and social agency when absolutely necessary.

Families that are dominated by relationships have an element of blinding impact. That is, these families are implanted in relationships that tend to mask their abilities to clearly understand and see the nature of their own behavior. Relationships are inclined to become overpowering and may prevent clear snapshots of family dynamics. The worker in such families has to take snapshots to be displayed for family members, not only to elucidate progress made during follow-up, but also at strategic points throughout the intervention process. The worker as facilitator should create bridges to understanding the entire picture of family inner workings, both images that are strong and clear as well as those that need further focusing and clarity.

The Jones family must be assisted by the worker to understand that there are three other dimensions—rules, roles, and rituals—that also are operating within their family dynamics. Perhaps the primary rule is to always continue quality interaction with one's parents and siblings. For example, Barbara Jones wants to ensure Carl's opportunity to visit with his biological father as a result of this preexisting rule in her own family of origin. Secondly, roles are likely to be rigidly defined by Barbara, as defined to her by her father and mother. Barbara is very much locked into expectations as to how she should function as a wife, mother, daughter, and sister. She may need to look deeper into her own expectations as to what might be best for herself and her family. Finally, rituals in the Jones family are demonstrated through the rigid manner in which Barbara struggles to obtain a college degree. The ritual attached to receiving a degree is ceremonial. Barbara has guilt feelings because she had to drop out of college to get married and because all of her brothers and sisters have college degrees. How well Barbara can attest to this reality, because she has always been present at every graduation ceremony, which no one in the family would dare miss. Barbara takes much pride in her siblings' successes in their educational and career pursuits, often exalting them. Still, not all of Barbara's siblings attended her wedding to Joe Jones, nor have they called to congratulate her about her current pregnancy. Barbara may need to gain insight into how rituals may not always serve the needs of all family members. Each new family system being formed will invariably develop its own rituals and set its own priorities about which rituals must be co-celebrated by all nuclear and extended family members.

FIGURE 5.1   A Modern Family Ritual

RITUALS AND THE JOHNSON FAMILY (SEE CASE STUDY SIX)

Engagement

The worker has been asked by Margaret Johnson to become involved with the family. This request grew out of Margaret's concern regarding the weekly Sunday dinners at the home of Eva Johnson, the paternal great-grandmother. Eva, age eighty-one, is extremely active as a volunteer in the community. Family members are seeking assistance from an outside individual to help with the discussion regarding Eva's overactive schedule at the local children's hospital. Several family members have hinted to Eva that she needs to slow down her busy schedule of activities, but she chides them saying that she has always been full of energy and "raring to go." Still, her family is worried about the demands she places on herself, particularly in meeting the needs of other family members, and have noticed that she looks tired at times.

In rituals-dominated families, such as the Johnson family, the worker has to be mindful that he/she must provide the opportunity for family members to discuss issues openly. The importance of this dynamic within the rituals-dominated family enables each participant to have input into designing each family activity. From these discussions rituals may be born and maintained. One must keep in mind that rituals within families that are rituals-dominated generally take place within the context of all family members being present. The only exception to this rule is when a family member is critically ill or dealing with an unforeseen event. In this case, Eva has agreed to meet with the entire family only if the meeting can be held at her house on a weekday evening and include the worker at dinner before the session. The worker has agreed to this arrangement.

Interviewing

In interviewing the Johnson family, the worker has to keep in mind the importance of focusing on issues that must be clarified. In revisiting these issues the worker is providing the opportunity for family members to experience the interviewing process, which is similar to the family's way of organizing itself and addressing its problems. That is, the worker will create a level of comfort for family members comparable to that experienced during historical rituals within the family. As the worker interviews family members he/she should concentrate on using the techniques of open-ended questions, summarization, paraphrasing, and seeking concreteness.

Open-ended questions should be useful within the context of the Johnson family, a multigenerational family. Asking open-ended questions allows information to be gathered from all family members present and should also help to bring about more open sharing of concerns within both nuclear and extended family systems. In summarization, the worker has the opportunity to have each family member hear again what has been shared, or if he/she has not been paying close attention, hear for the first time what issues are being raised. Moreover, corrections may be offered by family members regarding information perceived to be inaccurate. Paraphrasing gives the worker a chance to receive additional affirmation regarding his/her grasp and interpretation of concerns being shared within the family interview. To understand the specific issues that are rituals-oriented, the worker may need to seek more concrete details. That is, this approach enables additional descriptive information to be brought out in relation to specific activities or events, their origins, and their ongoing impact on family life.

Each of these techniques of interviewing may be utilized with the Johnson family, a rituals-dominated family. For example the worker should summarize information received in order to provide the Johnsons with an overview of the types of rituals existent within their family. Many families will be able to identify some of their rituals but may be unaware of other significant ritualistic activities that they would not perhaps classify as rituals per se. Utilizing other interviewing techniques highlighted above should help the worker to better understand the issues and dynamics of how rituals have evolved within the Johnson family, as well as how they impact each family member. These interviewing techniques should afford all family members an opportunity to share their perceptions and responses to family rituals and other unique ways of being as a family unit. The worker may need to reassure family members to be as open and honest as possible during this stage of intervention, fully realizing that some members may be more reluctant than others to criticize or reject family rituals for fear of being ostracized or labeled as being disloyal.

Assessment

A major task of the Johnson family, with the assistance of the worker, is to develop an accurate picture of family issues. That is, each family member must be able to perceive the primary reasons for the family's need for intervention. These major concerns may be broken down into three chief categories: weekly Sunday dinners at Eva's house; Christmas celebrations at Eva's house; and Eva's overextending herself and working too hard. A major concern, at present, in the Johnson family is the weekly Sunday dinner. The urgency of exploring the family dinner issue partially relates to Eva's advanced age, as well as to her focusing on the weekly family get-togethers as her primary source of self-fulfillment. The annual Christmas celebration also involves the gathering of all family members in Eva's home, even those who live in distant places. They come from afar to participate in this strong family ritual, and until now no family member has ever considered altering this tradition. The third and final issue involves work. The Johnson family members have always been extremely hard workers, an expectation of all family members that is frequently communicated at family gatherings. An example of this hard work may be observed through Eva's unwillingness to discontinue her volunteer work and her insistence upon cooking dinner for the entire family at her house every Sunday. The concern on behalf of her family is the amount of time that Eva presently has to spend in meal preparation. In earlier times Eva would prepare the meal in one day. But family members have noted that lately she takes longer and goes out of her way to prepare special dishes. What was a one-day event has turned into a weekly ritual that consumes much of her time. Also, the family feels that Eva's three half-days per week in the local hospital auxiliary gift shop is much too strenuous for a woman of eighty-one.

Planning and Contracting

In planning and contracting with a rituals-oriented family, the primary focus for the family is their concern about Eva's persistence in continuing the weekly family dinners. All members of the Johnson family have agreed that Eva is slowing down more yet refuses to reduce her activity level, especially the family dinner ritual wherein she cooks and serves the entire dinner single-handedly. When her family confronts her about working too hard and expresses concern about her seeming to be more fatigued, she retorts that a loss of energy comes with advanced age and states that she has planned accordingly for these changes. However, the family wishes to reshape responsibilities into workable goals that will satisfy everyone involved. They believe that they should be able to reach some compromise or consensus without canceling an important family ritual. For example, Eva's daughter-in-law, Clara Johnson, age sixty, has agreed to rotate the Sunday dinners to her home every other week. This recommendation has to be shared with Eva with the explanation that both parties are still able to meet their expectations.

As all family members come together to understand the nature of problem areas, they are continuing the family ritual of regular gatherings to discuss important issues in their lives, these concerns being largely oriented toward each other's well-being and happiness. Such an approach will increase the likelihood of Eva's embracing the intervention process, or any activity for that matter, that might afford the opportunity for all family members to come together. The worker must be aware that rituals sometimes persist, not so much because of the specific activities involved, but rather due to other factors such as family camaraderie, validation of feelings, and mutuality of interests.

Implementation and Action

In carrying out goals established for the Johnson family, the worker must ensure interaction by all family members with one another. In implementing the goal for Clara Johnson to host the family Sunday dinner twice a month, the worker is assisting family members to respond to a major family issue. Not only will this alleviate the pressure being placed upon Eva, but it will also allay anxiety on behalf of the family. The nature of this recommendation is simply to introduce a new ritual for the Johnson family. It should also be understood that some time may be necessary before Eva reaches full acceptance of this change. The worker may facilitate this process by helping the family to understand the real reasons that they agree to come together regularly as a family, that is, to share their love and concern for each other.

In regard to Eva's volunteer position, several options might be explored, including Eva's working only one half-day a week and her taking some time off from this job. But Eva has been instrumental in suggesting an alternative, a compromise that should satisfy both her and her family. Eva has agreed to share her job in the hospital gift shop with her best friend, May. This new arrangement means that Eva will now be working only six hours a week instead of twelve hours. The worker has discovered that Eva had initially been resistive to changing her hours because she had preferred to work all the morning hours that the gift shop was open. She had always considered herself to be in charge of the little shop during the morning hours, the busiest time, and enjoyed saying hello to all the staff that came by each day for their newspaper. Under the new arrangement, Eva and May will meet midweek to discuss specific job duties such as ordering supplies and restocking the shelves. Eva has even joked about never thinking that she would ever be involved in a job-sharing arrangement at her age.

During the implementation phase, the worker will work with the Johnson family as a facilitator or enabler with the goal of creating the opportunity for family members to have adequate dialogue. Therefore, the worker's primary approach is that of enhancing family dialogue and communication. Thus, family members will be able to share wishes and desires as well as explore the realities of their current needs. In the multigenerational Johnson family, the worker needs to ensure that family members from each family unit (e.g., Eva; her children; her grandchildren) have the opportunity to speak, are given ample time to express their views, and are encouraged to discuss alternatives with each other.

As with other families, the worker needs to clarify that the Johnson family must also understand the dynamics of rules, roles, and relationships within their family to better comprehend family functioning. The worker has the responsibility to assume the teacher's role and help the Johnson family understand how each of these dynamics, that is, rules, roles, and relationships, evolve and play themselves out within the family. To illustrate, the worker might point out the rule changes that have been proposed, wherein Clara Johnson will now take on the responsibility of hosting the weekly family dinner twice a month. A related issue involves role changes within the Johnson family. This change includes the request for Clara to take on the role of a family leader, which may someday result in her assuming Eva's vital position as the family matriarch. Still, one must realize that these changes may not occur without family agreement, including Eva's consent, and this new arrangement will need everyone's support and regular involvement to maintain the inherent ritual. In essence, the worker is helping the family to have greater clarity and appreciation for rituals by helping them to understand the interconnectedness of family rules, roles, and relationships in enabling family rituals to prevail. In the Johnson family this realization is crucial, for rituals exist as the basic fabric that holds the family together.

Termination

The termination phase represents the recognition of enhanced well-being as a consequence of the Johnsons' having addressed problematic issues. In other words, barriers confronting family members have either been removed, or family members have reached a level of functioning in which the ongoing intervention by the worker is no longer needed. The worker must be cautious at the point of termination because of having been such an integral part of family interaction, including being an invited guest at dinner. As such, the point of leaving must be approached via a transition period to enable the family to continue addressing issues after the physical departure of the worker. This step is critical in rituals-dominated families because the worker will have joined the family in an important role and in order to accomplish the tasks successfully may have become enmeshed. Therefore, leaving will have to be accomplished through a clearly defined and agreed-upon process. In a sense, leaving in and of itself becomes a ritualistic experience. As with all families and all family types, the worker must assist the family to realize that in order to bring about change, he/she has been a catalyst for helping the members to utilize many resources that were already present within the family. This mutual understanding helps to further clarify and implement the termination process.

Evaluation and Follow-up

The worker has the responsibility to assist in determining the level of functioning of the Johnson family. One important aspect of this process is ensuring mutuality, or mutual understanding between the family and the worker. For example, the Johnson family and the worker should agree that at this time Clara Johnson will assume partial responsibility for the weekly family dinner. Evaluation also includes the identification of resources needed for maintaining equilibrium in the family. For instance, the worker might suggest a resource to assist Eva in house-cleaning or someone to drive her to her volunteer job at the hospital gift shop. Perhaps the final step in evaluation and follow-up is the identification of future steps needed. Within the Johnson family these steps might include Margaret Johnson's eventual assumption of the family dinner as well as the family's recognizing and fully accepting her within this role.

Family members will be expected to understand that over time rituals will continue to shape and influence their family life. Therefore, family members should be able to express themselves freely regarding their future plans with the firm belief that rituals will most likely be a part of their existence together as a group indefinitely.

SUMMARY

The Four-R Model of Family Dynamics represents an approach to understanding how families function. All families are grounded in rules, roles, relationships, and rituals. This chapter explains and demonstrates the problem-solving process with application of the Four-R Model. Four families were presented and assessed throughout the intervention in accordance with the Four-R Model. It is the authors' view that all families, without exception, are guided by either rules, roles, relationships, or rituals as an organizing or unifying core. The responsibility of the worker is to help the family understand the impact of this unique way of being as a family system, as well as understand that the other three dynamics are also important variables in family coping. In essence, elucidation of the other variables contributing to family functioning should, in turn, enable any given family to continue to derive strength and direction from their intrinsic guiding force.

QUESTIONS FOR DISCUSSION

1. Describe the major issues within the Thomas family that make them rules-dominated.
2. Describe the major issues within the Romano family that make them roles-dominated.
3. Describe the major issues within the Jones family that make them relationships-dominated.
4. Describe the major issues within the Johnson family that make them rituals-dominated.

GROUP EXERCISE

Divide the class into small groups of three to six participants. Assign one of the four families to each group. Each group should take its assigned family through the problem-solving process. Identify in detail major issues within each step that will pertain to this particular type of family. Each small group should summarize the authors' discussion of challenges for the worker in each stage of intervention and then generate additional issues. The challenge here is to go beyond the authors' discussion. Each group will then present its findings to the class or write an individual reflection paper as a follow-up to this classroom exercise.

SIGNIFICANT TERMS

open-ended questions
closed-ended questions
seeking concreteness
furthering

providing/maintaining focus
summarizing
paraphrasing

ECO-MAP: A TOOL FOR FAMILY ASSESSMENT

The ecological map (aka, eco-map) is designed to assist the practitioner in assessing the structure and intensity of social interactions, relationships, and/or social support networks. The eco-map serves as a visual illustration of the connections vital to family coping and maintenance of family equilibrium. An eco-map may be used by the practitioner during the initial assessment of a family or it may be instrumental in helping both the practitioner and family members to understand relationship patterns and the flow of support in and among family members.

REFERENCES

Hepworth, D. H. & Larsen, J. (1993). *Direct social work practice: Theory and skills.* 4th Edition. Pacific Grove, Calif: Brooks/Cole Publishing Co.
Jones, D. M. (1992). Enmeshment in the American family. *Affilia: Journal of Women and Social Work,* 6(2), 28–44.
Minuchin, S. (1981) A method for organizing the clinical description of family interaction: The "family interaction summary format." *American Journal of Family Therapy,* 2(3), 131–141.

▶ 6

Families: Issues in Diversity

Throughout American culture, diversity has always been addressed. In every segment of society diversity can be observed. Whether one is looking at differences, variety, uniqueness, or nontraditional behavior, diversity is present. Attempting to be inclusive in all interactions must be the present goal for humankind. Webster's dictionary defines diversity as "quality, state, fact, or instance of being diverse," "difference, dissimilitude, and unlikeness." (Webster, 1983, p. 537). This definition is a mirror image of the authors' understanding of the vast nature of diversity. The context of the definition displays the essence of the Four-R Model, which aspires to describe family functioning in its unique forms.

This chapter will explore the uniqueness that exists within American family life. The topics to be explored are: ethnicity/culture; sexual orientation; diverse parenting; and women's roles and gender issues. These concepts are not by any means the only types of family diversity, but they are being discussed here to explore some of the complexities involved in evaluating ways in which families arrange themselves in and around diversity.

ETHNICITY AND CULTURE

Ethnicity and culture may be perceived as synonymous terms. In most instances, the similarity is justified; however, it is important to point out the differences between these two concepts. Ethnicity is one's identity with a given group over time, that is, across generations. For example, one may identify himself/herself as being Hispanic, African American, or Italian American. However, culture includes norms, mores, values, customs, and traditions of a particular group of people. The correlation between ethnicity and culture is further expanded by the unique intermingling of one's own cultural norms with those of other groups including those of the general society.

In social work practice with families, practitioners should understand the influences of ethnicity and culture within the context of family dynamics. Devore and Schlesinger (1991) developed a model of ethnic-sensitive social work practice that denotes that ethnicity is a source of cohesion, identity, and strength, as well as a source of strain, discordance, and strife. Similarly, family members will become aware that the unique and special traditions that unify them may simultaneously create distance, especially when they interact with persons outside their culture. The ethnic identification of a specific family will position the family for a connection with values, norms, customs, and mores that become intertwined with their perception of family life. The cultural traditions of a family may outline for the worker the manner in which the family carries out its responsibilities. When a practitioner uses the strengths of a culture, he/she is more likely to be perceived by the consumer/client as having respect and competence (Jackson-Hopkins, 1992). And as the worker is able to understand the differences and similarities within ethnic and cultural traditions, his/her ability to fully utilize the helping role will be tremendously enhanced.

Through examining ethnic and cultural traditions one may better understand the connection between a particular family and its identity. In the Hispanic family, for example, there is a strong kinship network that serves to connect the family members. This connection may be observed during times of crisis as well as during times of joy. The strong family network is implemented through religious traditions and practices such as birth, baptism, marriage, and coming-of-age celebrations. The majority of Hispanics (whether Mexican, Cuban, Puerto Rican, or South American) are Roman Catholic, but there is a growing number of Hispanics who are Protestant, both in the United States as well as in their countries of origin (Castex, 1994). Strong religious rituals provide the opportunity for regular interaction among family members. Whether it is a religious event such as a saint's feast day or a cultural event such as Cinco de Mayo, family members are given the opportunity for unification. These opportunities further strengthen solid family support systems.

In the African American family, culture is defined by generational teaching. This strong sense of history and shared beliefs have held the African American family together during times of slavery, racism, and oppression. The African American family has been described as a multigenerational kinship system organized around a family-based household spanning geographic boundaries to connect family units (Hill, 1973; Martin & Martin, 1978; Williams & Wright, 1992). Moreover, Hill (1973, p. 5) refers to this system of family support as "kin-structured networks." The cultural nature of African American families seems to contribute to the willingness of relatives to call upon one another for help and to maintain a feeling of reciprocity, a strong sense of "oneness" (Hall & King, 1982). African American families often come together as a community in religious worship services and celebrate family rituals around baptisms, weddings, wakes, and reunions.

Moreover, the African American family culture may be better understood through the Kwanzaa celebration which is celebrated between December 26 and January 1 of each year. Kwanzaa was founded in 1966 by Dr. Maulana Karenga (McClester, 1990). This celebration of African American culture is organized around seven principles (Nguzo Saba). These principles are: Umoja (unity); Kujichagulia (self-determination); Ujima (collective work and responsibility); Ujamaa (cooperative economics); Nia (purpose); Kuumba (creativity); and Imani (faith) (McClester, 1990). The celebration of Kwanzaa presents African American families with an opportunity to become closer to their identity as a people, to understand their African cultural heritage, and to solidify their sense of community and family life.

FIGURE 6.1 An African American Family

Another ethnic/cultural group is the Italian American family. In many American cities there is an Italian American community. Within these communities, sometimes referred to as "little Italies," there are restaurants and churches side by side. Festivals are often held during summer months as an expression of Italian cultural heritage. These events include food, games, street dances, weddings, religious services, among other community events. It is expected that Italian families will be present at these events, which are centered around cultural traditions passed on from one generation to the next. This is also demonstrated through the diversity of cuisine, as it is customary for each family to share recipes that are based on the place of origin of family members, such as Sicily or Northern Italy.

Having described families demonstrating ethnicity and culture as examples of diversity, the authors will now address the historical significance of these concepts to the social work profession. The social work profession has long had a commitment to equality. This commitment is part of the basic fabric of the profession. Values embracing the significance of ethnicity and culture undergird the historical development of social work as a profession. Leadership and advocacy have always been central to working with families in need. The nature of helping may be observed through the work of Jane Addams at Hull House. Through the settlement house movement, immigrant families were assisted in their adjustment to and assimilation into American society. Basic needs and other identified requests were responded to by social workers in their efforts to help families through challenging times. These services included English classes, food, housing, day care, employment, recreation, health care, counseling, and rehabilitation. Moreover, social workers have provided outreach to enhance mental health service delivery systems among Native Americans (Cooley, Ostendorf, & Bickerton, 1979) and have developed multiple intervention strategies for providing culture-specific practice for Native American clients (Miller, 1982).

History is reflected in the work of helping multiethnic populations through the era of the Great Depression, through World Wars I and II, to the Civil Rights movement, to the end of the Vietnam War in the 1970s, to the Boat People of the 1980s, to the 1990s conflicts in Somalia, Iraq, and Bosnia. The 1990s also brought about changes in the federal government's position regarding the provision of human and social services.

This change in federal welfare programs represents the refocusing of federalism to a states rights mode of governance. As this change occurs, poor people of all ethnic groups will need, perhaps more than ever before, the assistance of social workers for survival purposes. These changes will also impact middle-income families that historically would not have needed the support of social workers for basic subsistence. Middle-income families traditionally have had the foundation for basic needs but have used social work practitioners to assist in those issues preventing wholesome living experiences. These issues might include decreasing and/or eliminating marital problems, facilitating adoptions and foster care, and providing options for the care of older adult family members.

SEXUAL ORIENTATION

Social work has long had a commitment to understanding and advocating for the rights of gays, lesbians, and bisexuals, that is, those having a different sexual orientation. One of the cardinal values of social work is to respect the uniqueness and individuality of all persons (Hepworth & Larsen, 1993). The strong belief in this value has led to a required objective within the Council on Social Work Education Curriculum Policy Statement (1994). The rationale for this position by the CSWE is based on the belief of being nonjudgmental in assisting all groups of people. Social workers as a profession have always been accepting of any oppressed population within our society. Prior to 1974 the Diagnostic and Statistical Manual of the American Psychiatric Association classified homosexuality as a mental illness (Zastrow & Kirst-Ashman, 1993). Other groups, such as the American Psychological Association, have shifted their view about sexual orientation from a conservative to a more progressive, inclusive stance. Historically, persons with sexual views and lifestyles outside the norm have been ostracized and persecuted by members of society. Homophobia still prevails as a major obstacle for gays, lesbians, and bisexuals. This persecution has led to an invisible society that coexists within the larger society; this coexistence for purposes of survival has led to a bicultural experience, wherein persons may mask their sexual orientations at work, in their neighborhoods, and within their families of origin while they draw emotional support and strength from regular interaction within the gay community.

However, the Gay Rights movement initiated by the Stonewall bar incident in New York City (Hunt, 1974) helped to bring about changes in the manner in which individuals choose to share their sexual orientation. Even though some progress has been made through the Gay Rights movement, homophobia is still rampant and gay rights are denied in many American communities. For example, the state of Colorado and the state of Oregon have introduced laws that would rescind ordinances protecting the rights of gays and lesbians (Moss, 1994; Norblad, February 10, 1994). In Ohio, the city of Cincinnati repealed a local ordinance passed in 1992 that had granted equal rights in employment, housing, and public accommodations for gays and lesbians (Teepen, 1995). This law had originally included gays and lesbians as a Cincinnati minority group along with Appalachians and other minorities, but gays and lesbians were the only persons deleted from the law upon revision.

Robert Bray, an official of the National Gay and Lesbian Task Force, has stated that bisexuality appears to be more acceptable to the larger society than a gay or lesbian lifestyle (Gabriel, 1995). However, they are often rejected by both heterosexuals and homosexuals as not fitting in or staying in the closet. Some negative stereotypes against bisexuals have increased since they have been grouped together with gays and lesbians in gay rights initiatives in Colorado and elsewhere in the United States. Still, in Boston and San Francisco a new trend is the development of open bisexual communities by young people, modeled upon the urban gay and lesbian community (Gabriel, 1995). Social work practice with families must continue to target oppressive views and attitudes toward gay, lesbian, and bisexual citizens.

Persons with AIDS have also had a tremendous impact on perceptions of gays and lesbians, particularly gay men in American society. Gay males were the largest group first hit by the AIDS epidemic in the early 1980s, and unfortunately maintain much of the stereotype, despite safe sex practices and lower incidence rates within the gay community. Significant others of gays and lesbians with AIDS experience a deep level of grief, as they may be separated from their partner, who often returns home to die.

Other "family" issues may center around conflict with his/her own family of origin regarding their own possible contraction of the disease or discomfort during joint visitation by both extended families at the hospital or hospice. In some cases, the gay individual has had to retain an attorney to maintain visitation in the hospital, because relatives of the dying person may invoke the "blood or legal kinship" policy in regard to who is allowed to visit. The impact on the gay and lesbian community has been devastating, for most gay and lesbian individuals have lost one or more friends to AIDS. Those who have lost their significant other are often left alone, and because of homophobia and alienation from families of origin, may feel depressed and withdrawn. They may refrain from interaction with the gay and lesbian community, particularly association with other gay couples or like family groups, because without a partner they no longer feel comfortable within these social situations. Bisexual individuals may experience even greater problems relating to spouses or significant others, as these partners may fear contracting AIDS from them because of multiple or past sexual liaisons.

Many attitudes and policies have discouraged persons of different sexual orientations from having a family life or in any way partaking of full benefits offered by our society to other family groupings. Bell and

Weinberg (1978) noted that approximately twenty-five percent of all gay and lesbian individuals surveyed had been married at one time. Of these individuals more than one-third of lesbians were married previously, as opposed to one-fifth of gay men. Moreover, over half of all lesbians and gays responded that they had children from these marriages. Many older gay and lesbian individuals who have been married earlier and make midlife revelations regarding their sexual orientation and preference for a change in lifestyle often face banishment from their adult children's and/or grandchildren's lives. This experience is so painful that it leads many gay and lesbian couples into counseling, usually with their significant other/partner, to address family stressors and conflict over this fracture of family relationships.

Also, in the 1990s gays and lesbians are not recognized in the U.S. military forces due to the recent passage of the "Don't Ask; Don't Tell," policy wherein a gay or lesbian enlisted person may be discharged if he/she admits to being a homosexual. The law forbids discrimination by honoring the privacy of gay and lesbian military personnel, but this pretense assumes that the "secret" of one's sexual orientation is extraneous to job fulfillment (Kramer, 1993). Still, even mental health experts in the military would perhaps have to agree that marital and/or family support is often crucial to one's success on the job, as well as a sense of personal achievement. Similarly, military personnel are expected to refrain from confronting the issue of homosexuality, even if they suspect that the person is a gay or lesbian. This policy is clearly antifamily in its treatment of gays and lesbians, for to even admit that one has a different sexual orientation means losing one's job and tenure in the military. Thus, significant others of gays and lesbians must be concealed off military bases or seen in secret, which discourages any semblance of family living or family social support. The new policy in the armed forces communicates a "live and let live" attitude. That is, gays and lesbians may stay in the military throughout their careers as long as they do not tell anyone about their sexual orientation.

Moreover, gay and lesbian families have been forced to be creative in efforts to have children, due to the continuing oppressive views of society. For example, lesbian couples have used artificial insemination because of laws against adoption and laws that rule in favor of the father in cases of in vitro fertilization. Some lesbians have used sperm banks as a means of having children, although there is much controversy in society regarding legal rights of such parents (Sewell, 1994). In addition, more and more gay and lesbian parents are losing custody and/or visitation rights with their own biological children, due to their sexual orientation, particularly if they reside with a partner in a gay family configuration. Gays and lesbians who attempt to adopt or provide foster care generally face monumental obstacles and long waiting lists for children, often being offered young children of the opposite sex who are chronically ill (e.g., with AIDS) or have other terminal conditions.

Social work practitioners must continually update their knowledge of ongoing changes reflecting societal views of gay, lesbian, and bisexual families. By and large, gay and lesbian families do not experience rituals or legal sanctions for their relationships, nor do they receive equitable privileges in the areas of spousal or dependent benefits through employment. Such exclusion may lead to additional feelings of individual and/or family alienation. Updating information regarding current issues, trends, and policies by the practitioner is mandatory, based on the philosophy and values of acceptance and equality within the social work profession and within society as a whole.

DIVERSE PARENTING

Parenting is one the most important tasks in our society. Parenting includes the enormous responsibility of rearing children. Childrearing involves socialization, which enables children to move from childhood to adulthood and to vie within the world outside the family. Parenting is carried out by various constellations of individuals within society. In this section, the authors will address parenting by analyzing the following patterns of parenting: (1) grandparents as parents; (2) later-life parenting; (3) intergenerational family configurations; and (4) self-selected family groupings.

Grandparents as Parents

Grandparents as parents arose as an increasingly more common phenomenon in the 1990s. This increase in grandparents as the primary parenting figures in families may largely be attributed to current social ills such as substance abuse, economic depression, and early death of young parents due to chronic illness (e.g., AIDS), or violence. Substance abuse has prevented individuals from maintaining the focus that is necessary for parenting. In 1989 the National Committee for Prevention of Child Abuse approximated that between nine and ten million children were impacted by parents who were substance abusers and that some 675,000 children are abused each year by substance-abusing caretakers (Daro & McCurdy, 1991). These parents are often in and out of day treatment centers. Even though some of these persons are no longer institutionalized and participate in community-based outpatient programs, they must still rely on their own parents for childrearing. Moreover, a lack of training, which often leads to unemployment, deprives such persons of the economic support essential to caring for their own children. Therefore, their children are placed within the kinship network, most often with grandparents, instead of being placed in foster homes or institutional care. This trend is reflective of the family preservation movement, which was initiated in the 1980s and gained momentum in the 1990s. The Adoption Assistance and Child Welfare Act of 1980 (Public Law 96-272) was engendered out of concern that too many children were adrift in the foster care system and that a "least restrictive" environment should be provided for children involved with the child welfare system (Hartman, 1993). For many of these children the least restrictive environment was placement within the homes of their grandparents.

Likewise, during recent times of economic depression in the 1980s and 1990s more and more children, along with their parents, have been moving in with grandparents as a way to survive on limited financial resources. This is not astonishing, since the discrepancy between the poor and the rich spiraled more in the 1980s than at any other time in United States history, corresponding to the 1920s before the Great Depression (Philips, 1990). With the welfare reform movement of the 1990s, social workers have noted that many individuals have lost state and federal financial support for parenting and have resorted to pooling resources with their own parents for purposes of rearing their children. Due to downsizing in corporations, other parents have had to relocate, sometimes to distant parts of the country, just to save their jobs; consequently, for a variety of reasons, many turn to the grandparents to care for their children for extended periods of time.

Moreover, another reason that grandparents are parenting children of their offspring is that an increasing number of young parents die, due to such factors as AIDS, homicide, and natural causes. When parents die young, the children are more likely to be taken in by grandparents than by other relatives. Increasing rates of AIDS among women and children mean that grandparents are stepping in to take over childrearing responsibilities during the natural parents' extended illness and after they die. Children, many of whom have been left behind by intravenous drug-addicted mothers and fathers, may also be infected with the AIDS virus and thus require an excessive amount of care from aging grandparents.

Also, homicide is a major social problem that robs children of their parents. Young parents are more likely to be involved in drive-by shootings, domestic violence, and gang conflict in today's world. Perpetuators of these crimes are generally incarcerated for long periods, which deprives them from assuming their parenting role. It is estimated that up to eighty percent of all women in prison in the United States are mothers and that only eight to ten percent of these children left behind are in foster care (Fessler, 1991). Thus, one might surmise that when young parents commit or fall victim to crime, especially mothers, grandparents are generally approached first by the child welfare system for possible placement of the dependent children involved. Still other grandparents voluntarily assume the care of grandchildren because of the death of the biological parents from such natural causes as stroke, heart attack, or cancer.

Later-Life Parenting

Advanced medical technology and changing roles in society have led to persons' delaying childbirth. Women are postponing childbirth until after the completion of educational goals and/or the beginning of a career. Medical advancements (e.g., amniocentesis and ultrasound) have enabled more women to have successful birthing experiences well into their forties. Also, due to more liberal adoption standards, an increasing number of single women are adopting children later in life. Societal mores have changed to support women who decide to become parents later in life. It is much less of a stigma in the 1990s for an older unmarried woman to have or adopt a child and continue working at the same time. In 1990 it was estimated that more than half of the mothers of children under age six were in the labor force (Hofferth, Brayfield, Deich, & Holcomb, 1991).

Intergenerational Family Configurations

In many households, parents and grandparents live together and share the responsibility of parenting. Two major reasons for this parenting style are cultural tradition and economic retrenchment. These households must arrange among members how they will work together as parents. African American families have continued to return to family networks and intrafamily resources for parenting children with congenital and developmental disabilities and for addressing other needs required for coping (Daly, Jennings, Beckett, & Leashore, 1995). Likewise, Appalachian extended families often take turns sitting vigil and providing care for chronically ill or dying members both at the hospital and at home (Helton, 1995). Moreover, the 1970s television show *The Waltons* is a classic portrayal of a rural Appalachian intergenerational family. In this family the parents had primary responsibility for parenting but relied heavily on the wisdom and guidance of the grandparents, who lived under the same roof and figured as a constant, enriching force within the lives of the children. This family portrayal typifies families of the Great Depression era when families, not unlike many in the 1990s, lived together out of economic necessity.

Intergenerational living was a common pattern during World War II as young women, along with their children, moved in with parents-in-law when their husbands were serving their country in the military. While fathers were away, the mothers often worked in factories to assist in the war effort. Thus, grandparents were thrust into a shared parenting role. Similar patterns of family intergenerational coparenting reemerged during the Vietnam War. More recently, at the beginning of this decade the Gulf War called for both men and women to leave their families for the sake of military duty. Consequently, grandparents stepped in to share the crucial role of parenting, while mothers and/or fathers were serving in different parts of the world. During this last international conflict it was not uncommon to hear of fathers and their youngsters moving back in with their own parents or their spouse's parents while their wives served abroad.

Self-Selected Family Groupings

Some family configurations involve individuals who choose to share a household and resources, including parenting responsibilities. These individuals may be unrelated but choose to live under one roof for the well-being of all parties involved. Such individuals may come together as the result of unemployment, divorce, or the death of a spouse or significant other. These families often emerge out of the need for economic support, housing, parenting responsibilities, and emotional support. However, the emotional support may continue over the life span of these individuals, well beyond the initial crises that brought them together. Economics will most likely force more families to live together and share parenting roles as a result of not being able to live alone on dwindling public assistance funds. As public assistance programs are partially deleted, integrate work contingencies, or disappear for many young parents currently enrolled, they will increasingly be challenged to find alternative ways of parenting and survival. Stability for parenting may certainly be greatly enhanced by having another adult, with or without parenting experience, present within the home.

WOMEN'S ROLES AND GENDER ISSUES

The changing roles of women have been discussed and debated for centuries. Historically, women worked in the home and men had the "real job" and served as the major breadwinner. Still, women by the majority now work full-time or part-time. This increase of women in the workforce is a shift from the woman working in the home to working outside the home. Practitioners must be aware, however, that while the vast majority of women work out of necessity, a smaller number work because the opportunity exists or for reasons of self-fulfillment.

Society expects women to serve as the primary family member in charge of socialization of the children. Within this socialization role the concept of nurturing is imbedded. This role has changed significantly as more and more men are taking on the nurturing role with their children. This trend may be partially attributed to the fact that there is an increase in the number of single-parent fathers. It is estimated that up to sixteen percent of the 9.7 million single parents in the United States are men. The total number of single fathers grew from 390,000 in 1970 to 1,350,000 in 1990 (Webb, June 14, 1991). In such homes these men may take on the complete care of the children. Per Census Bureau figures, fifteen percent of all divorced or separated fathers have sole custody of their children while eight percent have joint custody. The number of fathers raising their children alone, following separation or divorce, has tripled between 1970 and 1990 (Greif, 1995). In addition, the number of divorced parents holding joint custody has increased. These two phenomena—single fatherhood and joint custody—have contributed to the changing roles of women within American society.

Also contributing to the changing roles of women are sexism and oppression. Women have historically been limited to prescribed roles

FIGURE 6.2 A Woman at Work

based on their gender. The attitudes and behaviors assumed by men to separate themselves from the "feminine" roles of women have led to further oppression of women by men in American society (Berger, Federico, & McBreen, 1991). Thus, the dichotomies engendered by this dual system of role assignment have led to discrimination against women. Graphic discrimination still persists within the working world in which women of the same age and with the same educational background earn forty percent less than men in comparable positions (Women's Wages, April 12, 1995). Equality does not exist in the workplace for males and females. But, this situation is fast changing as a result of changes in rules and regulations governing the labor market.

In some professions, such as medicine, clergy, and law, women almost always find themselves in lower-rank positions. These lower-rank positions are the result of perceptions of women's capabilities existent within the minds of those with power, usually men, as well the consequences of societal stereotyping. These perceptions of women are largely due to the socialization process. For example, girls are taught to be the nurse in play scenarios while boys are taught to be the doctor. Likewise, boys have traditionally been encouraged to think of "superheroes" in the comics as being their idols, while girls are persuaded to aspire toward famous ballerinas or songstresses as their role models. Such clichés would indicate the necessity of teaching children to be inclusive by exposing them equally to toys and other play materials and activities that would avoid gender stereotyping.

Another changing role of women relates to their commitment to eradicating the perception of themselves as mere sex objects. Women no longer want to be conceived of as just pretty faces to adorn billboards and perfume advertisements, but rather are demanding that they receive recognition for the diversity of their work roles, whether they are secretaries, soldiers, or space shuttle pilots. These changes in women's employment opportunities point to a growing recognition of women's right to choose work best suited to their needs as persons. It appears that there has been a cultural shift regarding the position of women in our society. This shift may be characterized as a movement from being dominated to being independent. This change influences parenting roles of women, enabling them to share roles and responsibilities with their spouse and/or significant others (Manns, 1981). These changes have brought about a new tradition in American motherhood, that is, more diversity and flexibility in the roles of women as nurturers and contributors in the workplace (Frankel, 1993).

Comparisons have been made regarding ethnic women's roles in responsibilities related to religious and traditional rituals, caring for the ill and dying, work, and seeking supportive services (McGoldrick et al.,

1989). With these comparisons, the bridge might be established to look at other factors, such as social bases of gender, social structures without gender, and gender-neutral authority and political power (Lorber, 1991). These issues should enable practitioners to create clearer visions for constructing a society that is both cultural and gender neutral. This would provide the possibility for a more egalitarian family system, which in turn should expand equality for all individuals in society.

SUMMARY

Diversity is a concept describing the variety of ethnic and cultural groups within American society. The responsibility of the social work practitioner is to uphold the NASW Code of Ethics. The value base of the code of ethics recognizes the importance of being inclusive in working with families. Social workers must be sensitive to cultural differences and highlight cultural strengths that may be utilized to enhance intervention. Moreover, it is the social worker's responsibility to enable families to understand the impact of culture on their functioning.

Diversity is a concept describing sexual orientation. Social work has historically been a forerunner in accepting and supporting those persons in society most often rejected. It is not surprising that social work took one of the first steps in embracing diversity in sexual orientation. Practitioners are held accountable by the NASW Code of Ethics to "start where the client is." Therefore, differences are encouraged to manifest themselves as deemed appropriate in order for individuals to have the highest quality of life possible. Families are encouraged to behave as defined by cultural traditions. These traditions serve as driving forces for family dynamics. Social workers need to be reminded of the issues confronting gay and lesbian members of society. By serving as an advocate for gay and lesbian parents, social workers may help to improve the quality of family life and also alleviate societal homophobia against the family unit.

Diversity is a concept describing a variety of parenting styles such as grandparents as primary parenting figures, later-life parenting, intergenerational parenting, and self-selected family groupings. Major social problems in our society have contributed to the necessity of creating new parenting patterns. Having an understanding of these problems, such as violence and substance abuse, will position the worker to better understand the various reasons for these parenting configurations.

Finally, diversity is a concept describing the changing roles of women in American society. Freedom is slowly emerging for women and allowing them to function in places heretofore prohibited to them. The increase of women in the workforce is only one of the major changes affecting women's opportunities. Not only are numbers increasing but women's workplaces are expanding in scope and degree of responsibility. These changes have had major influences on the roles of women in families. A more egalitarian attitude is arising to fortify women's positions in sharing family leadership roles.

QUESTIONS FOR DISCUSSION

1. Describe diversity within the context of your family of origin/current family grouping/community in which you live.

2. Describe the first time you were aware of persons with different sexual orientation in your friendship group, in your family, in your community.

3. Describe the most unique parenting configuration that you have encountered.

4. Describe how you perceive that women's roles have changed in your family.

GROUP EXERCISE

The class is organized as a debate team. The hottest or most controversial issue will serve as the target for discussion and analysis. One topic should be chosen and agreed upon by all class members (e.g., domestic violence, hopelessness, capital punishment, gang violence). Once the topic has been chosen, the class should divide themselves in ways that they feel will best address the issue at hand. For example, if the topic is capital punishment, half the class might advocate for and the other half might advocate against.

This exercise is designed to enable students to experience differences. As part of their discussion, students should refer to the NASW Code of Ethics (see Appendix).

SIGNIFICANT TERMS

significant other	CSWE
diversity	NASW Code of Ethics
oppression	Kwanzaa
racism	sexism

ethnicity
culture
homophobia
Diagnostic and Statistical Manual

intergenerational family
sexual orientation
later-life parenting

REFERENCES

Bell, A. P. & Weinberg, M. S. (1978). *Homosexualities: A study of diversity among men and women.* New York: Simon & Schuster.
Berger, R. L., Federico, R. C., & McBreen, J. T. (1991). *Human behavior: A perspective for the helping professions,* 3rd ed. New York: Longman.
Castex, G. M. (1994). Providing services to Hispanic/Latino populations: Profiles in diversity. *Social Work,* 39(3), 288–296.
Cooley, R. C., Ostendorf, D., & Bickerton, D. (1979). Outreach services for elderly Native Americans. *Social Work,* 24(2), 151–153.
Council on Social Work Education (1994). CSWE Policy Statement. In *Handbook of accreditation: Standards and procedures.* Alexandria, Va.: CSWE.
Daly, A., Jennings, J., Beckett, J. O., & Leashore, B. R. (1995). Effective coping strategies of African Americans. *Social Work,* 40(2), 240–248.
Daro, D. & McCurdy, K. (1991). *Current trends in child abuse reporting and fatalities: The results of the 1989 annual fifty state survey.* Chicago: National Center on Child Abuse Prevention Research, National Committee for Prevention of Child Abuse.
Devore W. & Schlesinger, E. G. (1991). *Ethnic sensitive social work practice,* 2nd ed. St. Louis: C.V. Mosby.
Fessler, S. (1991). *Mothers in the correctional system: Separation from children and reunification after incarceration.* State University of New York at Albany.
Frankel, J. (1993). The employed mother and the family context. *Focus on Women Series.* Vol. 14. p. 282. New York: Springer Publishing.
Gabriel, T. (1995). Bisexuality moving out into the open. *The Plain Dealer,* Sections 3-E & 6-E, June 26.
Greif, G. L. (1995). Single fathers with custody following separation and divorce. *Marriage and Family Review,* 20(1–2), 213–231.
Hall, E. G. & King, G. C. (1982). Working with strengths of black families. *Child Welfare,* 61(8), 536–544.
Hartman, A. (1993). Family preservation under attack. *Social Work,* 38(5), 509–512.
Helton, L. R. (1995). Intervention with Appalachians: Strategies for a culturally specific practice. *Journal of Cultural Diversity,* 2(1), 20–26.
Hepworth, D. H. & Larsen, J. (1993). *Direct social work practice: Theory and skills,* 3rd ed. Belmont, Calif.: Wadsworth Publication Co.
Hill, R. (1973). *Strengths of black families.* New York: National Urban League.
Hofferth, S. L., Brayfield, A., Deich, S., & Holcomb, P. (1991). *The national child care survey, 1990.* Washington, D.C.: Urban Institute.
Hunt, M. (1974). *Sexual behavior in the 1970's.* Chicago: Playboy Press.

Jackson-Hopkins, M. (1992). Cultural traditions and barriers that may hinder therapeutic change. In A. W. Edwards (Ed.), *Human services and social change: An African-American church perspective*, (pp. 109–116). Cleveland, Ohio: Inner City Renewal Society/Orange Blossom Press.

Kramer, M. (1993). Don't settle for hypocrisy. *Time*, July 26.

Lorber, J. (1991). Dismantling Noah's ark. In Lorber, J. & Farrell, S.A. (Eds.), *The social construction of gender*, pp. 355–369. Newburg Park, Calif.: Sage Publications.

McClester, C. (1990). Nguzo Saba (The seven principles). *KWANZAA: Everything you always wanted to know but didn't know where to ask*, 2nd ed. New York: Gumbs and Thomas.

McGoldrick, M, Garcia-Preto, N., Hines, P. M, Lee, E. (1989). Ethnicity and women. In McGoldrick, M., Anderson, C. M., & Walsh, F. (Eds.), *Women in families: A framework for family therapy*, pp. 169–199. New York: W.W. Norton.

Manns, W. (1981). Support systems of significant others in black families (pp. 238–251). In McAdoo, H. P., *Black families*. Beverly Hills, Calif.: Sage Publications.

Martin, E. P. & Martin, J. (1978). *The black extended family*. Chicago, Il.: University of Chicago Press.

Miller, N. B. (1982). Social work services to urban Indians. In Green, J. W. (ed.), *Cultural awareness in the human services*. Englewood Cliffs, N.J.: Prentice-Hall.

Moss, M. S. (1994) (Ed.), NASW backs custody fight, rights laws. *NASW News*, 39 (2), 6.

Norblad, A. (1994). Bar anti-gay laws is upheld. *The New York Times*, Section A, p. 20, February 10.

Philips, K. (1990). *The politics of rich and poor*. New York: Random House.

Sewell, D. (1994). Lesbian pair share thrill of motherhood. *The Plain Dealer*, Section D, pp. 1, 4, January 25.

Teepen, T. (1995). Anti-gay decision is cruel. *Atlanta Journal Constitution*, Section D, p.7, May 21.

Webb, B. (1991). USA snapshots; More Dads are single parents. *USA Today*, Section A, p. 1, Col. 1, June 14.

Webster's Deluxe Unabridged Dictionary, Second Edition, (1983). New York: New World Dictionaries/Simon and Schuster.

Williams, S. E., & Wright, D. F. (1992). Empowerment: The strengths of black families revisited. *Journal of Multicultural Social Work*, 2(4), 23–36.

Women's wages found to trail men's worldwide. (1995). *Boston Globe*, April 12, 28:5.

Zastrow, C. & Kirst-Ashman, (1993). *Understanding human behavior and the social environment*, 3rd ed. Chicago: Nelson-Hall.

▶ 7

Fields of Social Work Practice: Beginning Intervention with Families

In exploring fields of social work, four areas of beginning practice will be discussed, with an emphasis on family issues. These practice fields will include: social work with older adults; social work with children; social work with persons with developmental disabilities; and social work in communities/neighborhoods. In assessing six areas of practice most likely to be encountered by undergraduate social work students, consideration will be given to the following concepts: (a) definition of field of practice; (b) issues and problems; (c) service delivery systems; (d) case example, highlighting crucial social work roles.

As these select fields of practice are examined, emphasis will be given to the role of the family and their response to various issues at hand.

SOCIAL WORK WITH OLDER ADULTS

Description

According to the *Social Work Dictionary* (Barker, 1995, p. 12), older adults in the United States are defined as "people who have reached at least age 65." In describing older individuals or those who have entered the stage of late life, various practitioners utilize the terms *aged, older adults, senior citizens,* and *the aging* (Ginsberg, 1995, p. 297). Although much diversity exists in describing this client population, the authors will use the term *older adults* to apply to those clients sixty-five and over throughout the following discussion.

Issues and Problems

The primary issues experienced by older adults include health concerns, financial problems, abuse and neglect, disengagement, ageism, and community-living alternatives. These problems are further impacted due to a lack of preparation on behalf of practitioners. Therefore, these primary issues are absolutely necessary to consider in developing strategies for intervention. These issues have been influenced by a relative lack of attention being given to older adults within our society. This neglect has resulted in increased factors contributing to ageism and the overwhelming oppression of older adults. Gonyea (1994) notes that the general public now holds older adults accountable for economic downswings and rising costs of Medicare and Medicaid; she adds that many in our society view the older adult population as "well-off and reaping huge benefits from the state." Nothing could be further from the truth.

Still, families are traditionally responsible for the health care of its members. Being concerned about health is perhaps the chief priority among older adults. Health care is becoming increasingly more inaccessible to this client population. Also contributing to this unavailability of health care is a lack of adequate economic support for older adults. With the increase in health care costs and the decrease in earned income, older adults find themselves without the necessary means to obtain quality health care. In addition, society restricts the income of older adults, many of whom are single women and/or retirees without adequate retirement benefits. Likewise, fewer older adults are working in the 1990s, compared to previous decades. In 1900 two-thirds of men sixty-five and older were working; by 1950 this figure was estimated to be 45.8 percent. In 1980, the rate of labor force participation had been curtailed to 19.5 percent of men and 9.5 percent of women sixty-five and older (U.S. Bureau of Census, 1982) In 1993, 2.9 percent of the total workforce were men sixty-five and older; and 2.5 percent were women sixty-five and older (U.S. Bureau of Labor Statistics, 1993). Therefore, older adults must rely on family members—generally adult children—in their efforts to maintain independence.

Abuse and neglect of older adults are on the increase. They are vulnerable to their children, spouses, other relatives, or others in the community. Abuse and neglect take the form of physical hitting, verbal abuse, and abandonment, that is, being left alone. These responses take away the dignity and self-worth of older adults and make them susceptible to other problems. It is no wonder that depression is a common problem among older adults (Zastrow & Kirst-Ashman, 1993). Family members are usually strategically placed to observe diminishing functioning, both physical and psychological, of their older relatives. However, when they are so closely involved in the care of their parents or older adult relatives, their ability to perceive even minute changes may be compromised. Practitioners must, therefore, be able to observe diminishing functioning and immediately seek answers as to why these changes are occurring. Although the older person may be the primary source of information, the worker must turn to family members for further clarification and input.

Furthermore, disengagement is a phenomenon observed in the lives of older adults. This process occurs for a number of reasons, including poor health status and health care availability, limited income, abuse and neglect, idle time, feelings of uselessness, and ageism. Disengagement is a twofold process wherein the older adult is at least partially ready to reduce his/her involvement in society, and at the same time society dictates that the older person is no longer needed or useful to society (Zastrow & Kirst-Ashman, 1993). That is, the older person decides that it is time to reduce his/her main societal roles, largely centered around work and family responsibilities. Likewise, ageism or discrimination against older adults is an all-too-common problem in this country. Ageism often originates out of thinking that older persons can-

FIGURE 7.1   Older Adults

not contribute to society but should be left alone. Older adults are simply ignored and thus become isolated from the larger society. Ageism has also been perpetuated due to the continued embracing of a youth-oriented culture in America.

Community-living alternatives for older adults are important for social work practitioners to consider in serving this client population. These alternatives for persons sixty-five and older include day care centers; senior citizens' programs, assisted-living environments, group homes, high-rise apartment complexes, shared-living cooperatives, and nursing homes. Family members often must take difficult steps to ensure the continued health, safety, and well-being of their older adult relatives. If an older parent is no longer able to care for himself/herself, adult children are often placed in the painful dilemma of making ultimate decisions. Sometimes, this is the first major decision that a child has to make regarding a parent. Awareness of this role reversal might contribute to feelings of guilt, resentment, and other emotional discomfort in both the adult child and the parent. If placement outside the home is not imminent, the agony involved in decision making may be prolonged. As older adults are taken into their children's homes, sometimes as a last alternative because of climbing out-of-home placement costs, conflict may emerge around such issues as family governance, space, or childrearing.

Service Delivery Systems

As an individual moves toward his/her twilight years, an accessible and sufficient service delivery system is mandatory. In working with older adults, many social workers soon realize that shortages and gaps in services are not atypical. This creates a void for the older adult, because in 1991 seventy-four percent of all persons sixty-five and older lived with their spouses in their own homes (Ginsberg, 1995). As these facts are realized, communities are forced to create workable service delivery systems to meet the growing needs of older adults. This would indicate the need for agencies to coordinate services. One negative aspect contributing to the lack of a comprehensive service delivery system is that of diminishing income, forcing agencies to downsize programs and services. Older adults are frequently at an unfair advantage when agencies are forced to reduce or cut back services. While many older adults benefit from long-established programs, such as meals-on-wheels, transportation, and visiting nurses' home care, others require a broader range of health care, nutrition counseling, housekeeping services, neighborhood recreational programming, and ongoing in-home social services. For many older adults the receipt of these services is life-sustaining and tantamount to personal autonomy.

In reflecting on older adults it is important for the worker to keep in mind the necessity of interpreting services from the standpoint of how helpful they might be instead of their limited availability. For example, there are older adults in nursing homes who would not be there if adequate home care was available. Many services for older persons have been developed for maintenance reasons rather than to enhance overall well-being and quality of life. Thus, social workers must be persistent in evaluating and establishing priorities for quality care for all older adults whether at home or in residential care. This focus on enhancing the quality of life would not exclude a constant awareness of positive aging that is brought about largely by good health, active societal involvement, and strong social support networks. As the baby boomers move into their twilight years within the first couple of decades of the twenty-first century, services must be increased even more to meet the demand. Not only will there be increased numbers of older adults, but people will most likely continue to retire earlier due to the changing nature of the labor market. These changes will include downsizing, increased job requirements and credentials, competition, and forced corporate mergers.

Case Example (See Case Study Two—The Davis Family)
Minnie, the maternal grandmother, is suffering from Alzheimer's disease. She was recently diagnosed by the family physician after undergoing a series of tests. Some of Minnie's major symptoms are forgetfulness, erratic behavior, and confusion. John Davis recently was awakened by the smell of smoke and ran into the kitchen to find a pot of soup burning on the stove, unattended. Minnie had been trying to cook herself some lunch but had forgotten to watch the stove. John yelled at Minnie, telling her that she is going to burn down the house if she cannot think about what she is doing. Consequently, Minnie began to cry, ran into her room, and locked the door behind her; she stayed there until Marie Davis came home from work and pleaded with her to come out. This incident led to the first serious argument between John and Marie Davis. He expressed that he does not feel it is his role to take care of his mother-in-law. He defines his role as that of the principal "breadwinner" and not a "nursemaid." This argument led to the children's asking questions about why their grandmother was so upset.

After the parents explained what had happened, Henry immediately said that his father was a "mean bully." Terry said that Henry was overreacting, that their father was correct in protecting their grandmother from harming herself. John is reserved in describing his actions, whereas Marie is livid about the whole affair. She accuses her husband of not understanding Alzheimer's disease and of always having disliked her mother. She further remarked that her husband has been displaying chauvinism toward Minnie and her. Terry was upset with his mother because he understood his father's response as being protective and not abusive of his grandmother. Minnie, of course, does not fully understand what the uproar is all about, for she seems to have already forgotten the incident.

As a result of this family dispute, Marie has called the Franklin Street Neighborhood House for help. She has requested a visit from the social worker, Mrs. Long, to deal with family issues related to her mother's Alzheimer's disease. As per standard procedure for her program, Mrs. Long has agreed to schedule an in-home visit as soon as possible.

Mrs. Long visited the Davis family at 6 p.m. at their home and was greeted at the door by Henry. About that time, Marie drove up and got out of the car, beginning to apologize for being late, due to her supervisor's last-minute demands at the dry cleaning store. John is watching the evening news and Terry is listening to his radio in his room. Marie enters the house and asks the family to convene in the living room. John joins the family but does not turn off the television. Marie realizes that Minnie is still in her room and goes to get her. When Marie and Minnie return and are seated, the family interview begins.

Mrs. Long, the social worker, states that she is pleased that the family has requested assistance from the agency and asks to be introduced to each family member. After being introduced to the family by Marie, the worker then asks how she might be able to help them. Marie begins to talk of her concerns about her mother's health, yet appears reluctant to continue the discussion in the presence of Minnie and John. He adds that he is concerned about the safety of his mother-in-law and admits that he has recently yelled at her for that reason, but for that reason only. At that point, Mrs. Long turns to Minnie and asks her, "Do you know why I am here?" Minnie, in turn, replies, "I don't know you, but everyone is welcome in our home." Mrs. Long notices tears in Marie's eyes as her mother speaks.

Then the worker asks the children to share their views of the problem. Henry, the youngest child, states that he had become frightened when his grandmother began to cry and locked herself in her room. Terry states that he agrees with his father and does not see why he has to be there for the session anyway. John, at that point, looks at Terry and frowns.

After each person has spoken, Mrs. Long provides instructions that include having members of the family interact and talk with one another about what each member has shared, as well as any other issues that they want to bring up. John shares his frustration in attempting to help take care of Minnie, and in so doing, having been criticized for "scolding" her. Marie shares that it is hers and her family's responsibility to take care of her mother, regardless of the degree of difficulty. John states that he understands her concerns but feels that she spends all of her time either with her mother, with the kids, or at work. As he raises his voice in response to his wife, Minnie becomes tearful and goes to her room but then later returns.

As John and Marie continue to disagree, Mrs. Long intervenes and attempts to help the parents understand the basis of their own feelings and concerns and each other's views. Likewise, the children are brought into the family discussion, and all are encouraged to find common ground or issues that they all share. Although Terry is reluctant to speak further, both he and Henry are able to elaborate on their concerns. The worker points out that all family members want basically the same things. They want to take care of Minnie's needs and ensure her safety, happiness, and well-being. Marie makes it clear that she has no intention of placing her mother in a nursing home and asks the family for their understanding and support of this decision. The family members all seem to agree with the mother, yet want to understand Minnie's medical/emotional problems more fully.

Mrs. Long, the social worker, seizes this opportunity to make some suggestions for the family to ponder. She informs the Davises that there is a day activity program for older adults at her agency and that she would be glad to look into possible openings. She points out that full- and part-time involvement is available so that Mr. and Mrs. Davis would be able to arrange Minnie's participation at their convenience around their work schedules. Mrs. Long hands the Davises a pamphlet on the program, which they peruse and share with the children. Mrs. Long also suggests that she would be happy to provide more information on Alzheimer's disease and offers to bring the family a brochure from the Alz-heimer's Society.

Mrs. Long offers to come back in one week to meet with the family again and asks each member to write down any questions that come to mind during the week to share in the next meeting. As she prepares to leave, Mrs. Long goes over to Minnie and tells her how much she has enjoyed meeting her and compliments her dress. Minnie responds by thanking her for sitting and talking for a while.

SOCIAL WORK PRACTICE WITH CHILDREN

Description

Social work practice with children refers to supportive intervention given by the worker that will enhance the well-being of children. These services include traditional child welfare services (e.g., protection, foster care, adoption), but also entail a way of understanding dynamics impacting children. They also include the description of a framework for depicting a positive orientation or strength perspective in service delivery. The strength perspective provides the opportunity for children to be evaluated more holistically. Child welfare is defined by *The Social Work Dictionary* as "programs and ideologies oriented toward the protection, care and healthy development of children" (Barker, 1995, p. 57).

The authors' interpretation of generalist social work practice with children includes a strength perspective that focuses on the overall well-being of children, leading to a foundation by which to create healthy outcomes. This perspective supports children's rights to fulfill their maximum potential at home, at school, and in the community at large and to have a direct say about what is happening in their lives at any given time. This perspective provides a forum for supportive analysis of self-esteem, motivation, positive image, survival knowledge, and role adaptation.

Issues and Problems

One of the basic needs for children is safety. Safety has been defined as security in having one's physical needs met. Also, security encompasses a feeling of protection and a strong sense of well-being. As such, the worker has the responsibility to provide guidance and emotional support enabling children to have a wholesome self-image. Self-image is predicated upon the ability of the worker to assess environments that are fluid in nature. That is, environments are forever changing, thus creating dynamics that must be continuously assessed. The worker's ability to assess and make appropriate decisions determines the secure environment in which children must live, attend school, and thrive emotionally.

Children's issues and problems are described by parents and other authority figures. The worker's role is to describe issues and problems from the child's point of view. The worker must provide the vehicle by which children are heard. One author recalls having observed a poignant example of a child's assuming his right to input in decisions being made about his life. A foster care worker busied herself in arranging for a two-week period of respite care for a six-year-old-boy and his five-year-old brother, as the boys played in the adjoining playroom at the agency. The six-year-old, overhearing the phone conversation, came to the worker's desk, got her attention, and said, "Make sure you get us a good home." At that point, the worker discontinued the call and proceeded to have the boy describe to her his view of a "good home."

This example reiterates the fact that all children are looking for and deserving of "a good home." Children are capable of articulating and defining their own concerns if given the chance to do so. These concerns must be placed in the informational framework by which children will be given respect for their ideas. These ideas may then be organized into strategies on behalf of children. These strategies should be clearly presented so that they can be readily utilized by workers and others in helping positions. Children often have not been given the opportunity to be spokespersons for themselves, not even in their own families. The social worker in the 1990s must work to change this outdated approach to children's services. An updated approach is imperative and must invariably include children's views about and concerns regarding decisions being made about their lives. In this expansion of his/her approach to children, the worker has the responsibility to maintain the primary view and interpretation of the child's concerns. This approach should help to maintain integrity for the rights of those children in need of assistance. This process thus involves a strong protective and respectful position regarding all services being provided to children. A suggested method on behalf of the worker is that of maintaining an open mind and allowing children to interpret their daily experiences in their complicated living circumstances, both with their natural families and in child care placements outside the home.

Another set of issues for children relates to the social experience of the worker. Workers must be aware of their own feelings and experiences concerning issues such as child governance, family separation, education, and peer involvement. When workers are blinded by their own assumptions and/or biases, they will not be able to listen attentively or perceive the child's messages. Therefore, social workers in children's settings must continually self-assess and carefully evaluate their approach and decisions as they work with and on the behalf of children. This does not mean that workers cannot make decisions that appear to be in the child's best interests. But the point being made is that social workers must always be aware of their need to be child-centered in planning and implementing intervention strategies. When children's views can be heard and their input woven into the practice plan, the probability of protecting their self-esteem and fostering trusting relationships with these children over time will be much greater.

Service Delivery Systems

As children are identified for services, society has the responsibility to position agencies to provide requested or needed services. These services range from foster care to adoption; from short-term residential care to long-term institutionalization; from specialized foster care to maternal and infant care services; from service coordination for children in schools to advocacy and counseling for adolescents in the juvenile court system. These services and others are necessary to ensure the well-being of children in our society. From these descriptive characteristics in programming for children, one should realize that much diversity prevails in the nature and types of services available. Such services have been developed over time to respond to the range of requests made on behalf of children as well as those programs sanctioned by society on an involuntary basis (e.g., child protection services and juvenile probation). These requests for services may be made by parents, teachers, social workers, doctors, nurses, lawyers, clergy, and concerned citizens. Moreover, other programs have been designed to meet the unique and special needs presented by children and their families.

Services for children have also been created to meet the broad span of changing needs that youngsters exhibit as they grow, develop, and accommodate to their fast-expanding world. That is, as children move from early childhood to the school-age years, their worlds becoming increasingly complex and challenging, and this pattern will remain true throughout adolescence and their advancement to adulthood. Consequently, the service delivery systems of yesterday will not meet the needs of children in the 1990s. That is, services should be redefined and tailored to include the needs of children today and without exception should incorporate input from the mouths of children themselves.

In a relatively short period of time, social workers have experienced a child welfare system that has transitioned from orphanages and traditional foster care to innovative programs such as after-school prevention, community-based day treatment, and brief, collaborative intervention programs. Even though there has been expansion in the types of accessible programs, many gaps in services remain. That is, the need exists for program development that addresses the environmental circumstances of social problems such as rampant violence in our neighborhoods and communities. These violent acts are not always addressed as part of the problem scenario that receives attention in traditional, supportive child welfare services. One reason for this gap in service is a widespread lack of community understanding of the display of violence between and among children, as well as within their families. In addition, children respond in violent ways often in response to their own feelings of hopelessness or lack of control over their environment.

Therefore, social workers must always give credence to the importance of involving children in the development of programs. And this involvement should not be tangential or peripheral. Rather, children must be seen and heard, that is, there should be equity in children's involvement in this process. Children must be seen as equals and treated impartially where their best interests are concerned. Being viewed as equals would appear to be a variation from the attitudes toward children and their rights and responsibilities in more conventional child welfare programs. Giving children an opportunity to participate in decision-making efforts might elevate their level of investment in resolving their problems. It has long been proved that individuals are better able to help themselves when they have been involved in crucial decisions regarding programming that will affect them.

Another consideration in offering services to children is the multiservice agency. Almost every community in the United States has a local public welfare agency, and these agencies are perhaps the most readily identifiable service delivery system known to the general public. These agencies may be described as following the generic or umbrella human service model with a range of services under one roof designed to meet the social service needs of persons of all ages. The positive aspect of this type of agency is that of having all service programs, including public assistance and casework services, based at one centralized location. The limitation of this approach is the lack of flexibility or independence that often exists, as traditional public children's services or child welfare agencies exist as an aggregate of services within one large and complex bureaucracy. When programs such as day care, foster care, and child crisis intervention services are interwoven with other services within a large public service delivery system, they may lose some of their creativity and spontaneity in developing new and timely programs to meet societal demands. One way to add creativity is through the use of other community agencies to provide complementary, specialized services such as wilderness programs, "boot camps," or other innovative programs for children (Mixdorf, 1989; MacKenzie, 1993). Boot camps, often referred to as shock incarceration, demand that violators serve a brief term in a prison or jail in a quasi-military setting not unlike actual military boot camps or basic training regimens. It is estimated that some thirty states, ten local jurisdictions, along with the Federal Bureau of Prisons, have initiated some form of boot camp programs (MacKenzie, 1993).

Schools must also be considered as a critical component in the care of children. The educational system is intended to prepare young persons for life in today's complex and demanding society and thus should be considered integral to the well-being or welfare of children. Schools may have programs that enrich youngsters for a more wholesome living experience. This simply means that children are taught not only how to survive but also how to participate in the development of strategies for optimal personal growth and goal achievement. These strategies are reflected through classroom participation and other enrichment activities within the school setting. However, schools have not always taken the creative lead in establishing programs to meet the diverse needs of children. Many school systems throughout the country are in crisis and tend to lag behind other mainstream community institutions designed to assist children. This discrepancy may be attributed to a number of reasons, such as differences in philosophies about children's well-being, funding deficiencies, or a lack of community collaboration and/or support.

More and more children's programs in the community are positioning themselves on the cutting edge of service delivery by introducing ingenious services that give child consumers an increased say in program governance. Nevertheless, one should be aware that many traditionalist practitioners of social work have difficulty in adjusting to programs in which children have an equal role in setting and enforcing punishments and rewards. Still, the standard organizational structure of the public school system does not always lend itself well to children as "lay" leaders or collaborators in decision making. However, there are exceptions to the rule.

One example of program innovation is the school mediation program. School systems utilizing mediation tend to have less violent behavior than those not utilizing this strategy. Mediation programs are designed to have students mediate disputes and other conflicts among fellow students. The mediation team may address problems such as fighting, tardiness, truancy, drug paraphernalia, weapons, and mild arguments. Mediation provides youngsters an opportunity to enhance their self-esteem, to make important decisions affecting their peers and themselves, and to enrich feelings of autonomy and independence within the school environment. In such programs cutting edge services are clearly visible (Winner, 1990).

As such new program areas for children are being introduced, it is of vital importance that the social worker place this information within the context of family life for purposes of assessment and intervention planning. One must recall that all children are members of families. As such, these family members must be consulted and included in determining appropriate programs and services for their children. Programs that involve parents are much better situated to bridge the gap between the family and school. Special educational services, by regularly involving families in determining what school programming might best serve their child could, in actuality, serve as a model for expanding supportive and liaison services to families. Nonetheless, in all school settings, both school personnel and the family should stay mutually involved in the continued socialization of children and champion them in their preparation for the assumption of adult responsibilities.

Case Example (See Case Study Five—The Jones Family).
Carl Barker, age fourteen, has been having difficulties with the authorities. He and two of his friends have been caught throwing stones at store windows in the downtown area. He maintains innocence and places the blame on his two friends. However, Carl was observed by an off-duty police officer in the act of throwing a stone. Moreover, he has been skipping school often and is lagging far behind in his studies. Carl's mother, Barbara Jones, has been informed by the juvenile authorities about Carl's behavior. She explained to the authorities Carl's frustrations about his father's incarceration at the state prison. She interprets her son's behavior in choosing "bad" friends as a result of his own father's association with crime. Barbara has convinced the authorities that Carl is not a "bad" youngster but is experiencing self-esteem problems due to his father's absence. In addition, Carl is having problems relating to his new stepfather, Joe Jones.

Barbara has worked with the authorities in determining what should be done with Carl. They have decided to place Carl in the Juvenile Day Activity Center. The family worker from the Juvenile Day Activity Center has visited with Barbara and Joe as a result of Carl's infractions. The worker, after an assessment is completed, agrees with Barbara and Joe that Carl is not a "bad" youngster and feels that his problems can be adequately addressed through the center. This program is funded by the Juvenile Court and provides multiple services for youth and their families: (1) group intervention; (2) on-site schooling for children with emotional/behavioral problems; (3) family counseling; (4) recreational activities; and (5) individual counseling.

DEVELOPMENTAL DISABILITIES

Definition

Developmental disabilities are defined as those problems occurring in individuals at birth or before age twenty-two and also affecting three or more areas of functioning, including such skills as receptive and expressive language, mobility, cognition, and self-care. Functional areas might also include learning, self-direction, capacity for independent living, and economic self-sufficiency (DeWeaver, 1995, p. 712). These conditions generally last throughout the individual's lifetime and require multifaceted, long-term care. Types of developmental disabilities include cerebral palsy, Down syndrome, seizure disorder, mental retardation, and autism (Barker, 1995).

Issues and Problems

The primary issues confronting persons with developmental disabilities and their families include living alternatives, difficulties in family adjustment and coping, and education. One of the most significant problems facing the family may be the placement of a child with disabilities. Family members are often fearful of dying and leaving their special child behind, having no one to care for him or her. Workers need to be sensitive to this powerful feeling within families. Another aspect of this dynamic is the overwhelming thought that care needs for such a child will consume all the family's time and energy. Therefore, the specific issues confronting parents include that of fulfilling the care provider role as well as that of meeting the child's economic needs. The parents' fears may be broadened in today's world because prior to the 1960s most children with developmental disabilities were placed in institutional settings.

With deinstitutionalization, longer life spans of persons with disabilities due to the advances in medical technology, and national special education laws, parents now have more options for keeping their children within their own homes and communities. Still, parents are often hard pressed to locate and finance adequate resources to meet their child's specific needs. As these children age, along with their parents, families are then more challenged than ever before to create alternatives for family living.

In the 1980s more group homes opened for adolescents and young adults with disabilities. However, in many communities parents have had to collaboratively form coalitions with social workers and other professionals to combat resistance by community residents to the opening of such group homes in their midst. Likewise, as persons with developmental disabilities transition from sheltered workshops into their twilight years (generally at an earlier age than nondisabled adults), they often need the assistance of social workers with mainstreaming into such programs as senior centers and community residences for older persons.

Family adjustment and coping continue to be a major focus for social work practice with persons with disabilities. Families of these children have been emphasized in research and conjecture over the past thirty years or more. With the advent of deinstitutionalization in the 1960s, floods of persons with all types of developmental disabilities returned to their home communities. Consequently, social workers and other helping professionals shifted their focus away from institutional care services to family-focused intervention. Families of persons with developmental disabilities demanded attention and expanded programs enabling their children, some of whom had reached adulthood, to remain at home.

Olshansky (1962) was the first to explore in the literature the impact of rearing a child with a disability on the family. Olshansky, who accentuated parental adaptation, conjectured that all parents of children with disabilities experience chronic sorrow, which affects their reactions to their child and affects overall coping ability. Later, some professionals have compared coping with a child with disabilities to that of grieving over a loss (i.e., the loss of having an ideal child) (Wikler, 1981), while others highlighted the assessment of parental adjustment at critical periods of development. That is, parents might achieve some degree of acceptance after the child's initial diagnosis, yet once again experience coping difficulties when the child fails to reach or is delayed in accomplishing other major developmental milestones such as talking, walking, beginning school, attaining puberty, or reaching adulthood (Beavers et al., 1986).

Another major area of family coping centers around the reactions and adaptation of siblings of the child with disabilities. These issues were first addressed as persons with developmental disabilities returned home and again became a key focus within the family system. Younger children who have an older sibling with a disability may take on the role of an older child, that is, he/she may assume increased responsibility than would a child his/her age in a family without a child with special needs. On the other hand, when the youngest child in a family has a developmental disability, the parents may tend to overprotect this child to the point of neglecting the growth and development of other children in the family. In some families, siblings of the child with disabilities are more likely to seek approval and direction outside the family, feeling that the parents do not have time for him/her or as a protective measure designed to meet their emotional needs without adding more stress to the family (Freeman, 1987).

Perhaps the most difficult challenge for families of children with disabilities is that of how to locate and utilize resources within the educational system. All children diagnosed as having developmental disabilities are entitled to special education services through the public schools, either through self-contained classrooms wherein all students have disabilities, or in mainstreamed, "regular" classes where they may learn alongside children without disabilities. However, many parents remain on the fringes of their child's educational experience, going to their child's school only when requested by the staff to do so, while others are demanding more services and a deeper involvement of their children in all aspects of school life. Although special education has been mandatory in public schools since 1975, many parents feel disenfranchised and believe that school staff do not have a qualitative or holistic understanding of their child. Parents of preschool and younger children are beginning to expect more from public schools now that federal legislation has been passed to address the developmental needs of such youngsters within the context of the family system (Helton, 1994).

Service Delivery Systems

The service delivery system for individuals with developmental disabilities is especially complex, due to the tremendous need for these persons to have continuous services throughout their lives. A unique role to be performed by social workers is that of connecting families to community resources. This crucial social work role is often carried out within the context of case management and casework services. Another major task of the social worker is to discuss the specific type of service needed by a child and/or family. That is, some programs and services are specifically designed and geared toward serving persons with developmental disabilities; these might include sheltered workshops and the Special Olympics. On the other hand, there may be more generic services available, for example, through the local children's hospital, school district, or Big Brothers/Big Sisters organization that will best serve the needs of the person with developmental disabilities. It should always be the goal of the social worker to provide services within a least restrictive environment. That is, services should be designed to provide optimal benefit to the person with disabilities and his/her family.

Another area to be considered is the role of the worker in the diagnostic assessment of persons with developmental disabilities. Since the early 1970s these services have been largely been provided or coordinated by a national network of university-affiliated programs that assess and develop intervention plans for persons with disabilities. Freedman (1995) states that multiple and complex needs are intrinsic to persons with disabilities, who require continual guidance and monitoring. Therefore, an interdisciplinary approach is crucial to meet these ongoing and ever-changing needs. Disciplines needed are likely to include developmental pediatrics and family medicine; neurology; psychology; psychiatry; special education; speech pathology; occupational and physical therapy; nutrition; nursing; and social work. The social worker's roles often include those of service coordinator or case manager, family evaluator, parent support group leader, mediator, and parent advocate.

Moreover, social workers play a significant role in facilitating an appropriate school placement for the child with disabilities. Since 1975 there has been a national special education law that mandates equal public educational opportunities for school-aged children, within a least restrictive environment. This law requires that the parent or parents of any child identified as having a disability would be involved in establishing an Individual Educational Plan for the child in conjunction with the appropriate school personnel (Education for All Handicapped Children Act, 1975). Since 1986, preschool children must also be evaluated and placed in educational or developmental enrichment programs that provide not only an Individual Family Service Plan but also service coordination (Education of the Handicapped Amendments, 1986). The primary role of the school social worker or child welfare worker is to make sure that children entitled to either early intervention or public school–based services receive these services in a timely manner. Social workers must also ensure that family members of these children maintain an integral role in the planning and implementation of services. In addition to assuming the role of linking families to requested resources in the community, social workers may need to help families develop new programs such as cooperatives for respite care and transportation to health care. And it is just as important for the social worker to assist families in obtaining goals they themselves have set for the child.

Another role of the worker is that of enabling families to assess the capabilities of the person with disabilities within multiple environments. Such an awareness will assist the family member with disabilities to function as independently as possible within the community. For example, many a parent will recognize, upon observation, that their child may not be challenged enough by a T-ball coach or recreational leader to compete or do things for himself/herself. Social workers then must help parents to advocate for their child to be given maximum opportunities to prove themselves in such situations. To assist in this task, the social worker must be aware of the full range of programs available to this client group and their families. These might include sheltered workshops, job placement services, transitional living programs, group homes, legal guardianship services, respite care, the Special Olympics, and integrated recreational centers.

In addition, social workers must understand updated legislation developed to enhance the quality of services and accessibility afforded to persons with disabilities throughout our society. As persons with disabilities age and become increasingly involved within society, the necessity for them to develop an awareness of such legislation becomes more imminent. The Rehabilitation of Act 1973 was the first comprehensive federal legislation protecting the civil rights of persons with disabilities. Section 504 of this act protected persons against discrimination because of their disability in federal programs or any program receiving federal funding (Orlin, 1995). Moreover, the Americans with Disabilities Act of 1990 was passed to ensure equal opportunity for persons with disabilities, full participation within society, enhanced independent living opportunities, and economic self-sufficiency. Precisely, the Americans with Disabilities Act prohibits discrimination against persons with handicapping conditions in employment, state and local government services, public accommodations, and telecommunications (Orlin, 1995).

However, both clients and students with developmental disabilities have expressed frustrations about the loopholes in this law, because many small businesses (e.g., used-book stores, individually owned restaurants) with only a handful of employees do not have to comply with the law. This is especially discouraging, considering that minor changes might provide access ramps and adaptive rest rooms. And, as is the case with other legislation, it takes a while for consumers and the general public to learn about the rights and responsibilities entailed. Social workers must help persons with disabilities and their families to advocate for these rights and support them to be as proactive and autonomous as possible. Many families are so involved with the day-to-day struggles of their child with disabilities that they are unable to keep up with legislation that may expand opportunities made available for the child now and in the future. Social workers must continue to empower these families through direct counseling, as well as through referrals to advocacy organizations such as the Association for Retarded Children, Parents of Special Children, and Family First, so that families will also have a direct voice in proposed legislation to benefit their children. On the other hand, as the worker provides needed services he/she must also help to educate society at large about the rights of persons with developmental disabilities to live, work, and play as full participants in the communities where they live.

Case Example (See Case study Three—The Thomas Family)
Richie Thomas, age four, was born with congenital cataracts and is therefore legally blind. Richie is protected by the special education laws for young children. His mother, Beverly, has been informed by Richie's pediatrician that he needs to be enrolled in a preschool education program for children with disabilities so that he will be positioned to take advantage of all possible resources available. Beverly, an assertive parent, has already contacted the local school district to inquire about the placement of Richie. A school social worker has been assigned to coordinate Richie's interdisciplinary diagnostic evaluation and placement for preschool.
    The worker will assume the responsibility of addressing the needs of the child within the context of his family. Richie needs a specialized preschool program tailored to meet the ongoing needs of blind and/or partially sighted children. It appears that in part due to his visual challenges Richie also has verbal processing difficulties; thus, he has remained socially immature. The worker must guide and direct the mother in meeting Richie's needs. This interpretive role is extremely crucial because the goal is to empower the mother to assume major responsibility for obtaining resources for Richie over time. Moreover, the worker must assess the overall functioning of the family system and look carefully at the family's impact on Richie. Therefore, other family members' needs must also be addressed. In the Thomas family the worker will need to identify issues related to Beverly's being a full-time working mother and maintaining a household as a single parent as well. Moreover, the specific needs of Richie's siblings must be assessed and addressed in the Individual Family Service Plan.

COMMUNITY/NEIGHBORHOOD SERVICES

Definition

Community/neighborhood services are centralized social services provided in a particular community or locale. Community may be defined as a geographical area in which residents share an identity and agreed-upon or collective understanding of ownership. The ownership takes on the collective understanding of the residents (Barker, 1995, p. 69). The primary goals of community-based services are to be user friendly and holistic. Accessibility is key to the individual's opportunity to utilize those services being provided. When services are delivered based on specific geographical boundaries, the likelihood of residents' having some knowledge of their existence is greater than if services were delivered within the broader community.

Issues and Problems

Community-based services are delivered in the midst of problems and issues unique to that community, as well as those in the larger society. In most inner-city communities, drugs and violence are prevalent. However, these two issues are present in most communities, including suburbia. For example, domestic violence and child abuse cut across all socioeconomic lines. Therefore, it is of the utmost importance for community-based service programs to be aware of the violence factor within their midst. These agencies must strive to create and deliver programs that will effectively counter violent outbursts. Community dwellers must coalesce their efforts in supporting the agency's thrust, identifying and responding to the impact of violence in all its forms within the neighborhood. Violence cannot be adequately addressed without including the growth and development of gang activity. Gangs have the reputation of being violent and destructive, even to their own communities. Although this reputation exists, there are some gangs that are not violent or destructive, but rather, serve as a protector for the community of which the members are a part (Perkins, 1987).

In addition, young people are naturally drawn toward the same sex as part of the socialization process during late childhood and early adolescence. Therefore, it is expected that they will band together. The difficulty arises, however, when destructive behavior develops during this bonding phase. Social workers must keep in mind that children need to have places where they may gain acceptance and be able to prove their competence. Gangs exist in many communities as proving grounds where children may quickly find friendship, as well as seek direction and guidance from peers. Social workers must realize that community/neighborhood services have long stood as a safe haven, that is, a secure environment for fostering the growth and development of children through center-based and outreach services.

Service Delivery Systems

Community services for families are designed based on the unique needs of the community. Resources impact the percentage of time given to a specific service provided by the community/neighborhood center. Therefore, a patchwork approach to service delivery exists in most communities.

Within this approach, services are designed in size and scope, based on the needs identified through the goals of the community agencies. These programs might be selected through a strategic planning effort. As services are identified through a planning process, selection is determined by the governance structure of the agency. In reflecting the patchwork approach to service delivery, social workers must be informed regarding the development of such plans. Having this knowledge will position social workers to understand why some services are small in focus while some others are large in focus. An example of this dynamic might be an agency's decision to use twenty percent of its resources for services to the elderly and fifteen percent for the hunger center. In this example, concern for the elderly is given precedence because there is a sizable population of older adults living in this neighborhood and receiving services regularly at the community center. Therefore, a driving force for this agency might be services to older adults. However, one might also assume that hunger is an ongoing problem in the neighborhood.

Perhaps the most single pressing problem is the lack of economic support for services being delivered in the community. In times of economic retrenchment, neighborhood-based services tend to suffer drastically. That is, the focus is more likely to be given to services that reflect emergency or crisis needs. Social workers need to keep in mind that family services have long been the core focus of community-based services. The family has been the primary target population for intervention in such programs. Therefore, as resources decrease, families will continue to lose the support on which they have always been able to rely at centers near their own homes. These services have traditionally represented the entire spectrum from domestic violence to day care. These services have typically reflected the heart and soul of community-based services.

In community-based services, issues such as transportation and formal referral are generally not high priority items. This is related to the fact that residents may be able to walk to the agency for assistance, with or without an appointment. In addition, a formal referral mechanism is generally not needed because most services are present under one roof. Community centers attempt to offer the most requested services needed by the residents. Families are also referred by word of mouth through the informal network of neighbors and friends. This linkage system may be even stronger in ethnically and culturally diverse neighborhoods.

Another concern is the political context within a given community. Politicians may devise a method for censoring funds available to certain agencies. For example, a city council may have the authority to provide either a gang prevention program or a plan for sidewalk repair. If a positive relationship does not exist among agency directors, advisory groups, and council persons, the city council may decide to fund sidewalks versus crucial social programs so desperately needed by their constituents. In the above example, a related issue might be the denial on the part of the persons in power of the existence of gang violence within their community. Moreover, as elected officials come and go, the design of the patchwork of community services will change. One way to lessen the curtailment of services is through the continual networking of the agency directors with key decision makers such as councilpersons and the mayor.

Community/neighborhood-based services provide multiple programs for women. These services include day care, education, self-esteem programs, and maternal and infant health care. Women aspiring toward career development frequently seek health care through the local community-based agency. Their advancement and success are frequently predicated on the assistance offered through diverse services designed to meet family needs. An illustration of a woman's utilizing community-based services for families is shown in the following case example.

Case Example (See Case Study Five—The Jones Family)
Barbara Jones is a nurse's aide and is seeking to earn her registered-nurse diploma. She is in a support group located at the neighborhood center near her home. She has chosen to participate in this group as a way of addressing the issues confronting her as a full-time working person also enrolled in nursing school full-time. Through the support group she has managed to reorganize her responsibilities so as to reduce barriers that might block her success. Barbara has become close with two members of the group, one who attends her college and is majoring in nursing and the other, majoring in social work. Barbara and these two new friends sometimes study together in the library and occasionally go shopping together. Barbara has also used the agency to address her concerns regarding visitations with her former husband in prison. The agency provides a visitation program that Barbara has used for herself and her son. This program has specifically offered transportation to the prison where her former husband, Hugh Barker, is incarcer-

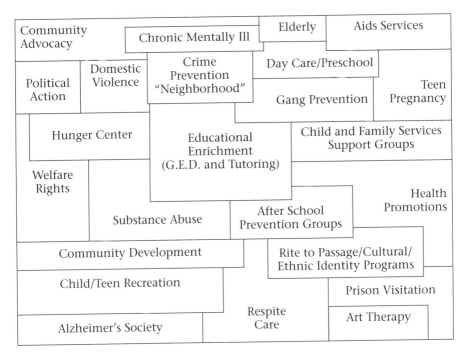

FIGURE 7.2   A Patchwork Approach to Community Services

ated. The support received from the group has positioned Barbara to cope with difficult times in family life. In addition, the group has helped Barbara to accept herself and to discontinue belaboring her own guilt about her siblings' having obtained college degrees, leaving her the only sibling without a degree. The competitive nature within her family relationships has all but diminished. She maintains that acceptance from group members has enabled her to achieve her successes thus far.

SUMMARY

Several fields of practice have been explored, including social work practice with older adults, social work practice with children, social work with persons with developmental disabilities, and social work in community services. The intent of highlighting these select areas of practice is to demonstrate the importance of family-focused social work. These fields of practice represent primary areas for the generalist practitioner. The generalist practitioner has the responsibility to be informed about significant areas of social work practice at micro, mezzo, macro levels. This knowledge is required for the generalist practitioner to have the necessary foundation for service delivery. Having this well-rounded core knowledge should enable the practitioner to meet a range of requests from consumers. The family remains the primary area by which the authors have explored various approaches to social work intervention.

QUESTIONS FOR DISCUSSION

1. Describe the major fields of social work practice known to you.

2. List the issues facing older adults that remain challenges for social work intervention.

3. Describe the issues confronting children during your childhood years versus problems of children during your adulthood.

4. Describe the roles of the social work practitioner in assisting persons with developmental disabilities and their families.

5. What type of program would you develop to address gangs in your community?

GROUP EXERCISE

Divide the class into four groups, each representing a field of practice. Students should be permitted to choose a field of practice. In the presentations, students should be encouraged to choose a field in which they have little experience or least knowledge. Each group will be assigned a field of practice discussed in the chapter and will be asked to describe the essence of the problems confronting families experiencing these issues. Identify ethical or value conflicts inherent in working with this specific client population. Recommendations toward steps to be utilized in addressing issues should outlined. Concrete suggestions toward assisting families in how to specifically address concerns should be offered. In these suggestions, please include resources that might be helpful.

After completing small group discussion, each group will share with the class the highlights of the group process. In addition, individual students will be asked to report at least one idea learned from examining a particular field of practice.

SIGNIFICANT TERMS

micro
mezzo
macro
older adults
child welfare
developmental disabilities
mental retardation
community

neighborhood center
disengagement
ageism
governance
twilight years
baby boomers
mediation
mainstreaming

REFERENCES

Barker, R.L. (1995). *The social work dictionary* , 3rd ed. Washington, D.C.: NASW Press

Beavers, J., Hampson, R., Hulgus, Y. & Beavers, R. (1986). Coping in families with a retarded child. *Family Process*, 25, 365–378.

DeWeaver, K. (1995). Developmental disabilities: Definitions and policies (pp. 712-720). In R. L. Edwards (Ed.), *Encyclopedia of social work*, 19th ed. Washington, D.C.: NASW Press.

Education of the Handicapped Amendments of 1986, P.L. 99-457, 100 Stat. 1145.

Education for All Handicapped Children Act of 1975, PL 94-142, 89 Stat. 773.

Freedman, R. I. (1995). Developmental disabilities: Direct practice (pp. 721-729). In R. L. Edwards (Ed.) *Encyclopedia of social work*, 19th ed. Washington, D.C.: NASW Press.

Freeman, H. (1987). Siblings. In Simon, R.(Ed.), *After the tears: Parents talk about raising a child with a disability*. San Diego: Harcourt Brace Jovanovich.

Ginsberg, L. (1995). *The social work almanac*, 2nd ed. Washington, D.C.: NASW Press.

Gonyea, J. G. (1994). The paradox of the advantaged elder and the feminization of poverty. *Social Work*, 39(1), 35–41.

Helton, L. R. (1994). Strengthening efforts for a family systems approach in early intervention with disabled infants and toddlers. *Social Work in Education*, 16(4), 241–250.

MacKenzie, D. L. (1993). Boot camp prisons in 1993. *National Institute of Justice Journal*, November, 227, 21–28.

Mixdorf, L. (1989). Experimental education and corrections: Teaching through action. *Corrections Today*, 51(5), 38–42.

Olshansky, S. (1962). Chronic sorrow: A response to having a mentally defective child. *Social Work*, 43, 190–193.

Orlin, M. (1995). The Americans with Disabilities Act: Implications for social services. *Social Work*, 40(2), 233–239.

Perkins, U. E. (1987). *Explosion of Chicago's black street gangs: 1900 to present*. Chicago: Third World Press.

U.S. Bureau of Census (1982). *Population profile of the United States: 1981.* (Population characteristics, Series p. 20; pp. 39–55). Washington, D.C.: U.S. Government Printing Office.

U.S. Bureau of Labor Statistics. (1993-a). Bulletin 2307; and *Employment and earnings,* January issue, p. 396.

U.S. Bureau of Labor Statistics. (1993-b). Bulletin 2307; and *Employment and earnings,* January issue, p. 398.

Wikler, L. (1981). Chronic stresses of families of mentally retarded children. *Family Relations,* 30, 281–288.

Winner, S. M. (1990). Law-related education grant, U.S. Department of Education, pp. 6–7.

Zastrow, C. & Kirst-Ashman, K. (1993). *Understanding human behavior and the Social Environment.* 3rd ed. Chicago: Nelson-Hall.

▶ 8

Trends in Policy and Practice

INTRODUCTION

Social work practitioners must always be aware of the changing environment. With environmental changes come shifts in policy and practice issues. These issues are connected to the societal changes as developed according to the current technological, political, and socioeconomic factors. To remain up to date in advancing information within the profession, generalist social work practitioners are being challenged to integrate that which is standard procedure with new and innovative ways of delivering services. Therefore, this chapter will include content that will enable the practitioner to focus on and gain insight into developing trends. Trends to be examined include foster care and adoption, family preservation, deinstitutionalization, health care, women in the workforce, children's day care, and licensure and regulatory statutes.

FOSTER CARE AND ADOPTIONS

Description

Foster care is designed to provide care and protection for children unable to live in their own homes or with other persons authorized to provide care. These authorities may include group homes, residential facilities, or other adults appointed by the courts. Foster care is still needed for children without adult protection today as much as in earlier times. The social worker must keep in mind that foster care is a necessity when families are in crisis and/or for some reason over the long term are unable to provide the required nurturance, governance, and support. Therefore, foster care should not be perceived unilaterally as just an alternative to adoptions.

Foster care grew out of apprenticing and indentured care for homeless youth (Barker, 1995). These homeless youth were under the supervision of merchants, craftspeople, and other community leaders for the sole purpose of providing assistance and guidance. In addition, vocations were often introduced during these living experiences. Such experiences provided the children involved with protection, nurturance, and potential lifetime vocations. This does not mean that children were provided just adequate care; rather, the intent was to enable children to have the necessary support for growth and development and to enhance their capacities for eventual autonomous living.

Essence of Trends

One important trend in foster care is the addition of single individuals as foster parents. This trend is increasing due to the lack of enough two-parent foster homes. Single individuals may provide needed homes for hard-to-place or hard-to-discipline youngsters. Hard-to-place children might include sibling groups, older children, biracial children, children with developmental disabilities and other special needs, and children with multi-emotional and behavioral problems.

Another trend is the placement of children in settings falling somewhere on the continuum between traditional foster care and independent living. Traditional foster care generally ends when the child turns eighteen, at which time the young person is expected to move into independence. The trend includes time reserved for young people to continue to receive monitoring and support after age eighteen. That is, these young people would still maintain ties with the foster care system while moving toward independent living. An example of this new type of fostering might be a young person moving into an apartment and remaining under the supervision of a foster care program. These young persons are given the opportunity to display their ability to be independently functioning adults. They may attend higher education, become employed, or follow a combination of working and going to school. The "testing period" is designed to provide the opportunity for the young person to prove his or her ability to be autonomous and function without continuous agency monitoring. This crucial time is devised to empower the young person to be self-sufficient and to experience comfort in doing so.

Another area of concern for social workers is adoption, which may be defined as the process of individuals taking on the legal responsibilities for the care of a dependent child. This agreement gives the child the right of ownership to family resources and likewise gives the parent the responsibility for complete care of the child (Barker, 1995). The rights and responsibilities are identical to those already present in families in which the parents have given natural birth. Related to this trend is that of joint custody, which is deemed to be in the best interest of the child (Ratcliffe, June 17, 1995). Also, a survey of judges and attorneys indicated that they supported joint custody as desirable in most divorce cases (Draughn, Waddell, & Selleck, 1988).

A trend in adoption services is that of gay and lesbian couples' being given the right to adopt children. This remains a controversial issue in some states or within some traditional ways of thinking. Still, as Ricketts and Achtenberg (1989) point out, psychological health and contentment would seem to lie in how such families live, not in how they are defined. Another trend is the adoption of the children of one's mate. An example of this trend might be the marriage or cohabitation of two persons who adopt one another's children. This phenomenon has increased due to the widening acceptance of differences in current family structure. An additional trend in adoption is that of "unified" adoptive families. Unified adoptive families may be defined as those families wherein the adoptive child has found his/her biological parents in later life. Consequently, there may be two set of parents or family systems, with many family members from each system choosing to interact and establish ongoing relationships. This trend is on the increase largely because in this era there is a strong desire for each individual to have a personal identity based on family of origin. This phenomenon has caused crises for many individuals involved in such arrangements. For example, questions may be raised by the adoptive parents centering around such issues as, "Am I losing my child?" On the other hand, questions might be raised by the natural parent(s) regarding the opening of old wounds. This may bring on feelings of self-judgment on the part of the biological parents, as well as a fear of indictment by society for having placed a child for adoption in the first place.

The social work practitioner must maintain a nonjudgmental attitude in working with all clients. However, this view takes on a special meaning when it comes to persons' having to address self-guilt as a result of difficult decisions made earlier in their lives. Some natural relatives, biological parents, and other family members may choose *not* to have a relationship with the adoptive individual, despite the fact that this person may have searched long and hard for his/her roots. The social worker must, therefore, assist the adoptee to accept and respect the biological parents' and/or family members' right not to become part of a unified adoptive system.

Significance for Social Work Practice

These trends in foster care and adoption are important for social work practitioners to understand because of the urgency within society to address broken relationships. This urgency relates to the necessity for establishing healthy relationships in those families where ties have somehow been severed. Strong family relationships cannot be established where tension is present. In an effort to alleviate tension the practitioner must grasp the wave of conflict and attempt to reduce the level of stress on all family members involved.

In working with foster and adoptive families, the worker must keep in mind the importance of networking with all parties involved such as foster parents, adoptive parents, and biological parents. This would indicate the worker's responsibility to be absolutely clear about his/her role. In considering the possibility of three different family systems coming together for therapeutic interaction, the worker has to remain in a neutral position, always focusing on the well-being of the child and on his/her future. This does not mean that the worker lacks the ability to focus on the parents or should in any way de-emphasize working with parents, but is merely a reminder that the worker must always protect the rights of the child as a unique and separate individual.

FAMILY PRESERVATION

Description

Family preservation can be defined as just that, preserving the family over time despite any disruption and also empowering family members to maintain mutual support for one another. These programs are tailored to keep children within their own families; therefore, they should not be removed through foster placement or other arrangements such as juvenile detention or residential placements (Barker, 1995). Primary goals for family preservation might include the enhancement of parenting skills, improving communication, and teaching anger management skills (Tracy, 1995).

Essence of Trends

Family preservation is in and of itself a current trend in keeping families together. This trend has developed in response to traditional methods of working with families whereby family members were generally separated in order to address problems. The current thrust in family preservation is

FIGURE 8.1   Family Sharing

to shorten the amount of time given to resolve family problems. From a socioeconomic standpoint, this trend originally grew out of the need to preserve agency funds. Programs were at first developed for a ninety-day intervention cycle. More recently, some intervention cycles have been decreased to sixty days; others have been reduced to forty-two- and/or thirty-day cycles. Some family preservation programs have effectively utilized multifamily groups involving peer and nonpeer help within and across families, wherein parents and child groupings from several family systems will meet with a family counselor for the purpose of problem resolution (Cassano, 1989). However, the social worker must always be aware that decisions ought to be made that reflect the integrity of family unity. The cycle of intervention deemed appropriate should be based on the amount of time needed as defined by the worker in collaborative planning with the family.

One example of family preservation involves a social worker's efforts to maintain a father and teenage daughter with mental retardation at home together. The worker assisted the daughter to be able to take care of her own personal hygiene each day. The worker showed the young woman how to put the soap on the bath cloth and wash herself thoroughly. The father up until that time had not been able to accomplish this task. Prior to the worker's involvement, the father had struggled incessantly to help his daughter learn how to take care of herself. Little improvement was made in this effort until the social worker intervened and modeled how the young woman might carry out personal hygiene responsibilities on her own.

A trend that is reenergizing family preservation is that of multi-family group intervention. In this intervention, two or more family members are encouraged to interact with one another for joint problem-solving. Moreover, group techniques and family communication theory are utilized. One important aspect of this method is that it gives family members the opportunity to problem-solve across family lines or boundaries. An example of this method might be a mother's correcting the son of another family involved in the group because of his truancy. The goal is for a positive response to take place regardless of who is interacting with whom. The response from this young man might result from his perception that the other mother perhaps has a more objective view of his situation. With his own parents, the young man may have always been locked into verbal exchanges that have prevented a positive response from those involved.

Significance for Social Work Practice

Beginning social work practitioners must have at least a working knowledge of family preservation programs. This is a necessity to communicate and understand new techniques that have been designed to preserve and maintain families. Social workers must be able to participate in case consultation with other community service providers on an ongoing basis. In today's environment, social workers will most likely find themselves in team conferences developing strategies and techniques centered on keeping families together. The urgency of being informed is key to social workers' being able to advocate on behalf of the families they serve. Social workers must be brokers of resources enabling families to maintain their existence within the community. Resources that might be provided include counseling, transportation, referral, mentoring, parent education, and childrearing. These supports enable families to continue to cope with the continual challenges of family living.

DEINSTITUTIONALIZATION

Deinstitutionalization is defined as the release of clients from an institution because it has been decided that these individuals can now survive in the outside world. These persons are deemed to have the skills to function and to problem-solve in the community at large. The increase in deinstitutionalization is largely due to a decline in economic support for maintaining persons in institutions or residential facilities.

Essence of Trends

The movement toward deinstitutionalization started in the l960s with the development of community-based mental health programs and programs for persons with developmental disabilities. The 1970s brought a more aggressive move of returning clients to their home communities. The visibility of these individuals grew as family members attempted to respond to the complex needs of these returning family members. The quick return of these members, often without advance planning or notice, informed the greater community of the challenging service needs of these diverse client populations. These individuals included persons with mental retardation and developmental disabilities, persons with chronic mental illness (e.g., schizophrenia), older adults, and dependent children. These groups, of course, added to the already growing homeless population. In the 1980s and 1990s, there has been a continued policy of returning clients to their home communities. Furthermore, the AIDS crisis has contributed to economic drain, thereby perpetuating the inclination toward deinstitutionalization and increasing the need for community health care.

Significance for Social Work Practice

The decline in economic support for human services is important for social work practitioners to understand. This knowledge will enable workers to better support the planning process on behalf of their clients. As these trends are understood, the worker will be able to enhance clients' well-being by being able to describe adverse conditions being faced by these displaced individuals. These persons are victims of a declining social fabric. That is, societal structures for assisting such persons economically have diminished to a new low. As welfare structures decline, social workers must develop new ways of assisting families whose members need ongoing, intensive community-based services. Thus, social workers must help families to understand that problems related to deinstitutionalization are also impacted by macro issues; that is, they should not blame themselves for a decline in resources that makes it difficult to maintain family members at home. Due to recent economic downswings, all families have faced greater obstacles in caring for their own.

The trend of deinstitutionalization has emphasized the importance of case management as a practice technique. The social worker as case manager must ensure that services are provided to the client in a timely and comprehensive manner. The case manager, first of all, is a coordinator for all services being provided to the client system; such services might include child care, employment, health care, transportation, educational support, home nursing services, and counseling. In monitoring service delivery, the social worker must network with all agencies or programs involved and keep abreast of issues or difficulties facing the client at any time. Thus, another important role of the case manager is that of identifying gaps in service delivery and aiding agencies to collaboratively provide services to fill these gaps. This effort often leads the case manager to advocate for and help with the development of new programs to meet clients' needs in the community.

HEALTH CARE

Description

Health care is the effort to treat and prevent illness and to promote the health and well-being of all individuals. Health care has gone through a dramatic overhaul toward efforts for major reform. In the past, health care has been provided by health care professionals working independently or in varied health care facilities existing throughout the community. Those delivering health care services included private physicians' offices, hospitals, public health departments, outpatient services, and nursing homes. Social work practitioners have long been involved in the delivery of health care services to clients both at micro and macro levels of practice. In fact, the social worker role has long been perceived by other health care professionals as vital to supporting the emotional adjustment of clients and particularly crucial to their assimilation back into family and community life after hospitalization. Moreover, social workers assist clients in locating appropriate health care services and take an active role in advocating for changes in health policy to accommodate more individuals and serve their health care needs more efficaciously.

In the 1980s and 1990s health care delivery began to change its focus by supporting delivery systems that could compress the course of treatment as well as focus more on prevention and health education. Health maintenance organizations (HMOs) were developed as prepaid programs to meet the total health needs of an individual and/or family. Out of this HMO movement sprang managed health care programs. Managed health care is "a formal network of health care personnel, third-party funding organizations, and other fiscal intermediaries who provide for virtually all the health and mental health care an individual or family might need in exchange for regular premium payments" (Barker, 1995, p. 224).

Essence of Trends

Managed care increases the opportunity for clients to choose the desired physician or health care network. The physician has to belong, of course, to the managed care collective of providers, as compared to the HMO wherein one physician also prescribes needed services offered by a range of subspecialists, generally under one roof. The latest managed care move enables consumers to have more choices in selecting physicians, thereby eliminating the dread fear of visiting an unknown physician. This movement has the potential of giving back to families the concept of the family doctor. That is, every family member sees the primary care physician, regardless of the presenting problem. After seeing the primary care physician, he/she will then be referred to subspecialists as needed. The philosophy behind managed health care is that the connection between the physician and family members is maintained over time. This continuity of care suggests that there might be increased opportunities for the development of stronger and more trusting relationships between the physician and family members. In this approach to health care delivery, education and prevention efforts are paramount and are viewed as critical to keeping family members better informed and promoting optimal use of health care services.

Through the managed care trend, social workers are able to focus directly on one organizational structure with some assurance that families will be served by the same physician and/or fixed set of care providers. Having this confidence, social workers may be able to spend time on other family problems requiring acute attention rather than spending endless hours brokering health care services or arranging transportation to multiple, perhaps distantly located, health facilities.

Significance for Social Work Practice

Social workers will need to investigate managed care systems and take a more active role in carving out their position within this new modality. The significance for social workers is that they must take the initiative to adapt their roles in meeting needs of clients within existing service delivery systems, while maintaining quality of care and incorporating new health care mandates. Through this approach, workers might actively involve themselves in advocacy for new human service programs within agencies and redefine or reframe current services to fit within the managed care network. Another dynamic in this whole process is the need for social workers to commandeer and maintain advocacy positions to promote community-wide organizational and program planning efforts in health care at local, state, and federal levels.

Another significant factor in managed health care is the opportunity for social workers to educate clients regarding new developments in health care and related fields of practice. Social workers also will be required to provide educational services to the client regarding the usage of these new health care programs. The ongoing supportive social work role is essential for continuity of care. For example, an adolescent girl being treated for anorexia will still be able to receive counseling services from a social worker through the managed care network within the mental health service delivery system. Likewise, a visiting home care social worker providing support to maintain a frail older person in his/her own home would continue to have a central role under managed care.

WOMEN IN THE WORKFORCE

Description

Increasing numbers of women enter the workforce annually. These women include single, married, separated, and divorced, of all ages. To examine this trend further, one should note that in 1970, 42.6 percent of the labor force were women; by 1991, 57.4 percent were women; and it is predicted that by the year 2005, 63.5 percent will be women (Gottleib, 1995). By comparison, in 1993, 57.9 percent of all women were in the workforce (U.S. Bureau of Labor Statistics, 1993).

Despite the above trend, women continue to be viewed through stereotypic "glasses" within the working world. They are not perceived as equals in terms of being able to contribute as much as their male counterparts. This attitude is, in part, due to the socialization process in American society wherein females are looked down upon as the weaker and/or second sex. Therefore, in families women are too often considered more suited for the nurturing role as opposed to being suited for the more assertive power broker's role. The governance role is given to the male rather than the female in most American families. However, social workers need to keep in mind that gender is not the determining factor for the governing or nurturing position in a family, but, rather, the person who is best suited or positioned for the role. For example, men can also be nurturing and may be able to take on the assigned role as the primary nurturer in the family. Likewise, the female can take on the primary role as power broker or breadwinner in a family.

In family intervention, social workers should invariably promote and support positions being assumed by the most capable person, whether male or female. This approach should also be modeled and reflected when decisions are being made about positions in the workforce. Social workers must serve as strong advocates for this approach. No longer can women be perceived and treated as just "homemakers, housewives, and mothers" or as "built-in caretakers of the children." The realities of women's expanded roles in the workplace are dispelling these stereotypes, but there is still much advocacy and empowerment to be done by the social work profession on behalf of women.

Essence of Trends

Although women's contributions to the workforce are significant, most women still remain in gender-segregated occupations. In these jobs they are employed as secretaries, nurses, child care workers, sales/retail workers, and social workers (Gottlieb, 1995). These occupations continue to pay less than jobs occupied by men. As stated earlier, women earn only sixty cents for each dollar earned by men (Women's wages, 1995). This disparity in pay between women and men continues to widen and remains inequitable. This reality persists regardless of changes reflecting the advancement of women's rights in other aspects of American life. However, neither the expanded visibility of women in the workforce nor their increased coverage in the media has impacted the dissimilarities in salaries and overall opportunities for career advancement.

In the classic professions of medicine, law, politics, business, and education, women have made some gains, but these have been small, nonetheless, given the proportion of women in the general population. Tokenism unfortunately still affects women in many of these major areas of professional employment. In some high-profile positions, women have proved to be effective and exemplary in crucial leadership roles; however, no real change has occurred for the masses. This is perhaps largely due to a double standard that remains within the context of our society.

Another important dynamic is that of delayed childbirth. Women are now more likely to enter the workforce and establish their career positions before having children. This trend is contributing to the increase of women, especially younger women, in the workforce. Society in general seems to expect women to stay home after they give birth and not go back to work, or seek employment. Some women, of course, accept this moratorium and leave the job market shortly before and/or after childbirth. However, many of these women plan such a hiatus knowing full well that they have already solidified their careers and thus may expect to return to their jobs after having their baby, without a loss in status or career momentum. In 1990 more than half of the mothers of children younger than six were in the labor force (Hofferth, Brayfield, Deich, & Holcomb, 1991).

Moreover, women are able to deliver babies later in life due to advanced medical technology. Advanced medical practice has allowed women, therefore, to be examined and monitored so that any pregnancy risk factors may be discovered and addressed. Having the opportunity to establish their positions within a career base before having children positions women to resume the competition and self-actualization that are conducive to career success.

Also contributing to women's remaining in the job market and/or having a choice about when to have a child is the Family and Medical Leave Act passed in 1993. This legislation allows for men or women to stay home and take care of newborn babies or other family members. By exact definition, the Family and Medical Leave Act allows men or women to take up to twelve weeks of unpaid leave each year, with health care coverage intact, to care for a sick family member, newborn, or newly adopted or foster child (Barker, 1995, p. 130). Because of this legislation, women may remain in the workforce while their spouse stays at home to care for a newborn or other relative. Moreover, another advantage for women is that an increasing number of employers are providing in-house or collaborative day care arrangements in the community. These provisions enable women to have their children nearby during the work day. Consequently, they may visit the center and perhaps have lunch with their children. Moreover, being in such close proximity allows women to interact with the staff regularly, thereby monitoring the care their children are receiving and learning firsthand about any issues that might arise.

Significance for Social Work Practice

Social workers must always keep in mind the NASW Code of Ethics as a driving force in addressing the status of women in the workforce. Women must be seen, first and foremost, as individuals and must be assessed for their contributions to the workforce and society. The Council on Social Work Education mandates that social work students receive "content on patterns, dynamics and consequences of discrimination, economic deprivation and oppression concerning women" (CSWE Curriculum Policy Statement, p. 40). Social workers, therefore, must serve as strong advocates on behalf of women in the workforce, as well as within society at large. Social workers must continue efforts to increase the range of choices afforded to women, including accessible health care, alternative child care arrangements, improved salaries, and expanded opportunities for employment and promotion.

Social work practitioners must be informed of current issues impacting women. These issues reflect current views of society that in turn contribute to policy decisions regarding the place of women in the workforce. The position of women does not reflect equity with other workers in similar positions. As social workers become better informed, they are more likely to reflect added sensitivity and competence in approaching the needs of women. In welfare reform efforts, women have been encouraged to discontinue receiving public assistance, but jobs are simply not being created to meet their needs. This would indicate major inconsistencies in recommended policies and the establishment of programs to implement these stated policies. Consequently, a double bind exists that women on welfare find perplexing and disheartening. When jobs are not generated for women who would choose to work rather than stay on public assistance, it appears that society continues to severely penalize them with the perpetuation of the "welfare dependency" stereotype.

Therefore, social workers must take the lead in diminishing such views, because many women begin to unconsciously believe this stereotype, which may then prolong their reliance on the system. As a profession, social work must help women to unlearn negative roles that have developed as a result of societal oppression and perceive themselves as viable candidates for inclusion throughout the workforce. As Sidel (1984) pointed out, women need assistance in breaking away from the "pink collar ghetto" and in being able to compete for higher-paying, traditionally male-dominated blue collar jobs. Social workers must take the initiative to refute welfare myths and support the creation of training for jobs wherein women can compete for a higher status and wage. This process will first involve helping society, especially key policymakers, to think differently about women's roles as workers, both inside and outside the home.

CHILDREN'S DAY CARE

Description

Day care may be defined as physical care for children when their parents or guardians are unavailable. Children's day care may be divided into three major categories: (1) freestanding, for-profit day care centers; (2) nonprofit, institutionally affiliated centers; and (3) continuum programs offering a range of child care/educational services spanning day care through the early childhood grades.

Freestanding, for-profit day care for children are those programs designed to bring a profit for owners of such facilities. Nonprofit day care centers are usually housed in or affiliated with community/neighborhood hospitals and government offices. Continuum day care programs are those that are developed as an ongoing educational process organized around a philosophy of the child moving from day care to preschool, to kindergarten, and perhaps into the early primary grades (e.g., first, second, third grades) within the same system. Such programs have built in the philosophy of enhancing continuity in a child's life, thereby contributing to the emotional stability of both child and family.

Essence of Trends

The emphasis in day care is moving toward continuity of care over time. Many parents attempt to place their children in programs wherein their needs might be addressed over a period of several years. Stability and self-confidence appear to be greater in children who spend several years within the same environment and philosophy of care. With such continuum care programs, parents are freed from having to establish new relationships with persons providing care for their young children. So the parents do not have to periodically adjust to a new philosophy or model of care. Moreover, freedom from this obligation to continually seek child care allows the family more opportunities for supporting their children's other needs or perhaps attending to other family issues.

Another trend is that of families' searching for programs that provide holistic care. Parents are generally concerned not only about the cognitive development of their children but also about their emotional and ethical development. Through this comprehensive approach, programs often address an orientation to social problems reflective of environmental conditions. An example of this focus is the "good touch/bad touch" training that aims at exposing children to the risks of sexual and/or physical abuse. Some children's day care programs also introduce children to age-appropriate content on substance abuse, family violence, and human sexuality. Staff may explore children's attitudes and provide appropriate content through techniques such as play therapy, art therapy, or bibliotherapy (i.e., using select children's books written to help children understand and cope with major life challenges). These techniques may help children to experience a greater knowledge of issues and problems existing in the world around them through the use of familiar materials and approaches.

Another growing trend is the development and expansion of licensed "day care homes." In this type of arrangement, parents who mistrust outside day care programs may choose to create their own day care or find individuals with similar views. Thus, cooperatives are formed to address the joint need for day care. The cooperative is designed to pool resources as well as combine comparable attitudes toward the educational process and/or child development. That is, a particular child care philosophy is agreed upon by those persons participating in the network. Networks developed through this process generate additional consumers through formal referrals and word of mouth. Cooperatives can provide a more cohesive working relationship among family members. Sometimes a family will create its own cooperative child care program wherein grandparents, aunts, uncles, cousins, nieces, nephews, and other surrogate relatives will collaboratively work toward caring for all children within the extended family system. Cooperative day care programs may also be established around philosophical and religious views. An example would be families affiliated with a fundamentalist religion creating a day care consortium reflecting these values and views.

Federal legislation since the mid-1970s has been passed to offer a variety of supports, both direct and indirect, to children of working parents. These include income tax credits for mid- to high-income families and funding provided to states for poor working families (Chilman, 1993). The Child Care and Development Block Grant, introduced by the Omnibus Budget Reconciliation Act of 1989 (U.S. General Accounting office, 1990), provided states with funds, seventy-five percent of which were earmarked to provide child care for low-income working parents with children under thirteen and twenty-five percent of which were allocated for providers and for improving quality of care. This legislation also provided $1.5 billion in matching funds to the states to assist low-income working families or parents in job training programs. Moreover, in 1992 Head Start received substantial increases in federal funding to provide all-day, all-year programming, buildings for housing health care services to siblings of children enrolled, and literacy and educational programs for parents (Chilman, 1993; Children's Defense Fund, 1992).

Significance for Social Work Practice

Social workers must inform themselves about the general rules and regulations regarding what is permissible practice in society in delivering child care. Any individual has the right to create home child care programs. These programs may not necessarily reflect the views of a worker's personal value base but may be reflective of acceptable and standard policy in the field of child care. Thus, workers must help families to be aware of the full range of child care options that may be available within the community.

The social work practitioner has the responsibility to ensure that minimum standards be met. The importance of meeting these standards determines the quality of care for children. Quality of care implies that the program is oriented toward fostering age-appropriate socialization and positive self-esteem. Without proper monitoring of programs, the needs of children will most likely not be met in day care. A lack of developmental stimulation may contribute to insufficient social skills which are so essential for wholesome childhood development.

Child care programs with rich financial resources can provide the most up-to-date tools and educational foundations. However, all programs must be monitored for quality of care. Social workers must especially pay careful attention in assessing whether quality services are being delivered in smaller, perhaps less recognized programs in the community. Many small-scale child care providers with fewer financial resources may still offer services equal to or in some cases superior to larger programs in their ability to nurture, encourage, and enrich the lives of children. Social workers may be positioned in community advocacy roles that enable them to help such programs compete for the resources necessary to meet and/or maintain basic standards for child care.

Social workers need to develop broader roles allowing them to become more involved in the entire spectrum of early intervention for children. These roles are necessary for social workers to be able to interpret program needs for decision makers. This involvement will enable them to support an inclusive environment to empower both children and families. Having this role places workers "at the table" with other principal providers of services for children, such as teachers, child psychologists, and nurses. By being involved with other members of the early childhood education team, workers may be better positioned to address the psychosocial needs of children and families affected by economic retrenchment, curtailment, and/or consolidation of services. This role also allows social workers to have a more direct influence on the development of children and the involvement of families.

Social work practitioners possess unique understanding of children and their families. They may be able to interpret and guide the thinking of families, as well as function when necessary as spokespersons for families. This holistic approach to service delivery in early childhood educational settings is vital to meeting the complex financial, emotional, and social needs of children and families.

THE IMPACT OF SOCIAL WORK LICENSURE AND OTHER REGULATORY STATUTES

Description

The phenomenon of licensure is highly visible within the context of society. A license is required for almost every public service job within society. These jobs range from dogcatcher to doctor, from hair stylist to social worker. Professional licensure is required and considered as a standard in almost every major profession within our society. Licensure has always been a requirement for professions such as law, medicine, and nursing. In recent years, licensure for social workers has been on the increase. Licensure and/or regulation of professional social work practice is now required in approximately forty-eight states, Washington, D.C., Puerto Rico, and the Virgin Islands (American Association of State Social Work Boards, 1993). Licensure is required primarily as a protection for consumers. Licensure determines who can deliver services and sets the scope of practice at a given level. That is, the level of practice is generally determined by the degree of education and years of practice experience in social work.

Essence of Trends

Licensure is one of the most important growth areas for social work practice today. This importance is related to the growth of licensure within the profession. Growth is indicated by the number of states requiring licensure for professional social work practice. This trend will continue to develop in the future as professions attempt to enhance the delivery of services often while competing with each other for consumers and limited resources. Licensure is also designed to protect the public from a lack of qualification and unethical behavior among practitioners. A growing concern from members of society is the quality of services delivered by professionals. The demand from citizens has pushed policymakers to support requests on behalf of their constituencies. These requests include supporting licensure from the belief that licensed persons have at least met minimum qualifications for their profession. These qualifications are expected to provide practitioners with the foundational values, knowledge, and skills significant to their profession. To ensure thoroughness in values, knowledge, and skills, a quality assurance effort must be present and enforced.

Quality assurance is maintained through the requirement of initial examination upon licensure, and thereafter monitoring may be assured through continuing education requirements as a contingency for licensure renewal. In addition, social work boards in some states are given the responsibility to license and renew licenses on behalf of the government and the profession. This important task contributes to the overall enhancement of the profession. Enhancing the profession leads to the ultimate goal of improving the well-being of the general population. As the era of licensure expands, the philosophy of the movement, in and of itself, has to be addressed.

Philosophically, licensure grew out of the need to regulate the productivity of social workers. The thinking is that regulation will protect and raise the quality of work delivered by practitioners. However, the great debate around licensure is related to whether one license or certification is better than another. The question here is not whether one license is better than another; the rationale for licensure or certification is the area of consumer protection afforded by such legislation. That is, having licensure or certification enables the social work practitioner to provide and implement services to meet consumer needs.

The range of licensure extends from the Associate Arts (AA) to the Bachelor of Arts (BA)/ Bachelor of Social Work (BSW), to the Master of Social Work (MSW), to the doctoral degree (Ph.D./DSW). Licensure based on these degrees, however, may be complicated in some states whereby related-degree individuals are being permitted to obtain social work licensure. Each state regulates through the state legislature the eligibility of social workers for certification within the profession. The actual licensing or regulatory law then determines all specifications for licensure at various levels of practice. Some states license only masters level social workers while others license all ranges based upon degree preparation. Regulatory boards are designed differently from one state to another. For example, the state of Ohio has combined counselors and social workers into a joint counselor and social worker board.

Significance for Social Work Practice

Some states have long-standing regulations for social work practitioners. Other states have added levels of certification or licensure in recent years. The added regulations continue to impact the social work profession. The significance of this impact has greatly influenced decision making of workers providing services to clients. This impact also provides the developmental process designed to create the foundation and fabric for accountability and high-quality service delivery. The accountability factor has significantly changed the face of social work practice. The significance of licensure enables individuals to work in specific areas of practice. The varied licenses are helpful and protective of the well-being of all family members. Licensure authorizes social work practitioners to deliver a broad range of professional services within the community.

The importance and thrust of licensure relate to the fluid nature of all clients, including families. That is, the needs of clients change over time, thereby requiring practitioners to be flexible in their efforts to fulfill the requests of all concerned. An example is that a licensed independent or clinical social worker would have both the skill and jurisdiction to deliver services to families experiencing marital problems, child abuse, domestic violence, or substance abuse. This same professional might also provide the community with education, consultation, and planning services around the problem of family violence. Licensure provides an added incentive toward this goal and increases motivation for the worker to do the best possible job. Therefore, motivation is in part an outcome for the recognition of being a licensed service provider. It is honorable to have a license from the standpoint of the consumer network. That is, consumers prefer to have a provider who has recognition as a quality professional. Professionals and consumers alike must continually be aware that having a license does not automatically mean that a social work practitioner has the values, knowledge, and skills necessary to deliver quality services. The consumer can feel comfortable, however, in knowing that having a licensed professional moves them closer to assurance that the service provider at least has the minimum qualifications for professional service delivery.

Having licensure empowers social work practitioners to compete in the labor market with other professionals. Licensure elevates the social work practitioner to a position on a par with other regulated professions. With the arrival of changes in the health care delivery system and the expansion of private practice in social work, credentialing will be the primary tool determining who will deliver services and what services will be delivered. Social work practitioners must be aware that families being served will be directly influenced by their breadth and depth of understanding the nature of the credentialing process. Likewise, practitioners must expand their knowledge regarding the growth and development of families through the process of continuing education. This would in turn empower families to continue to carry out essential functions through the intervention of skilled and acknowledged practitioners.

SUMMARY

Trends in policy and practice influence families in areas related to foster care and adoption, family preservation, deinstitutionalization, health care, women in the workforce, child care, and social work licensure. These trends reflect the importance of delivering a broad range of services to families. This broad range establishes boundaries for social work practitioners in determining how and what services can be delivered. Services to families cross many fields of social work practice and involvement. The practitioner, therefore, should understand a working definition for each trend, be able to identify the essence of each trend, and understand the significance for social work practice.

QUESTIONS FOR DISCUSSION

1. Describe the major social work trends influencing families.
2. List two to four emerging components of each trend.
3. Describe how each trend will impact your area of interest in social work practice.

(These questions may be answered within the context of the class as a whole, or the instructor may break the class into small groups of three to five persons to process the responses.)

GROUP EXERCISE

Divide the class into groups of three to five members. Each group should be given one of the following policy or practice issues and asked to present the current concerns and challenges for practitioners:

unified adoptive families
Each student in this small group should imagine that he or she is an adoptive child, now grown up; consider the pros and cons of creating a unified adoptive family network. Include in your discussion ethical and value dilemmas. Be detailed in outlining problems and challenges.

family preservation
Have students address the pros and cons of family preservation. Each student in this small group should present his or her views on why families should always be kept together. [In addition, students should consider the impact that limiting the number of days for family intervention might have on the long-term success of family preservation.] Students should consider whether any child care institution will be needed in this era of family preservation.

longevity
Discuss the policy implications of living longer, that is, social security, health care, retirement age. Students should be divided into small groups of three to five students. Identify the current trends and issues confronting practitioners in attemping to assist older adults. Project ahead to the year 2030 and imagine what problems will be confronting practitioners and consumers.

licensure

Divide the class into groups of three to five students. Have students describe the importance of having licensure as practitioners. Specifically, what are the benefits to the consumer? What are the benefits to the professional? What are the benefits to the society? What will the major challenges be for social work licensure in the future? Use concrete examples in your presentations. Do not forget to address any ethical or value conflicts that may develop in small group deliberations.

SIGNIFICANT TERMS

unified adoptive family	developmental disabilities
family preservation	managed care
health maintenance organization	children's day care
longevity	licensure
deinstitutionalization	regulatory statute

REFERENCES

American Association of State Social Work Boards (1993). *Social work laws and board regulations: A state comparison summary*. Culpeper, V.A.: American Association of State Social Work Boards (AASSWB).

Barker, R. L. (1995). *The social work dictionary*, 3rd ed. Washington, D.C.: NASW Press.

Cassano, D. R. (1989). Multi-family therapy in social work practice—part I. *Social Work with Groups*, 12(1), 3–14.

Children's Defense Fund (1992). *Legislative year in review*. Washington, DC: Author.

Chilman, C. S. (1993). Parental employment and child care trends: Some critical issues and suggested policies. *Social Work*, 38(4), 451–460.

Council on Social Work Education (1994). CSWE Policy Statement. In *Handbook of accreditation: Standards and procedures*. Alexandria, V.A.: CSWE.

Draughn, P. S., Waddell, F. E., & Selleck, L. R. (1988). Joint custody: Perceptions of judges and attorneys. *Journal of divorce*, 11(3–4), 21–34.

Gottlieb, N. (1995). Women overview (pp. 2518–2588). In Richard Edwards (Ed.) *Encyclopedia of Social Work*, 19th ed. Washington, D. C.: NASW.

Hofferth, S. L., Brayfield, A., Deich, S. & Holcomb, P. (1991). *The national child care survey, 1990*. Washington, D.C.: Urban Institute.

Ratcliffe, R. G. (1995). Bush signs bill establishing joint custody. *Houston Chronicle*, Section A, p. 29, Col. 1, June 17.

Ricketts, W. & Achtenberg, R. (1989). Adoption and foster parenting of lesbians and gay men. *Marriage & Family Review*, 14(3–4), 83–118.

Sidel, R. (1984). *Women and children last: The plight of poor women in affluent America.* New York: Penguin Books.

Tracy, E. M. (1995). Family preservation and home based services (pp. 973–982). In Richard Edwards (ed.), *Encyclopedia of Social Work,* 19th ed. Washington, D.C.: NASW.

U.S. Bureau of Labor Statistics (1993). Bulletin 2307; and *Employment and earnings,* monthly, January issues.

U.S. General Accounting Office (1990). *Deficit reductions for fiscal year 1990: Compliance with the Omnibus Budget Reconciliation Act of 1989, P.L. 101-239.* Washington, D.C.: U.S. Government Publications Office.

Women's wages found to trail men's worldwide. (1995). *Boston Globe,* April 12 28:5.

▶ 9

Implications for Social Work Practice with Families
Current and Future Challenges

In this final chapter social work with families, including current and future challenges, will be explored. The areas for exploration will include; 1) a review of the Four-R Model of Family Dynamics and future adaptations; 2) recommendations for research; 3) practice with families in a multicultural society; and 4) longevity and the impact of better health. These four areas will serve as a bridge between current and future ways of understanding and working with families.

THE FOUR-R MODEL OF FAMILY DYNAMICS AND FUTURE ADAPTATIONS

The Four-R Model includes four dimensions for understanding families: rules, roles, relationships, and rituals. This model was developed by the authors through their extensive work with families in multi-practice environments and through the teaching of social work practice to beginning professionals. The authors have concluded that one of these family dimensions or guiding forces occupies a central position in any family. Each dimension is present within every family, but only one dimension will serve as the primary force behind family functioning. Once identified, the guiding force serves as a springboard for the beginning practitioner. This springboard should enable the worker to focus on governance, nurturing, and communication as a major task for understanding the family as a system. The predominant dimension or guiding force within the family will determine the process or mechanism by which governance, nurturing, and communication will be operationalized. The operationalization of the concept will constitute the instrument/channel to be used by the social work practitioner in working with the family.

An initial task for the worker will include his/her identifying issues of concern. Through the identification and close examination of these issues, the specific guiding force may be clarified. The identification of the guiding force is dynamic and ongoing, as is the case in all social work assessment. The guiding force within a family may change over time and be influenced by such factors as aging, marriage, education, change of employment, birth of children, cultural assimilation, health status, and death.

The future of the Four-R Model will especially be influenced by such factors as the increase of women in the workforce, the extended life span, and the increase of multicultural families and blended families. As the social work practitioner becomes informed about these influences, in conducting the assessment he/she will need to consider the impact of dynamic changes within society. The social work practitioner has the responsibility to assist families through any difficult transition or adaptation over time.

The Four-R Model may be used to help the practitioner understand the role of women in the workforce. Women who tend to be relationships-oriented may move toward being more rules-dominated after entering the workforce. This shift is related to the need for women to perhaps be more direct in their behavior within the workplace. Being more direct may be related to the effort to handle responsibilities. When rules are in operation within a family, less time may be needed for task completion. Rules generally predetermine responsibilities for all family members, both workers and nonworkers. In the future there is likely to be an even greater increase in women entering the workforce. Therefore, one might expect a shifting of women toward being more rules-dominated as an outcome of environmental conditions. In addition, there will most likely be a shift in family roles as women continue to enter the workforce in large numbers. The fluid nature of families and family dynamics may make it more difficult for the practitioner to determine the exact guiding force or dimension that is operating within a family.

The Four-R Model might also be used to understand the extended life span of individuals. Medical technology has largely contributed to the extended life span. The vast majority of older adults are healthy;

they live longer and are often able to remain in their own homes or semi-independent living situations into advanced age. The Four-R Model should assist the worker in interpreting shifts within family dynamics related specifically to longevity. As individuals live longer, they may adapt to the ruling dimension, given various circumstances in their lives. For example, in a person's younger days, he/she may be rules-oriented within the family, but in living longer may shift toward becoming more rituals-oriented. That is, the person may tend to do the same thing at the same time, in the same way, over and over again. This behavior may relate to an older person's ways of maintaining control within the family. Another example would be an older adult's insisting that someone in the family visit the graves of deceased relatives on their birthday and/or major holidays. This is required family behavior, on behalf of the older person, who utilizes these rituals to assist in solidifying his/her governing position as the family matriarch/patriarch.

Another aspect of an extended life span is the factor of retirement. Retirement is further influenced by the ages of various family members and the fact that family members may be retiring at different times. This dynamic is present whether one is married or single. That is, retirement will introduce new variables and issues regardless of present or prior marital status. An example is the "bossy" person in the work setting who may then shift to being a relationships-oriented person in retirement. This shift relates to the need to be structured or rigid within the work setting, but the need to rebuild a repertoire of friends during retirement.

The Four-R Model of Family Dynamics can also be used to help the worker understand the increase of multiculturalism and family functioning. The world is increasing in the number of multicultural families. This increase is inevitably leading to new patterns of family dynamics; thus, new barriers are being introduced as a result of multicultural families' relocating into the communities of urban, rural, small town, and suburban America. The recommendation to the worker is that he/she must be fully informed about the various ethnic cultural groups in the community in which he/she works. The importance of having knowledge regarding these groups is related to understanding and interpreting the guiding dimensions within the Four-R Model and its adaptation to family-specific ways of being.

The Four-R Model might be used in multicultural families to address myths and stereotypes regarding cultural values, traditions, and behaviors. An example of this might be the use of the Four-R Model to interpret how the roles of women might be subservient within the context of the family. The general American society may look down on these cultures wherein women would seem to be entrenched in the roles of mother and housekeeper. These roles may be reflective, however, of

FIGURE 9.1   Multicultural Awareness

deeply ingrained cultural traditions, but as women are introduced to other cultures and broader societal opportunities their behavior may shift toward a more egalitarian position. With this occurrence, there may be shifts in family roles. Thus, these women may choose to enter the job market or seek educational opportunities. The social work practitioner should keep in mind that this shift in roles may cause conflict within some families.

Moreover, the Four-R Model should help the practitioner to understand religious traditions within the multicultural family. With a clearer understanding of rituals, stereotypes may be removed from the descriptive language about a specific culture. Rituals are designed to assist families in carrying out traditions that reflect the historical experiences and belief systems that have grounded their families over time. These family rituals may shift and take on different meaning as multicultural roots find a comfortable space within the context of the prevailing culture. Social work practitioners may take on the role of assisting families to find that comfortable zone wherein they may remain rooted in their cultural identity and heritage. For example, a woman giving up her veil or other traditional dress does not necessarily mean she has given up her involvement in family traditions and rituals.

Finally, the Four-R Model can be used to better understand blended families. With the divorce rate being almost fifty percent, there is also an automatic growth of blended families. Having knowledge of blended families through the application of the Four-R Model should position the social work practitioner to understand the fluid nature of family dynamics brought about by such factors as divorce, remarriage, and step-parenting. Blended families may join together a person who has grown up in a rules-dominated family and a person who has grown up in a rela-tionships-dominated family. Also, one or both partners may have been involved in another adult family relationship wherein their guiding force differed from their partner's dominating family dynamic.

What happens when these two persons come together? The chal-lenge of the social work practitioner is to combine the dynamics in order to have a better understanding of the primary characteristics of each dimension; this process should assist the worker in bridging the two fam-ily units together. It has been noted that a major problem of social work practice in this modern age is whether social work practitioners should give more credence to family structure or to family functioning (Vosler, Green, & Kolevzon, 1986). This task is of vital importance as the growth of blended families continues in society. This situation can be more chal-lenging for the social work practitioner when there are dependent chil-dren involved and where visitation and/or joint custody has to be worked out. In assessing these merged family systems, the social worker may uti-lize standard interventive tools such as genograms and eco maps. There-fore, social work practitioners may seize the opportunity to create a new practice area—connecting two families with two different orientations into one and then supporting them well beyond divorce mediation into "integrative dynamics" counseling. That is, social workers need to offer their services to blended families over the long term.

RECOMMENDATIONS FOR RESEARCH

Perhaps the most important research focus may be testing the utility of the Four-R Model itself. Family researchers have pointed out that although many instruments and paradigms exist for the assessment of family functioning, social work practitioners often use idiosyncratic indi-cators in evaluating their practice with families (Reichertz & Frankel, 1993). Researching the effectiveness of the Four-R Model in understand-ing overall family dynamics should add considerably to research method-ology. This is the initial phase necessary to build a foundation to be used by others in understanding families. Students might be asked in class to share information about their own family dynamics as they relate to the

Four-R Model. The focus here might be either their family of origin or their current family system. The next logical step might be to have students test the Four-R Model with families with whom they are involved in field practicum.

Another possibility might be to have social work practitioners from the community test the Four-R Model with their own families, as well as with their clients. Having practitioners test the model may allow the opportunity for them to first examine their own family of origin or current family and then explore the model further with their own clients. The Four-R Model is predicted to be relevant with all family groupings. Accepting this premise, practitioners should conduct a research project with various ethnic and cultural groups. The outcome of this study might provide comparison data among these groups, including both recent immigrants and those cultural groups that have assimilated into the prevailing culture.

Since the assumption is that the Four-R Model is relevant to all family groupings, it might provide additional knowledge if tested internationally. Cultures differ by countries and even within countries based on such variables as political affiliation, socioeconomic status, historical traditions, religious beliefs, and geographical variations. The importance of international testing relates in part to the fact that technology in communication is quick and easy. In using distance learning and other technological advances, the world has become much smaller. Therefore, it will be vital to determine how the Four-R Model would be applicable when applied to various populations in other parts of the world.

The last area to be considered for research might be to examine the impact of the Four-R Model of Family Dynamics in assessing and intervening with blended families. The focus of this research might be to understand the impact of the Four-R Model upon the individual within the blended family. One research strategy might be to utilize a longitudinal approach that would study family dynamics at various intervals. This type of research, for instance, might yield a better understanding of family adaptation; effect of distance versus local residence of an absent parent; the remarriage of one parent versus the single status of the other; and the birth of a child within the blended family.

PRACTICE WITH FAMILIES IN A MULTICULTURAL SOCIETY

In the coming years, it is predicted that world populations will be predominantly ethnically diverse and/or composed of persons of color. This reality will have a strong impact upon American society and culture.

Multicultural groups are expected to grow rapidly and dominate society as we know it. The Four-R Model of Family Dynamics can also be used as a tool for understanding the historical traditions, values, and world views of these multicultural groups. It is particularly important for practitioners to have knowledge of cultural traditions of other groups to prevent distortion based on one's own perceptions (Jackson-Hopkins, 1992).

Cultural assimilation will occur as multicultural groups adjust to and redesign the fabric of American culture. Therefore, families may take on different configurations largely due to the integration and merging of cultural traditions and lifestyles. Impacting the shape of families will be such factors as intermarriages, combined religious worship, and other unique traditions inherent to family groupings within a multicultural society. Once they blend together beyond cultural boundaries, these individuals will form transcultural configurations. As multicultural groups begin to merge and advocate for equity for all, families will begin to force social institutions to change. These new social institutions must reflect the tenor of the multicultural environment. For example, a unique attribute of cultural and ethnic groups is their use of informal networks, for instance, extended families and neighbors for resources such as child care and care for older adult relatives. Consequently, these multicultural groups, both unilaterally and collectively, are predicted to demand societal and/or institutional subsidies in return for the indigenous, ethnic-sensitive kinship and community care that they themselves have developed.

LONGEVITY AND THE IMPACT OF BETTER HEALTH

The extended life span will impact the functioning of families. Usually, longevity evokes an image of good health. This assumption may or may not be true depending on one's perspective. However, medical technology is bringing about a more healthy society. One also needs to recognize that with increased longevity a person might be ill for a long period of time and still have a quality life, thereby contributing to the well-being of the family. Longevity should provide opportunities for increased intergenerational interaction wherein third-generation family members may have more quality time with first-generation family members. Thus, there will be more opportunity for the transmission of family rituals through face-to-face contact, rather than through family stories or photograph albums handed down by one's parents or grandparents.

As Carter and McGoldrick (1989) have indicated, all families have a life cycle of their own. Therefore, as persons live much longer, the family dynamics of rules, roles, relationships and rituals will inevitably be affected. For instance, as the authors have observed, it is not atypical for great-grandparents to assume parenting roles during retirement. This trend might be expected to prevail into the next century, with older adult heads of households living longer and families maintaining their structure within the community. Also with increased longevity, couples may find themselves living much longer, without having the responsibility for parenting or grandparenting. With families living so much longer, social workers must realize that they may need more assistance in meeting their needs within multilayers of family networks. The oldest family members at or near the top of the family tier may tend to find themselves not being utilized as much as younger family members.

As people live longer, society has to reshape its social institutions. At present, institutions are generally not designed to accommodate the needs of an aging population. Social work practitioners must provide input and leadership in redeveloping such institutions. In this transitional state, practitioners' contributions can be taken from their experience in assisting families with multiple and complex life issues. The new issues confronting practitioners and consumers are areas of concern largerly based upon the impact of a multicultural world and advances in medical technology. The future opportunity for redesigning helping systems to support families is now an imminent concern.

As human beings live longer, new roles will emerge in response to the extra time given. With added years, additional time is available to make contributions unheard of before. Complicating the additional time factor is that these persons are more likely to have good health, that is, they are likely to have no serious illness. The question for practitioners is to try to discern what new responsibilities may be introduced into an already busy work environment. The present retirement age may well not be acceptable for healthy individuals living into their late seventies and eighties. It is important to realize that longevity may provide new roles for older adults, which will in turn enhance their quality of life.

Another component of longevity is the need for new and creative living arrangements. It is quite possible that in the future great-grandparents, grandparents, and parents may be living together under one roof. This opportunity will bring new questions to be raised in order to determine the quality of life of such families. Social work practitioners may intervene to aid family members in raising the questions that will help them to describe the best living arrangement for optimal well-being. Some questions raised might center around how to share resources, who will be head of the household, who will care for grandchildren and great-grandchildren, how family rituals will be shared and practiced, and who will take charge of intergenerational storytelling.

These areas will most likely contribute to new foundations for day-to-day living. These new foundations will undoubtedly contribute to the fabric of new or expanded social structures.

One cannot overlook the possibility that self-selected families will continue to develop. These families will represent all types of individuals coming together out of their joint need to be family-centered for purposes of economic and emotional support. For example, three widowed and/or divorced grandmothers might share a household out of their need to pool resources and share social and emotional support. This arrangement might be beneficial to young families within the kinship network, as they seek child care arrangements. Child care might be carried out by these individuals as their health permits or if other social or work obligations will not interfere.

Another example of the effects of longevity might be the development of new structures to support intergenerational family constellations. These constellations may be needed to respond to the increasing number of families of multigenerations sharing the same household. As individuals continue to live longer, new support mechanisms will be developed to assist all family members with ongoing emotional and financial needs. A family support foundation might be established in response to the growing request of individuals seeking support as a result of longevity and economic shortfalls. Such support might be used, for instance, for helping family members experiencing the loss of a spouse, a financial crisis such as bankruptcy, lack of health care, or the need for educational advancement.

SUMMARY

The Four-R Model of Family Dynamics is designed to explore family structure and functioning holistically, that is, from micro, mezzo, and macro perspectives. Because of its holistic and generalist perspective the Four-R Model of Family Dynamics may be adapted to examine issues facing families today and in the future. As society becomes multicultural, additional programs and services must be developed to address these diverse needs. The social work practitioner's need to understand family rules, roles, relationships, and rituals will be greater than ever before. Moveover, longevity might close the gap between the discrepancy in the life spans of men and women. Consequently, social work practitioners should have ample opportunity to create innovative programs addressing this phenomenon. As the needs of the family change over time, societal institutions must also change to meet these dynamic needs. Through this reciprocal interaction, the family will continue to flourish as the primary source of governance, nurturance, and self-actualization throughout the life span of the individual.

QUESTIONS FOR DISCUSSION

1. Name a specific area of family work in which you might conduct research utilizing the Four-R Model of Family Dynamics.
2. Identify your cultural/ethnic affiliation. Describe the use of the Four-R Model within the context of your worldview and cultural value system.
3. Using the blended family as an example, how would you apply the Four-R Model in understanding transitions and challenges?

GROUP EXERCISE

Arrange the class in a circle. Have each class member describe the diversity within their community. How is their family similar to or different from their prevailing family type? Remind class members to listen as each person shares without making comments or judgments. After the completion of the presentations, divide the class into small groups of three to five members. During the small-group discussion, participants should talk about the issues shared in the larger group, such as guiding forces (Four-R Model), family structure, cultural diversity and ethical dilemmas.

SIGNIFICANT TERMS

longitudinal research	self-actualization
family foundation	semi-independent living
family life cycle	divorce mediation
longevity	integrative dynamics counseling

REFERENCES

Carter, B. & McGoldrick, M. (1989). *The changing family life cycle*. 2nd ed. Boston: Allyn & Bacon.

Jackson-Hopkins, M. (1992). Cultural traditions and barriers that may hinder therapeutic change (pp. 109–116). In Edwards, A. W. (Ed.), *Human services and social change: An African-American church perspective.* Cleveland, Ohio: The Inner City Renewal Society/Orange Blossom Press.

Reichertz, D. & Frankel, H. (1993). Integrating family assessment into social work practice. *Research on Social Work Practice,* 3(3), 243–257.

Vosler, N. R., Green, R. G., & Kolevzon, M. S. (1986). The structure and competence of family units: Implications for social work practice with families and children. *Journal of Social Service Research ,* 9(2/3), 1–16.

Appendix

Glossary

ADA—(Americans With Disability Act) Legislation passed in 1990 to ensure equal opportunity in employment and public accommodations for all persons with developmental disabilities.

advocate—A person speaking on behalf of someone else.

ageism—Stereotyping and oppression of older adults.

alliance family—Persons choosing to live together in a family configuration without being related by blood.

assessment—Evaluation or examination of information/data shared by the client during intervention.

assumption—An impression not grounded in truth or reality.

authority—The act of having control, power, or direction.

baby boomers—Persons born after World War II, that is, between 1946 and 1960.

birth order—The position of one's birth within the family.

bibliotherapy—Therapy using books.

blaming—Always placing the fault for one's behavior onto others.

blended family—A family unit comprising natural family members and those who enter by marriage.

blocking—An incongruent communication pattern whereby an individual disrupts and impedes communication.

blood ties—To be related by blood kinship.

body language—A person's nonverbal signals used in communication through the utilization of facial expressions, gestures, and body positioning.

boot camp—A juvenile program patterned after a military basic training camp.

bottom-up approach—An egalitarian orientation toward decision making and governance.

boundary—A parameter that separates a system from its environment.
broker—An individual who links clients with resources.
caretaker—A family member who provides nurturance and emotional support for other members.
case management—The process of coordinating and monitoring services across a network of delivery systems.
childrearing—The art of bringing up children.
children's day care—A program designed to provide care for children when parents or legal guardians are not available.
child welfare—Looking out for the well-being of children.
closed-ended questions—Inquiries that seek specific answers in an interview.
collective self-development—The art of improving the existence of all individuals within a group, for example, the family.
communication—Exchange of information between a sender and a receiver.
community—A geographical area wherein people share similar values, interests, goals, and services.
community living alternatives—Living arrangements for persons sixty-five and older that include day care centers, assisted living environments, group homes, high-rise apartment complexes, shared living cooperatives, and nursing homes.
compromise—The act of meeting another person halfway.
conflict resolution—The art of settling disagreements.
congruent communication—Clarity between what is being said and what is being felt. This is the highest level of communication.
consensus—Agreement reached through mutual exploration of the best interests of the group.
contracting—Developing goals and objectives that are agreed upon by both practitioner and client in an effort to bring about planned change.
CSWE (Council on Social Work Education)—An organization with the primary responsibility for accrediting schools of social work in the United States.
cultural assimilation—The adaptation of an individual from one culture to another.
culture—Customs, values, traditions, norms of a people.
cyclic grieving—Reacting to loss over the long term with acute reactions at crucial developmental or transitional periods.
deinstitutionalization—The movement of individuals from institutions to community settings.
developmental disabilities—Multiple delays in the development of an individual that have an onset before age twenty-two, affect three or

more areas of functioning, and are likely to exist throughout one's life span.

disengaged relationships—Family relationships in which members are so isolated and distant from one another that they are unable to reach consensus.

disengagement—An older adult's pulling away from society as society concurrently pulls away from the adult.

diversity—Aspects of individual that differ from those of others.

division of labor—The sharing of responsibilities with each person taking on a separate task.

dominance—The act of having control.

double bind—The inability to comment on a discrepancy.

DSM—Diagnostic and Statistical Manual.

eco-map—An assessment or intervention tool that enables the practitioner/client to understand the configuration of social support systems available.

economic retrenchment—An era of limited financial resources and/or economic opportunities.

Education for all Handicapped Children Act—Federal legislation passed in 1975 to ensure equal educational opportunities for school-age children with developmental disabilities in public school systems.

empowerment—Helping individuals to help themselves reach their ultimate potential.

engagement—The process of entering the client system and connecting for purposes of increasing well-being.

enmeshed relationships—Family relationship whereby members are so close to one another they are unable to perceive problems or make unique contributions toward problem resolution.

environment—All phenomena within one's surroundings that affect growth and development.

ethnicity—One's identity with a given group over time across generations.

evaluation—The art of assessment and analysis.

explicit—Openly and outwardly expressed or displayed.

extended family—Relatives of an individual comprising grandparents, aunts, uncles, cousins.

external resources—Programs and services outside the family system.

family—Persons choosing to live in the same household and taking the responsibility for caretaking and socialization for all members.

Family and Medical Leave Act—Legislation, passed in 1993, allowing men or women to stay home and care for a newborn baby, a sick family member, or a newly adoptive or foster child for up to twelve weeks of unpaid leave from work each year, with health coverage intact.

family dynamics—Those concepts that guide family functioning.

family functioning—The family's ability to problem-solve and cope with day-to-day problems.

The family foundation—An organization developed by family members to assist one another in time of financial need.

family life cycle—The developmental stages of family relationships ranging from single adulthood to marriage through retirement.

family of origin—Birth family.

family preservation—The effort to maintain family relationships over time regardless of level of functioning or transition.

family sculpture—A family therapy exercise designed to graphically display how family members typically relate to one another.

family structure—The way in which a family organizes itself.

family values—Those standards, ethics, and beliefs by which the family functions and governs itself.

follow-up—The phase of intervention designed by the worker to recontact and reassess the client's coping abilities after termination.

Four-R Model of Family Dynamics—A conceptual framework for evaluating families by examining rules, roles, relationships, and rituals.

furthering—Facilitating and moving the interviewing process forward.

gangs—An indigenous group of youngsters who come together because they share common goals and objectives.

gender—Sex of an individual.

gender-delivered role—A role that society has sanctioned for an individual based on his/her gender.

generalist—A term used to describe an individual having broad-based practice skills.

genogram—An assessment diagram depicting family lineage.

goals—Broad plans of action.

governance—Setting and enforcing rules within the context of the family.

guiding force—The dominant pattern of a family's behavior that governs and steers overall family functioning.

health maintenance organization (HMO)—A prepaid program developed to meet total health needs of an individual/family; such programs often have their own medical facilities staffed by physicians with multiple specialties and other health care professionals.

hierarchy—The way a system is organized to include higher and lower rankings.

holistic—Total picture/view of any situation.

homeostasis—The natural balance that a system seeks in order to maintain itself.

homophobia—Fear of homosexuality.

implementation—Bringing about action; the doing of practice.

implicit—Hidden, discreet, understood without saying.

incongruent—When actions and feelings are inconsistent.

individualism—Striving for independence and autonomy in one's life.

input—Energy coming into a system.

in-school mediation—A program utilizing students to address and resolve conflict within the school community; judgment by peers.

integrative dynamics counseling—Extended counseling to assist divorced individuals to continue to relate to one another and support one another in regard to childrearing and other issues requiring mutual attention.

intergenerational family constellation—A household in which parents and grandparents live together and share the responsibility of parenting.

internal family resource—The emotional support and guidance provided from within the family to all members.

interviewing—The dynamic process of gathering information from the client.

irrelevant—Inability to show any relationship to what is taking place.

joint custody—A legal arrangement wherein both parents maintain and share the legal responsibility for a child or children.

Kwanzaa—An African American cultural celebration organized around (seven principles): Nguzo Saba: Umoja (unity): Kujichagulia (self-determination); Ujima (collective work and responsibility); Ujamaa (cooperative economics); Nia (purpose); Kuumba (creativity); and Imani (faith).

kinship network—One's relatives.

later-life parenting—Having children through natural birth or adoption into one's middle-age years.

leadership—The process of taking charge.

licensure—A permit enabling practitioners to legally deliver services.

longevity—Extending the life span; living longer.

longitudinal research—Research that examines phenomena usually at intervals over a period of time.

macro—An orientation toward working with large systems.

mainstreaming—Integrating individuals with special needs or circumstances, of any age, into the regular population of persons receiving services.

managed care—A formal network of health care personnel and resources that provides for all health and mental health care needs of an individual/family in exchange for a health care premium; such a program may be contracted with an individual/family or health care institution.

mediator—One who intercedes to facilitate communication and understanding.

mental retardation—Having an IQ below the normal range, that is below seventy.

mezzo—Working with small groups and family networks.

micro—Direct practice with individuals.

multicultural society—The inclusion of all cultural and ethnic groups within society.

mutuality—Bilateral understanding; both parties have clarity regarding issues.

myth—An assumption that has no basis in reality.

NASW Code of Ethic—A set of standards and values that guide the practice of professional social workers.

neighborhood center—A place in the community, with geographic boundaries, providing multiple services to persons of all ages.

nuclear family—A family consisting only of father, mother, and children.

nurturing—Providing care and emotional support.

objectives—Specific goals or plans.

offspring—One's children.

older adult—A person who has reached at least sixty-five years of age.

open-ended questions—Inquiries allowing for multiple answers and elaboration.

oppression—The state of being controlled and limited.

output—Energy leaving a system.

parameter—Boundary or limit.

paraphrasing—Restating information in one's own words.

placating—Always agreeing with the view of others even at the expense of one's true feelings.

planning—Formulating goals and objectives.

power—The ability to act.

process recording—A word for word written description of an interview, also depicting emotional reactions of the worker and including an assessment and plan of action.

providing/maintaining focus—An interviewing technique whereby the worker provides structure to the interview and guides the client in staying on topic.

racism—Stereotyping and feeling superior to others based on ethnicity or race; discrimination against those who are different.

rapport—The emotional linkage or bond between worker and client.

reciprocal—Mutual exchange; two-way interaction.

regulatory statute—A legal standard or certification permitting one to practice a profession.

relationship—The degree of connectedness within a family based on kinship ties.

resources—Individuals and institutions that the family relies upon to meet its needs.

role—A set of behaviors expected of an individual.

ritual—The tendency to repeat the same behaviors over time; systematic or methodical repetition of behaviors.

rule—Regulation established for governance; monitoring.

seeking concreteness—An interviewing technique whereby the worker guides the client to state information clearly and specifically.

self-actualization—Being all that one can be.

self-selecting family grouping—A configuration in which individuals choose to share a household and resources including parenting.

semi-independent living—Transitional living within the community whereby an individual needs some ongoing monitoring or service delivery system; semiautonomous living.

service delivery system—A network of agencies or programs providing assistance to clients.

sexism—Prejudice toward an individual because of gender.

sexual orientation—One's identification: homosexual, heterosexual, or bisexual.

sibling—Brother or sister.

significant other—An individual to whom one turns for social and emotional support.

snapshot approach—The process by which the practitioner utilizes multiple visual images of family functioning to develop holistic understanding of family dynamics.

socialization—The process by which persons acquire the knowledge, skills, and values empowering them to participate competently within society.

storytelling—Sharing family history and experiences across generations.

structure—Organization and guiding principles.

subsystem—A part of the whole.

summarizing—A technique in interviewing whereby the worker repeats and pulls together information using words shared by the client.

super-reasonable—Expression of ideas without any regard for underlying feelings.

system—Elements comprising the whole that are reciprocal with defined boundaries.

termination—The process of ending service delivery.

top-down approach—An orientation wherein all decisions are made by individuals at the highest level of a system or organization.

trend—A pattern or current movement within society.

twilight years—The sunset of one's life; late life years.

unified adoptive families—Families wherein the adoptive child has found his/her biological parents in later life, leading to the two family systems choosing to interact and establish ongoing relationships.

values—Standards, ethics, or mores that guide one's behavior and ways of thinking.

The NASW Code of Ethics

PREAMBLE

This code is intended to serve as a guide to the everyday conduct of members of the social work profession and as a basis for the adjudication of issues in ethics when the conduct of social workers is alleged to deviate from the standards expressed or implied in this code. It represents standards of ethical behavior for social workers in professional relationships with those served, with colleagues, with employers, with other individuals and professions, and with the community and society as a whole. It also embodies standards of ethical behavior governing individual conduct to the extent that such conduct is associated with an individual's status and identity as a social worker.

This code is based on the fundamental values of the social work profession that include the worth, dignity, and uniqueness of all persons as well as their rights and opportunities. It is also based on the nature of social work, which fosters conditions that promote these values.

In subscribing to and abiding by this code, the social worker is expected to view ethical responsibility in as inclusive a context as each situation demands and within which ethical judgment is required. The social worker is expected to take into consideration all the principles in this code that have a bearing upon any situation in which ethical judgment is to be exercised and professional intervention or conduct is planned. The course of action that the social worker chooses is expected to be consistent with the spirit as well as the letter of this code.

In itself, this code does not represent a set of rules that will prescribe all the behaviors of social workers in all the complexities of professional life. Rather, it offers general principles to guide conduct, and the judicious appraisal of conduct, in situations that have ethical implications. It provides the basis for making judgments about ethical actions before and after they occur. Frequently, the particular situation determines the ethical principles that apply and the manner of their application. In such cases, not only the particular ethical principles are taken into immediate consideration, but also the entire code and its spirit. Specific applications of ethical principles must be judged within the context in which they are being considered. Ethical behavior in a given situation must satisfy not only the judgment of the individual social worker, but also the judgment of an unbiased jury of professional peers.

This code should not be used as an instrument to deprive any social worker of the opportunity or freedom to practice with complete professional integrity; nor should any disciplinary action be taken on the basis of this code without maximum provision for safeguarding the rights of the social worker affected.

The ethical behavior of social workers results not from edict, but from a personal commitment of the individual. This code is offered to affirm the will and zeal of all social workers to be ethical and to act ethically in all that they do as social workers.

The following codified ethical principles should guide social workers in the various roles and relationships and at the various levels of responsibility in which they function professionally. These principles also serve as a basis for the adjudication by the National Association of Social Workers of issues in ethics.

In subscribing to this code, social workers are required to cooperate in its implementation and abide by any disciplinary rulings based on it. They should also take adequate measures to discourage, prevent, expose, and correct the unethical conduct of colleagues. Finally, social workers should be equally ready to defend and assist colleagues unjustly charged with unethical conduct.

SUMMARY OF MAJOR PRINCIPLES

I. *The Social Worker's Conduct and Comportment as a Social Worker*

   A. Propriety. The Social worker should maintain high standards of personal conduct in the capacity or identity as social worker.

B. Competence and Professional Development. The social worker should strive to become and remain proficient in professional practice and the performance of professional functions.
C. Service. The social worker should regard as primary the service obligation of the social work profession.
D. Integrity. The social worker should act in accordance with the highest standards of professional integrity.
E. Scholarship and Research. The social worker engaged in study and research should be guided by the conventions of scholarly inquiry.

II. The Social Worker's Ethical Responsibility to Clients

F. Primacy of Clients' Interests. The social worker's primary responsibility is to clients.
G. Rights and Prerogatives of Clients. The social worker should make every effort to foster maximum self-determination on the part of clients.
H. Confidentiality and Privacy. The social worker should respect the privacy of clients and hold in confidence all information obtained in the course of professional service.
I. Fees. When setting fees, the social worker should ensure that they are fair, reasonable, considerate, and commensurate with the service performed and with due regard for the clients' ability to pay.

III. The Social Worker's Ethical Responsibility to Colleagues

J. Respect, Fairness, and Courtesy. The social worker should treat colleagues with respect, courtesy, fairness, and good faith.
K. Dealing with Colleagues' Clients. The social worker has the responsibility to relate to the clients of colleagues with full professional consideration.

IV. The Social Worker's Ethical Responsibility to Employers and Employing Organizations

L. Commitments to Employing Organizations. The social worker should adhere to commitments made to the employing organizations.

V. *The Social Worker's Ethical Responsibility to the Social Work Profession*

M. Maintaining the Integrity of the Profession. The social worker should uphold and advance the values, ethics, knowledge, and mission of the profession.

N. Community Service. The social worker should assist the profession in making social services available to the general public.

O. Development of Knowledge. The social worker should take responsibility for identifying, developing, and fully utilizing knowledge for professional practice.

VI. *The Social Worker's Ethical Responsibility to Society*

P. Promoting the General Welfare. The social worker should promote the general welfare of society.

THE NASW CODE OF ETHICS

I. *The Social Worker's Conduct and Comportment as a Social Worker*

A. Propriety—The Social worker should maintain high standards of personal conduct in the capacity or identity as social worker.

   1. The private conduct of the social worker is a personal matter to the same degree as is any other person's, except when such conduct compromises the fulfillment of professional responsibilities.

   2. The social worker should not participate in, condone, or be associated with dishonesty, fraud, deceit, or misrepresentation.

   3. The social worker should distinguish clearly between statements and actions made as a private individual and as a representative of the social work profession or an organization or group.

B. Competence and Professional Development—The social worker should strive to become and remain proficient in professional practice and the performance of professional functions.

   1. The social worker should accept responsibility or employment only on the basis of existing competence or the intention to acquire the necessary competence.

2. The social worker should not misrepresent professional qualifications, education, experience, or affiliations.
3. The social worker should not allow his or her own personal problems, psychosocial distress, substance abuse, or mental health difficulties to interfere with professional judgment and performance or jeopardize the best interests of those for whom the social worker has a professional responsibility.
4. The social worker whose personal problems, psychosocial distress, substance abuse, or mental health difficulties interfere with professional judgment and performance should immediately seek consultation and take appropriate remedial action by seeking professional help, making adjustments in workload, terminating practice, or taking any other steps necessary to protect clients and others.

C. Service—The social worker should regard as primary the service obligation of the social work profession.
  1. The social worker should retain ultimate responsibility for the quality and extent of the service that individual assumes, assigns, or performs.
  2. The social worker should act to prevent practices that are inhumane or discriminatory against any person or group of persons.

D. Integrity—The social worker should act in accordance with the highest standards of professional integrity and impartiality.
  1. The social worker should be alert to and resist the influences and pressures that interfere with the exercise of professional discretion and impartial judgment required for the performance of professional functions.
  2. The social worker should not exploit professional relationships for personal gain.

E. Scholarship and Research—The social worker engaged in study and research should be guided by the conventions of scholarly inquiry.
  1. The social worker engaged in research should consider carefully its possible consequences for human beings.
  2. The social worker engaged in research should ascertain that the consent of participants in the research is voluntary and informed, without any implied deprivation or penalty for refusal to participate, and with due regard for participants' privacy and dignity.
  3. The social worker engaged in research should protect participants from unwarranted physical or mental discomfort, distress, harm, danger, or deprivation.

4. The social worker who engages in the evaluation of services or cases should discuss them only for the professional purposes and only with persons directly and professionally concerned with them.
5. Information obtained about participants in research should be treated as confidential.
6. The social worker should take credit only for work actually done in connection with scholarly and research endeavors and credit contributions made by others.

II. The Social Worker's Ethical Responsibility to Clients

F. Primacy of Clients' Interests—The social worker's primary responsibility is to clients.

   1. The social worker should serve clients with devotion, loyalty, determination, and the maximum application of professional skill and competence.
   2. The social worker should not exploit relationships with clients for personal advantage.
   3. The social worker should not practice, condone, facilitate or collaborate with any form of discrimination on the basis of race, color, sex, sexual orientation, age, religion, national origin, marital status, political belief, mental or physical handicap, or any other preference or personal characteristic, condition, or status.
   4. The social worker should not condone or engage in any dual or multiple relationships with clients or former clients in which there is a risk of exploitation of or potential harm to the client. The social worker is responsible for setting clear, appropriate, and culturally sensitive boundaries.
   5. The social worker should under no circumstances engage in sexual activities with clients.
   6. The social worker should provide clients with accurate and complete information regarding the extent and nature of the services available to them.
   7. The social worker should apprise clients of their risks, rights, opportunities, and obligations associated with social service to them.
   8. The social worker should seek advice and counsel of colleagues and supervisors whenever such consultation is in the best interest of clients.
   9. The social worker should terminate service to clients, and professional relationships with them, when such service and

relationships are no longer required or no longer serve the clients' needs or interests.

10. The social worker should withdraw services precipitously only under unusual circumstances, giving careful consideration to all factors in the situation and taking care to minimize possible adverse effects.

11. The social worker who anticipates the termination or interruption of service to clients should notify clients promptly and seek the transfer, referral, or continuation of service in relation to the clients' needs and preferences.

G. Rights and Prerogatives of Clients—The social worker should make every effort to foster maximum self-determination on the part of clients.

1. When the social worker must act on behalf of a client who has been adjudged legally incompetent, the social worker should safeguard the interests and rights of that client.

2. When another individual has been legally authorized to act in behalf of a client, the social worker should deal with that person always with the client's best interest in mind.

3. The social worker should not engage in any action that violates or diminishes the civil or legal rights of clients.

H. Confidentiality and Privacy—The social worker should respect the privacy of clients and hold in confidence all information obtained in the course of professional service.

1. The social worker should share with others confidences revealed by clients, without their consent, only for compelling professional reasons.

2. The social worker should inform clients fully about the limits of confidentiality in a given situation, the purposes for which information is obtained, and how it may be used.

3. The social worker should afford clients reasonable access to any official social work records concerning them.

4. when providing clients with access to records, the social worker should take due care to protect the confidences of others contained in those records.

5. The social worker should obtain informed consent of clients before taping, recording, or permitting third party observation of their activities.

I. Fees—When setting fees, the social worker should ensure that they are fair, reasonable, considerate, and commensurate with the service performed and with due regard for the clients' ability to pay.

1. The social worker should not accept anything of value for making a referral.

III. The Social Worker's Ethical Responsibility to Colleagues

J. Respect, Fairness, and Courtesy—The social worker should treat colleagues with respect courtesy, fairness, and good faith.
   1. The social worker should cooperate with colleagues to promote professional interests and concerns.
   2. the social worker should respect confidences shared by colleagues in the course of their professional relationships and transactions.
   3. The social worker should create and maintain conditions of practice that facilitate ethical and competent professional performance by colleagues.
   4. The social worker should treat with respect, and represent accurately and fairly, the qualifications, views, and findings of colleagues and use appropriate channels to express judgments on these matters.
   5. The social worker who replaces or is replaced by a colleague in professional practice should act with consideration for the interest, character, and reputation of that colleague.
   6. The social worker should not exploit a dispute between a colleague and employers to obtain a position or otherwise advance the social worker's interest.
   7. The social worker should seek arbitration or mediation when conflicts with colleagues require resolution for compelling professional reasons.
   8. The social worker should extend to colleagues of other professions the same respect and cooperation that is extended to social work colleagues.
   9. The social worker who serves as an employer, supervisor, or mentor to colleagues should make orderly and explicit arrangements regarding the conditions of their continuing professional relationship.
   10. The social worker who has the responsibility for employing and evaluating the performance of other staff members should fulfill such responsibility in a fair, considerate, and equitable manner, on the basis of clearly enunciated criteria.
   11. The social worker who has the responsibility for evaluating the performance of employees, supervisees, or students should share evaluations with them.
   12. The social worker should not use a professional position vested with power, such as that of employer, supervisor, teacher, or consultant, to his or her advantage or to exploit others.

13. The social worker who has direct knowledge of a social work colleague's impairment due to personal problems, psychosocial distress, substance abuse, or mental health difficulties should consult with that colleague and assist the colleague in taking remedial action.

K. Dealing with Colleagues' Clients—The social worker has the responsibility to relate to the clients of colleagues with full professional consideration.

1. The social worker should not assume professional responsibility for the clients of another agency or a colleague without appropriate communication with that agency or colleague.
2. The social worker who serves the clients of colleagues, during a temporary absence or emergency, should serve those clients with the same consideration as that afforded any client.

IV. The Social Worker's Ethical Responsibility to Employers and Employing Organizations

L. Commitments to Employing Organization—The social worker should adhere to commitments made to the employing organization.

1. The social worker should work to improve the employing agency's policies and procedures, and the efficiency and effectiveness of its services.
2. The social worker should not accept employment or arrange student field placements in an organization which is currently under public sanction by NASW for violating personnel standards, or imposing limitations on or penalties for professional actions on behalf of clients.
3. The social worker should act to prevent and eliminate discrimination in the employing organization's work assignments and in its employment policies and practices.
4. The social worker should use with scrupulous regard, and only for the purpose for which they are intended, the resources of the employing organization.

V. The Social Worker's Ethical Responsibility to the Social Work Profession

M. Maintaining the Integrity of the Profession—The social worker should uphold and advance the values, ethics, knowledge, and mission of the profession.

1. The social worker should protect and enhance the dignity and integrity of the profession and should be responsible and vigorous in discussion and criticism of the profession.
2. The social worker should take action through appropriate channels against unethical conduct by any other member of the profession.
3. The social worker should act to prevent the unauthorized and unqualified practice of social work.
4. The social worker should make no misrepresentation in advertising as to qualifications, competence, service, or results to be achieved.

N. Community Service—The social worker should assist the profession in making social services available to the general public.
1. The social worker should contribute time and professional expertise to activities that promote respect for the utility, the integrity, and the competence of the social work profession.
2. The social worker should support the formulation, development, enactment, and implementation of social policies of concern to the profession.

O. Development of Knowledge—The social worker should take responsibility for identifying, developing, and fully utilizing knowledge for professional practice.
1. The social worker should base practice upon recognized knowledge relevant to social work.
2. The social worker should critically examine, and keep current with, emerging knowledge relevant to social work.
3. The social worker should contribute to the knowledge base of social work and share research knowledge and practice wisdom with colleagues.

VI. The Social Worker's Ethical Responsibility to Society

P. Promoting the General Welfare—The social worker should promote the general welfare of society.
1. The social worker should act to prevent and eliminate discrimination against any person or group on the basis of race, color, sex, sexual orientation, age, religion, national origin, marital status, political belief, mental or physical handicap, or any other preference or personal characteristic, condition, or status.
2. The social worker should act to ensure that all persons have access to the resources, services, and opportunities which they require.

3. The social worker should act to expand choice and opportunity for all persons, with special regard for disadvantaged or oppressed groups and persons.
4. The social worker should promote conditions that encourage respect for the diversity of cultures which constitute American society.
5. The social worker should provide appropriate professional services in public emergencies.
6. The social worker should advocate changes in policy and legislation to improve social conditions and to promote social justice.
7. The social worker should encourage informed participation by the public in shaping social policies and institutions.

▶

Supplemental Exercises

As a demonstration on how to incorporate various family intervention tools, the following exercises are provided: eco-map, family sculpture, family communication exercise, family systems exercise, genogram, process recording, and family intervention contract. These tools are useful in assisting students in enhancing their skills in family assessment, intervention planning, and the provision of concrete supportive services to families.

JONES FAMILY ECO-MAP ANALYSIS

Based on the eco-map on the following page, Barbara Jones and her new husband, Joe, have a strong relationship. Likewise, Barbara has a strong relationship with her teenage son, Carl. This relationship is becoming more stressful and tenuous due to Carl's recent involvement with the Juvenile Court System. Complicating this relationship is the decrease in communication between Carl and his stepfather. Joe senses Carl's reluctance to open up and share feelings but continues to reach out to his stepson. Carl's reluctance may, in part, be related to his perception of his stepfather's role in the family and Carl's anxiety about the impending birth of the new baby. Due to his recent involvement with the authorities, Carl is under the supervision of the Juvenile Court, which has mandated a thirty-day grounding and curfew. Consequently, he has to be home each evening by 9 p.m., which has curtailed his freedom to go out with his friends and to play baseball at the local neighborhood center.

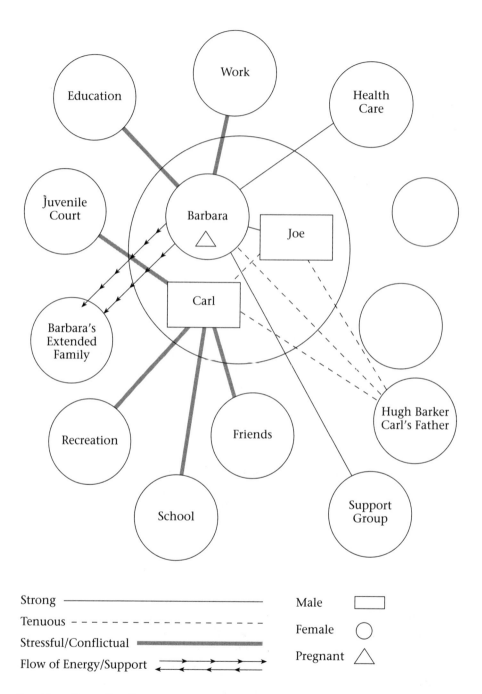

Eco Map: Jones Family

Carl's situation has been complicated further by his having skipped school, placing him behind in his studies. Carl very much wants to visit his natural father, Hugh, in prison and is in conflict with his mother and stepfather about this plan. Meanwhile, his father, Hugh, has been placing increased pressure on Barbara and Joe Jones to arrange the visit.

Barbara is highly influenced by her family of origin and their expectations of her. In fact, Barbara feels that she always reaches out to her parents and siblings, without exception, while they often seem to ignore some of her important concerns and/or fail to provide her with a mutual exchange of assistance. Barbara's problems are futher exacerbated by her stringent and demanding work schedule as a nurse's aide and her heavy class load as a full-time college student. Barbara often feels overstressed by her competing roles as spouse, mother, worker, homemaker, and student. However, Barbara has been receiving much support from her involvement in a women's support group at the local neighborhood center. Barbara strongly values proper health care and thus maintains a close relationship with her primary care physician and makes it a priority.

ECO-MAP EXERCISE

Instructions

Construct an eco-map of your own family or one of the case studies other than the Jones Family. In all instances, be sure to describe relationships that are tenuous, conflictual, nonreciprocal, strong, weak, or nonexistent. You may develop your own symbols and descriptors for showing other types of relationships but be sure to clearly define these symbols.

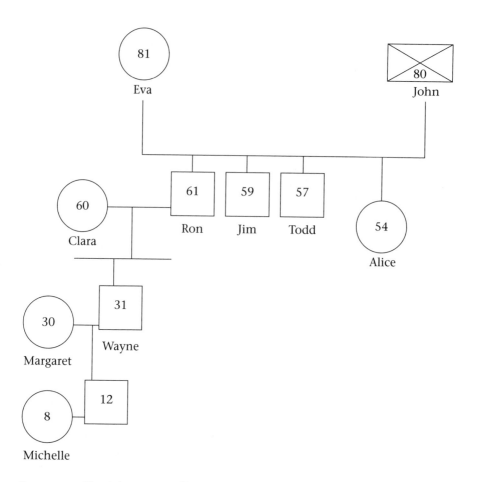

Genogram: The Johnson Family

ANALYSIS OF JOHNSON FAMILY GENOGRAM

The Johnson family is tri-generational. The family matriarch is Eva John-son, a widow whose husband, John, died three years ago. Eva and John had four children, three sons and one daughter, Ron, Jim, Todd, and Alice.

Ron is married to Clara and they have one son, Wayne. Wayne is married to Margaret and they have a son, Eric, and a daughter, Michelle.

GENOGRAM INSTRUCTIONS

Draw a genogram of your own family or one of the families from the text, other than the Johnson Family. You may wish to develop symbols/codes to use as descriptors as long as these are clearly defined and highlighted in your instructions for the genogram.

PROCESS RECORDING OF ROMANO FAMILY SESSION

Indentifying Information:

This family interview was conducted on (date; time) by Ms. C., social worker, at the home of Victor Romano. The Romano family (those persons present for the interview) includes: Victor Romano (age 58), the father; Julia Romano (age 54), the mother; Mario Romano (35), the older son; (Della, 34, Mario's wife, is out of town due to illness in her own family); Angelo Romano (age 33), the younger son; Veronica Romano (25), the older daughter; and Frances Romano (20) the younger daughter; Sue Wheeler (age 29), Angelo's fiancee.

Please note the following codes: Ann Carey, worker; Victor Romano, Victor; Julia Romano, Julia; Mario Romano, Mario; Angelo Romano, Angelo; Veronica Romano, Veronica; Frances Romano, Frances; and Sue Wheeler, Sue. Please note that gut level feelings refer to the reflections and feelings of the worker.

Family Interview

Ann: Hello, everyone. I am Ann Carey, from the Community Counseling Center.

Victor: Hello, I am Victor. I think you know my wife and son already (looking alternately at Julia and Mario).

Ann: Yes.

Julia: Thank you so much for coming, Ms. Carey. We appreicate your help. Let me introduce the rest of the family. This is my son, Angelo; Mario, you know already; next to him is Veronica; then there is our youngest, Frances.

Angelo: Mother!

Julia: Oh, yes, and this is Sue Wheeler, Angelo's fiancee.

Victor: Right!

Gut Level Feelings

I can sense the tension here. I cannot believe she did not introduce Angelo's fiancee.

Ann: Thank you for calling our Center, Mrs. Romano.

Julia: Well, I felt I had to do something (looking at Mario).

Ann: Please go on.

Julia: Well, you see, Victor is having difficulty. . . .

Victor: (Interrupting) I knew you would blame it all on me! If my children would only stay *in their place* and mind their own business!

Ann: Please, my wish is to hear from each of you separately so that I may be able to gain a fuller understanding of your concerns.

Gut Level Feelings

Tempers are flaring. I can see that it may be a challenge to get each family member to express his or her own views without interrupting one another.

Victor: I lost my job, you see . . . and this family should listen to me first!

Julia: We do, Victor.

Victor: Not really. I feel like a stranger in my own home!

Mario: Dad, you don't mean that.

Ann: Please, I would first like to hear each of you express your views of the problem. Mrs. Romano?

Julia: You know, my husband means well, but he is home all day now . . . and he sometimes interferes with my routines.

Victor: So that's your gripe!

(No one speaks.)

Ann: Let's try to hear from everyone okay?

Yes, as I said, I want each of you to voice your concerns, first. Then, we will have all of you discuss your issues with each other. Angelo, what are your concerns?

Angelo: This is hard. . . .

Ann: Please go on.

Angelo: I am tired of this whole family looking down their noses at Sue (Sue nods in agreement as she stares at the floor).

Ann: What do you mean, Angelo?

Angelo: You see . . . Sue is not Catholic . . . but I love her. We plan to be married next summer. No one has accepted her in this family.

Gut Level Feelings

I sense that this revelation by Angelo is a major point of contention within this family. Sue seems embarrassed and hurt, which is understandable.

Veronica: That's not true! Sue and I have been best friends for two years. She is more like a sister to me.

Frances: Great!

Ann: (Looking directly at Sue) Sue, would you like to say something?

Sue: Not really . . . well, Angelo and I . . . (breaks into tears).

Ann: Yes, go on . . .

Sue: We are getting married and we do love each other (looking at Angelo). That's all that should matter to anyone.

Victor: My family traditions matter more than anything else. All of my children have been taught *that* since they were small (looking around the room).

Julia: Victor, I think that we could listen more to Sue's side.

Angelo: Yes, Dad. We are getting married, regardless. I have always loved and supported all of you. You are my family.

Victor: I do not need your support nor your money (looking angrily at both Angelo and Mario).

Mario: Dad, you are not being fair about this! I gave Mom that extra money for baby-sitting Junior. You can use the money right now. I know the family needs it.

Victor: I am still the father! I am the head of this family. I have never planned on letting my sons or anyone else support me.

Gut Level Feelings

What a difficult task it is to keep family members from interrupting each other. They need some help with communication. I am clear about that. They just don't seem to listen to one another. Several family members seem to always want the floor.

Julia: Victor, please . . . we are a close family. They're just trying to help us out.

Frances: I think this whole situation is ridiculous! I thought my college would be paid for. Now look at me (frowning at her father)!

Ann: Frances, would you go on?

Frances: Dad and Mom have always been there for me. Now I may have to get a job at school just to finish.

Victor: Absolutely not! I forbid it!

Veronica: Frannie, you are not being realistic. We all have to pitch in now and help out in any way we can.

Frances: Sure . . . (looking toward the window).

Ann: Okay. I believe that I am beginning to sense how each of you sees the family problems. You have begun to share some feelings with each other that perhaps until now had been unspoken. At this point, let's continue with this sharing.

Gut Level Feelings

I hope they don't all start talking at once. I sense that I will need to work hard to keep the interactions focused.

Victor: It all started when my company downsized and laid me off, along with two other top executives . . . and I have a family here to look out for.

Julia: (Reaching over to take Victor's hands) We know that Victor. But you don't always seem to recognize that we are all affected by this crisis.

Victor: No, I don't think any of you understand *my* position in all of this. I am the father. I must always be able to take care of all of you.

Angelo: Yes, that is true. But it's only fair that you let us help you financially . . . at least until you are back on your feet.

Julia: And we do appreicate your offer . . . but . . . (looking at Victor).

Victor: But, sons are not supposed to take care of their parents.

Ann: Mr. Romano, your family seems really supportive and they seem concerned about you. It is out of this deep concern that they have offered their assistance.

Victor: Well . . . maybe. But there are other problems in this family destined to tear us apart (looking at Sue).

Gut Level Feelings

The family members seem to be listening to one another and at least not interrupting each other. Yet, I see that we must focus on one problem at a time.

Ann: I see, but what I want you to try to do is focus on one issue at a time. Can we go back to the impact of Mr. Romano's layoff?

Julia: Okay. I have my routine tasks around the house and I am very organized, especially about my kitchen. Now that Victor is home, he wants to help out with the dishes . . . and recently has forced Junior [Mario's four-year-old son] to eat lunch every day at the same time, 12 noon. You know how children are. Junior is not always hungry then, as he always eats a late breakfast.

Victor: I thought this was my home too?

Julia: You are missing the whole point Victor.

Mario: Dad, Mom is right. And Junior is large for his age. We do not want him to be an obese child.

Victor: That's absurd. I care deeply about my family. I am just trying to help out. You don't know how I feel about all of this.

Veronica: Dad, please listen to what everyone is saying. We love you, as much as always. That could never change. We're all in this together.

Gut Level Feelings

Finally, they're staying on topic and seem to be responding to what everyone is saying. Perhaps now we can move toward closure for today. I can't believe Victor used the phrase "I care deeply for my family." I think I am beginning to get through to him.

Ann: (Looking around the room, making eye contact with everyone). I am beginning to realize how much strength exists within your family. And, I sense that your respective roles are vital to your family make-up and your strength. However, some additional flexibility may be necessary.

Frances: I am sorry, Dad. I will pull my load at school and check out work/study at school next term.

Veronica: And I can check out the possibility of working part-time during income tax preparation.

Sue: Great, Veronica. Maybe we could work together on that.

Ann: (Smiling at Veronica and Sue.) Thanks. (Pause.) (Looking at Mrs. Romano first, and then around the room) I want to thank you again for asking for my assistance. You do have several problems that need attention, but I sense that you're off to a good start. I might reiterate that I perceive this to be a strong family, and you seem to really care about each other. I would like to continue to meet with you, if all of you are willing.

Julia: Victor?

Victor: Fine. Maybe it will help.

Ann: Excellent. I will see you next Wednesday evening, okay? I hope that all of you (looking around the room) will be able to attend. (The family members nod or chime "Yes").

Gut Level Feelings

At least they are willing to have me back again. That shows some commitment and some progress. I believe there is much potential for this family to resolve some of their challenges, one problem at a time.

Assessment

The Romanos, an extended family system, are strongly roles-dominated. Victor Romano has recently lost his executive position after many years of dedicated service to the company. This event seems to have shaken the family's sense of security and well-being. Victor has always been an excellent provider and still places much value on his role as head of the family, as well as the family breadwinner. Julia Romano, a homemaker, values her role as the family matriarch, including her childrearing duties and child care responsibilities involving her grandson, Junior. She seems sensitive to her husband's issues but does not want to relinquish her primary role as homemaker.

Mario, a physician, and Angleo, an attorney, have done well in establishing their careers, and they are loyal sons. They seem to be sincere in helping the family out during this financial crisis. Mario does seem to have some legitimate concerns about his son's eating schedule while at the grandparents' house. Some agreement will have to be negotiated concerning this matter, but the family seems somewhat open to resilience and compromise. They have also begun to listen each other's concerns.

Angelo's betrothal to Sue has caught the family off guard. The family had not anticipated any member marrying non-Catholic. But Veronica and Sue are already best friends and this relationship could provide an important link toward integrating Sue into the family. Moreover, Veroncia and Frances, still at home, are each willing to work to earn funds to complete their education.

In summary, although roles prevails in the Romano family, family members have already begun to take some important steps toward understanding how other significant family dynamics may aid them in regaining equilibrium and in turn enhance overall family coping.

Family Intervention Plan

1. Meet with family in one week.
2. Continue to focus on the impact of Victor's layoff on family functioning.

FAMILY SCULPTURE EXERCISE

Instructions

Select one of the family case studies displaying one of the four family types (rules-dominated; roles-dominated; relationships-dominated; rituals-dominated). Create a family sculpture using members of the class. Consider the dynamics provided in one of the four families. Think of such concepts as systems theory (e.g., boundary, subsystems, dyads, homeostasis), modes of communication, family roles, family expectations, power structure, and any other issues you consider to be important. After you have discussed the above dynamics, you should "sculpt" the family by showing with connecting strings (twine or rope) or positioning of family members (e.g., placater, blamer, etc.). Close relationships may be demonstrated by using a shorter section of string to connect family members or by placing family members physically close to one another. Family conflict or emerging changes in relationships may be identified by creating pressure on the string, that is, pulling it tighter between family members. The resistance of one family member may be demonstrated by continual movement, which may result in breaking the string or separating from the family configuration. A reminder is that the resistance can be demonstrated by having a family member move farther away from an individual or away from the entire family system.

FAMILY COMMUNICATION EXERCISE
(SATIR'S MODEL)

Using the example of the Culliver family select members of the class to play each family member/mode of communication. Have each role player act out in front of the class how each mode of communication may be demonstrated in a mock interaction among members of the Culliver family.

FAMILY CONTRACT EXERCISE

Instructions

Examine the following contract developed for the Thomas family, a rules-dominated family. Select one of the other family case studies and develop a contract for intervention.

Contract for Intervention—The Thomas Family

We believe that we as a family need help. We agree to meet weekly with Ms. Social Worker to work on our problems. We understand that these family meetings will be held at our home and will begin promptly at 6 p. m. We agree that we will take the responsibility to make sure that all family members attend and that everyone is on time for meetings.

Moreover, we agree to work on the following goals:

1. We agree to share our feelings (e.g., anger, sadness) with each other by stating how we feel at any given time.
2. We agree to respect one another by taking time to listen to each other's concerns.
3. We will discuss family rules weekly and evaluate as a family whether the rules need to be revised to meet current family needs.
4. We will develop one new family ritual (e.g. a weekly family activity), which involves all family members.

Signed

_____ Beverly Thomas

_____ Samantha Thomas

_____ Lewis Thomas Jr.

_____ Richie Thomas

_____ Ms. Social Worker

Today's Date_____

FAMILY SYSTEMS EXERCISE

Using the model developed by Pincus and Minahan (1973) create a systems analysis of one of the four family case studies. Identify the following systems: change agent; client; target; and action.

Before beginning this exercise, you may want to refer to the following definitions:

Change Agent: the professional or helper whose goal is to bring about planned change; the person, persons, or agency providing assistance to the client system.

Client System: the specific system receiving help (individual, family, group, community). The client system requests help from the practitioner and agrees to receive intervention, starting with the development of a contract for services.

Target System: Those individuals or systems that the change agent needs to change or influence to facilitate goals. Target systems are to be identified collaboratively by the practitioner and client system.

Action System: Persons with whom the change agent or practitioner works on behalf of the client system. These persons are brought in to assist in the accomplishment of goals.

Instructions

You may draw a diagram using circles (separate and overlapping) to show various interactions and/or relationships. For example, the client system circle may overlap the target system circle to demonstrate that the client may also be targeted for planned change.

▶ Index

accentuation, 39
accountability, 66, 75, 81, 156
Achtenberg, R., 141
action stage, *see* implementation and action stage
Addams, Jane, 98
adoption, 101–104, 139–142, *see also* child welfare
Adoption Assistance and Child Welfare Act (1980), 103
advocacy organizations, 131
advocate role, 56
African American family, 96–97, 104
ageism, 114, 115–116
aging, *see* older adults
agrarian economy, 4
AIDS epidemic, 100, 102, 103, 145
alliance-based family, 38, 39, 101–102, 105, 141
American Association of State Social Work Boards, 155
Americans with Disabilities Act (1990), 131
assessment stage, 51–54, 65–66, 72–74, 79–80, 87–88, 129, 204
assumptions, in family communication, 15–26

baby boomers, 117
Bales, R., 34
Barker, R. L., 113, 120, 126, 132, 140–142, 146, 150
bartering system, 4
Beavers, J., 127
Beckett, J. O., 104
Bell, A. P., 100–101
Bennett, L. A., 42
Berg-Cross, L., 41
Berger, R. L., 9, 107
Bernard, J., 34
Bickerton, D., 98
birth order, and family roles, 20–21
bisexuality, 100
blaming mode of communication, 6, 7–8
blended family, 38–41, 78–85, 165
bloodlines, 16–17
Bogulub, E., 21
boot camps, 123–124
bottom-up approach, 52–53
boundaries, 10, 12, 16–17, 32
Bray, Robert, 100
Brayfield, A., 104, 149
Brigham, J. C., 1
broker role, 56

Brown, J. E., 32
Bureau of Labor Statistics, U.S., 114, 148

caretaking, 29–30
Carr, P., 41
Carter, B., 167–168
case management, 145–146
Cassano, D. R., 143
Castex, G. M., 96
celebration rituals, 43
Census Bureau, U.S., 2, 106, 114
change agent system, 10
Child Care and Development Block Grants, 153
childrearing
    day care and, 151–154
    by grandparents, 102–104, 105, 168
    intergenerational, 5, 21, 104–105, 168–169
    later-life, 104, 150
    and self-selected family groupings, 105
    and sexual orientation, 101–102, 141
    and sharing of hierarchy, 19
    socialization and, 19, 106, 107, 148
Children's Defense Fund, 153
child welfare, 120–126
    and developmental disabilities, 126–132
Chilman, C. S., 153
client system, 10
closure of relationship, 58
collective self-development, 30
communication
    clarity in, 22–23, 38
    modes of, 6–9
    one-way versus two-way, 18
    openness of, 17–18, 38, 65
    and relationships, 38
community/neighborhood services, 132–135
congruent mode of communication, 7, 8–9
contracting stage, 54–55, 66–67, 74, 80–82, 88–89
control, assumption of, 20
Cooley, R. C., 98
cooperative day care programs, 152–153
coordinator role, 56
Council on Social Work Education (CSWE), 99
Culliver family, 7–8, 16, 17–18, 20, 22, 23, 25
culture, 95–99
    ethnicity versus, 96
    influences on, 96
    and multiculturalism, 163–164, 166–167

Daly, A., 104
Daniels, C., 41

Daro, D., 102
Davis family, 10–11, 17–19, 21, 23–25,
    117–120
day care, child, 151–154
Deich, S., 104, 149
deinstitutionalization, 126, 144–146
developmental disabilities, 126–132,
    143–146
Devore, W., 96
DeWeaver, K., 126
Diagnostic and Statistical Manual, 99
disability, *see* developmental disabilities
disengagement, 115
diversity
    in communication patterns, 15–18
    cultural, 95–99
    defined, 95
    ethnic, 95–99
division of labor, 36
Draughn, P. S., 141

eco-maps, 92–93, 165, 195–197
education, *see* schools
Education for All Handicapped Children Act
    (1975), 130
Education of the Handicapped Amendments
    (1986), 130
enabler role, 56
engagement stage, 49–50, 63–64, 71–72, 78,
    86
enmeshment, 81
Ernst, C., 20
ethnicity, 95–99
    culture versus, 96
    influences on, 96
    and women's roles, 107–108
evaluation stage, 59, 70–71, 77–78, 84–85,
    91
expectations, 36, 55, 66
extended families, 2–5
    African American, 96–97, 104
    grandparents as parents in, 102–104, 105,
        168
    Hispanic, 96
    intergenerational configurations in, 5, 21,
        96–97, 104–105, 168–169
    as relationships-dominated, 39–41, 78–85
external resources, utilization of, 56–57, 59

facilitator role, 56, 67, 75
family
    assumptions regarding, 15–26
    diversity in communication and, 15–18
    needs served by, 1–2, 29–30
    as system, 10–11, 206–207
Family and Medical Leave Act (1993), 150
family of origin, 141
family presentation program, 50
family preservation, 142–144
family sculpture, 205

family structure
    changes in, 2–5
    extended family, *see* extended families
    nuclear family, 2–3, 5
    power structure and, 15–16, 18–22
    and rules, 32
    strengths of relationships and, 22–25,
        38–39
    top-down communication and, 15–16
fathers
    at head of family, 15–16, 18–19, 21–22
    single, 106
Federico, R. C., 9, 107
Fessler, S., 103–104
follow-up stage, 59, 71, 78, 84–85, 91
formatting, 55, 67
foster care system, 101–102, 103–104, 121,
    139–142, *see also* child welfare
Four-R Model of Family Dynamics, 29–92
    and blended families, 39–41, 78–85, 165
    effectiveness of, 165–166
    and future adaptations, 161–165
    intervention strategies based on, 49–60,
        63–92
    and longevity, 162–163, 167–169
    and multiculturalism, 163–164, 166–167
    relationships in, 38–41, 78–85
    rituals in, 41–45, 86–91
    roles in, 34–38, 71–78
    rules in, 32–34, 63–71
Frankel, H., 165
Frankel, J., 107
Freedman, H., 129
Freeman, R. I., 128
Friedan, Betty, 19
furthering technique, 64, 72

Gabriel, T., 100
gangs, 133
Garbarino, J., 2
Gay Rights movement, 99–100
gender-delivered roles, 35
gender stereotypes
    and birth order, 20
    and family power structure, 15–16, 18–19,
        21–22, 148–149
    in roles, 34–35
    and social workers, 150–151
genograms, 198–199
Ginsberg, L., 113, 116
goals
    congruent communication as, 8–9
    in implementation stage, 56
    reshaping problems into, 55
    in rituals-dominated family, 89–90
    in rules-dominated family, 66
    termination as, 57
Gonyea, J. G., 114
Gottlieb, N., 148, 149
governance, 32–34, 65–66, 79, 148

grandparents
  as parents, 102–104, 105, 168
  role of, 5, 21
  see also older adults
Green, R. G., 21–22, 165
Greif, G. L., 106

Haley, J., 19, 49, 51
Hall, E. G., 97
Hanson, S. M. H., 22
Harris, O., 32
Hartford, M. E., 57, 58
Hartman, A., 103
health care, 146–148
health maintenance organizations (HMOs),
  146, 147
Helton, L. R., 104, 128
Hepworth, D. H., 57, 64–65, 99
Hesse-Biber, S., 19
hierarchy, fathers in family, 15–16, 18–19,
  21–22
Hill, R., 97
Hispanic family, 96
Hofferth, S. L., 104, 149
Holcomb, P., 104, 149
homeostasis, 9, 12
homicide, 103–104
homophobia, 99, 100
homosexuality, 99–102, 141
Hsu, J., 41
Hull, G. H., Jr., 9, 32, 34
Hunt, M., 99

implementation and action stage, 55–57,
  67–69, 75–77, 82–83, 89–90
independent living, 140
Individual Educational Plan, 130
Industrial Revolution, 4–5
input, 9
intergenerational family
  African American, 96–97, 104
  childrearing in, 5, 21, 104–105, 168–169
internal family resources, 59
intervention strategies, 49–60, 63–92
  assessment stage, 51–54, 65–66, 72–74,
    79–80, 87–88, 129, 204
  contracting stage, 54–55, 66–67, 74,
    80–82, 88–89
  engagement stage, 49–50, 63–64, 71–72,
    78, 86
  evaluation stage, 59, 70–71, 77–78, 84–85,
    91
  follow-up stage, 59, 70–71, 78, 84–85, 91
  implementation and action stage, 55–57,
    67–69, 75–77, 82–83, 89–90
  interviewing stage, 50–51, 64–65, 72,
    78–79, 86–87
  planning stage, 54–55, 66–67, 74, 80–82,
    88–89

termination stage, 57–59, 69, 77, 83–84,
  90–91
interviewing stage, 50–51, 64–65, 72, 78–79,
  86–87
in vitro fertilization, 101
irrelevant mode of communication, 7, 8
Italian American family, 98

Jackson-Hopkins, M., 96, 167
Jalali, B., 41
Jantzen, C., 32
Jennings, J., 104
Johnson family, 44–45, 86–91, 198
joint custody, 106, 141
Jones, D. M., 81
Jones family, 39–41, 78–85, 125–126, 135,
  195–197

Karenga, Maulana, 97
King, G. C., 97
kinship bonds, 4, 96–98
Kirst-Ashman, K. K., 9, 32, 34, 99, 115
Kolevzon, M. S., 21–22, 165
Kramer, M., 101
Kravetz, D., 35
Kwanzaa, 97

Laird, J., 41–42
Lamb, M. E., 20
Larsen, J., 57, 64–65, 99
leadership
  and birth order, 20–21
  in family, 20, 52–53
  in relationships-dominated family, 79
  in roles-dominated family, 72–73
  in rules-dominated family, 65
Leashore, B. R., 104
least restrictive environment, 128–129, 130
lesbianism, 99–102, 141
Levick, S. E., 41
Lewis, J. M., 22
licensure, 154–157
Lorber, J., 108

MacKenzie, D. L., 124
macro level, 146
mainstreaming, 127
managed health care, 146–148
Manns, W., 107
Martin, E. P., 97
Martin, J., 97
Maslow, A. H., 1
McBreen, J. T., 9, 107
McClester, C., 97
McCurdy, K., 102
McGoldrick, M., 107–108, 167–168
mealtime rituals, 43
mediation, in schools, 124–125
mediator role, 56, 57, 67
men

and sexual orientation, 99–102
as single parents, 106
as traditional heads of family, 15–16, 18–19, 21–22
micro level, 146
military service, 101, 105
Miller, N. B., 98
Minahan, A., 10, 206–207
Minuchin, S., 81
Mixdorf, L., 124
Moore, L. L., 38
Moss, M. S., 99
multiculturalism, 163–164, 166–167
multifamily group intervention, 144
mutuality, 50, 54–55, 84, 91

NASW Code of Ethics, 108, 150, 183–193
Native Americans, 98
neighborhood centers, 133–135
nonverbal communication, 6–7, 17–18, 51
Norblad, A., 99
nuclear families, 2–3, 5
nurturing, 30

objectives, 55
older adults, 113–120
with developmental disabilities, 127
and Four-R Model of Family Dynamics, 162–163, 167–169
and longevity, 162–163, 167–169
see also grandparents
Olshansky, S., 127
Omnibus Budget Reconciliation Act (1989), 153
open-ended questions, 72, 79, 87
openness of communication, 17–18, 38, 65
oppression, 106–107, 114
Orlin, M., 131
Ostendorf, D., 98
output, 9, 12

parameters, 35
paraphrasing technique, 64–65, 87
parenting, *see* childrearing
Parsons, T., 34
Perkins, U. E., 133
Philips, K., 103
Pincus, A., 10, 206–207
placating mode of communication, 6, 7
planning stage, 54–55, 66–67, 74, 80–82, 88–89
Powell, B., 20
power structure
family, 15–16, 18–22, 38, 148–149
and relationships, 38
in roles-dominated family, 72–73
priorities, 55, 67, 81–82
process recording, 199–203
providing/maintaining focus, 65

rapport, in engagement stage, 50
Ratcliffe, R. G., 141
regimentation, 35
regulatory statutes, 154–157
Rehabilitation Act (1973), 130–131
Reichertz, D., 165
Reiss, I., 2
relationships, 38–41
characteristics of, 38–39
and clarity in communication, 22–23, 38
family dominated by, 39–41, 78–85
in rituals-dominated family, 90
in roles-dominated family, 76
in rules-dominated family, 68
religious participation, 43, 164
respect, and communication, 38
retirement, 163
Richards, L. N., 22
Ricketts, W., 141
rituals, 41–45
family dominated by, 44–45, 86–91
in relationships-dominated family, 85
in roles-dominated family, 76–77
in rules-dominated family, 68–69
types of, 41–44
Robinson, J. D., 3
roles in family, 34–38
birth order and, 20–21
characteristics of, 34–36
childrearing, 19, 35, 106, 107, 148
family dominated by, 36–38, 71–78, 204
of family worker, 56–57, 67, 72
physical presence and, 23–24
power and, 15–16, 18–22
in relationships-dominated family, 85
in rituals-dominated family, 90
in rules-dominated family, 68
socialization and, 19, 34–35, 106, 107, 148
Romano family, 36–38, 71–78, 199–203, 204
rules, 32–34
development of, 32–33
of engagement stage, 50
family dominated by, 33–34, 63–71
in relationships-dominated family, 84–85
in rituals-dominated family, 90
in roles-dominated family, 76

Satir, Virginia, 6–7, 16, 51
Schlesinger, F. G., 96
Schmiege, C. J., 22
Schneewind, E. H., 41
schools
and care of children, 124
and children with disabilities, 128–129, 130
and day care, 151–154
mediation programs, 124–125
Schwartz, W., 58
self-esteem, 1, 30
Selleck, L. R., 141
senior citizens, *see* older adults

service delivery systems
  child welfare, 122–126
service delivery systems *(Cont.)*
  for individuals with developmental dis-
    abilities, 128–132
  for older adults, 116–120
  through community/neighborhood cen-
    ters, 116, 133–135
Sewell, D., 101
sexism, 106–107
sexual orientation, 99–102, 141
Shaefor, B. W., 52
shared values, 24–25
siblings
  birth order of, 20–21
  of child with disabilities, 127–128
  power hierarchy among, 18–19
  roles among, 19
Sidel, R., 151
significant others, 100–101
single-parent families, 3
  fathers as heads of, 106
  foster care and, 140
  rules and, 32, 33–34
  strength of, 21–22
Skill, T., 3
Slater, P. E., 34
snapshot approach, 54
socialization
  and birth order, 20–21
  in childrearing, 19, 106, 107, 148
  and drive for independence and individu-
    alism, 25
  to external environment, 30–32
  and family intervention, 49–50
  family role in, 1–2
  and gangs, 133
  and gender roles, 34–35
  and power structure in family, 18–19
  and roles in family, 19, 34–35, 106, 107,
    148
social work practice, 113–136
  in child welfare, 120–126
  in community/neighborhood services,
    116, 132–135
  current and future challenges of, 161–170
  with older adults, 113–120
  for people with developmental disabilities,
    126–132
  trends in, 139–157
sperm banks, 101
spirituality rituals, 43
Stachowiak, J., 6–7
Steelman, L. C., 20
Strauss, J. S., 41
structure, *see* family structure
Subrahmanian, C., 41
substance abuse, 102–103

subsystems, 9–10
summarizing technique, 64, 79, 87
super-reasonable mode of communication,
  6–8
Sutton-Smith, B., 20
systems
  defined, 9
  family, 10–11, 206–207
systems theory, 9–12

target system, 10
Taschman, H. A., 6–7
teacher role, 56
Teepen, T., 99
termination stage, 57–59, 69, 77, 83–84,
  90–91
Thomas family, 33–34, 63–71, 131–132
Toman, W., 19
top-down approach, 15–16, 52–53, 66, 72–73
Tracy, E. M., 142
trust, 22, 38
Tseng, W., 41
twilight years, 116, 117, 127

Udry, J. R., 34
understanding, and communication, 16–18
unemployment, 3, 5, 36–38, 71–78, 102–103
unified adoptive families, 141

values, shared, 24–25
Vosler, N. R., 21–22, 165
Voydanoff, P., 35

Waddell, F. E., 141
Webb, B., 106
Weinberg, M. S., 100–101
welfare programs, 98–99, 103
White, D., 9–10
whole family process, 41
Wikler, L., 127
wilderness programs, 123–124
Williams, S. E., 97
Williamson, J., 19
Winner, S. M., 124–125
Wolin, S. J., 42
women
  changing roles of, 105–108, 148–151
  childrearing roles of, 10, 19, 106, 107, 148
  community/neighborhood-based services
    for, 135
  earnings of, 107, 149
  and sexual orientation, 99–102
  in the workforce, 105–106, 148–151, 162
Woollett, A., 9–10
Wright, D. F., 97

Zastrow, C., 99, 115